THE PERFECT GIRL

LORNA DOUNAEVA

ALSO BY LORNA DOUNAEVA

The McBride Vendetta Series

FRY

Angel Dust

Cold Bath Lane

For Mum and Dad. Thank you for sharing your love of books with me and providing me with endless inspiration.

ACKNOWLEDGMENTS

A big thank you to Denis Dounaev, Mimi Dendias, Rory Matheson, Rob Barker, Nicola Welch, Lorna Day and Gemma Gatford.

Editors
Hayley Sherman
Maria Dounaeva

Cover
Coverquill

Copyright © 2019 by Lorna Dounaeva

All rights reserved.

No part of this book may be reproduced in any form or by any electronic or mechanical means, including information storage and retrieval systems, without written permission from the author, except for the use of brief quotations in a book review.

THE PERFECT GIRL

PROLOGUE

I prong the bee with tweezers and press its point against my bare flesh. My teeth clench as it barbs my skin. Then I shudder as the venom revives me. I look down and see the discarded insect jerking about on the floor. It flaps its tiny wings, but it's lost the strength to fly. It tries repeatedly to take off, but its life force is fading. It has given itself for me and now I will watch it die.

1

The cakes taunted him from behind the glass counter. Jock could almost taste the sugar on his tongue as he admired the sticky swirls of jam, cream and butter icing. Behind him came the melodic sound of spoons chinking against china. Middle-class voices uttered words like 'frightful!' and 'jolly good!' and chastised children with names like 'Ophelia' and 'Byron'.

He waited in a state of heightened agitation. His stomach rumbled accusations as waitresses scurried by in their flirty fifties-style dresses, but he wasn't good at getting served. The table by the window had just become available so he mooched over and sat down, setting up his laptop on the lacy white tablecloth. Presently, a waitress came over and took his order of Yorkshire tea and a slice of Battenberg. She had a little snub nose and a smile as wide as her face.

"Are you here for the May Fair?"

"No, just visiting."

"Ah, you're on holiday?"

"Kind of."

"Where are you staying?"

"I'm renting a room at the Dragon."

"Lovely." She glanced across the street at the run-down pub. Hard to believe that this place, with its fine china and fancy table cloths, was just across the street. "Hey, you see Dylan over there? He lives at the Dragon."

He couldn't have helped but notice the heavily freckled bloke with the spiky hairdo; a bog brush, they used to call it when he was a kid. That was about the last time he had seen anyone with such a haircut.

Before he could respond, she was hollering across the room. "Hey, Dylan! This gentleman's staying at the Dragon!"

Dylan looked at him with interest. "Are you divorced?"

"No."

He was embarrassed to be shouting across the tea shop.

"Separated?" His Welsh accent was as strong as hers.

"No. I'm single actually."

"Are you?" Dylan looked dubious. "What are you doing at the Dragon then?"

"He's on holiday," the waitress said.

Dylan looked even more dubious. He got up and walked over to Jock's table, surveying him with interest.

"A working holiday," Jock amended.

"What are you working on?" Dylan tried to get a look over his shoulder.

"Nothing." He closed the laptop.

"Well now you've really piqued my interest. If you don't tell me, I might have to tickle it out of you."

Jock looked at the waitress.

"He really would, too."

"Alright, I'm a writer."

Dylan's eyes lit up. "What's your name, then?"

"Jock Skone."

"Never heard of you. Have you, Angie?"

She shook her head. They both looked disappointed.

Jock knew he should leave it at that, but his pride wouldn't let him.

"I write under a pseudonym."

"Really?"

"Yes, I'm J.K. Jeffries."

"Oh my godfathers!" Dylan spluttered. "I always thought she was a woman!"

"Well I do write for women."

Dylan seemed to think this was hilarious. "He's J.K. Jeffries!" he said loudly, for anyone who hadn't heard.

Everyone in the shop turned to stare, the old ladies in particular. Dylan just couldn't let it go. He was like an annoying little dog, yapping at his heels. Writing women's fiction was nothing to be ashamed of, he reminded himself. He had been called the Agatha Christie of his generation. They had even made TV adaptations of a couple of his novels.

He turned back to his laptop, but Dylan continued to hover.

"Oh, I'm sorry, I'm distracting you, aren't I?"

"No, not at all."

He kept on typing. Within minutes, he had fallen into a trance-like state, the laptop wobbling as his fingers flew over the keys. He worked with a frenzy, the words gushing out of him like blood from an open vein. By the time he came to, Dylan had wandered off and his tea was as cold as a puddle.

He had been so engrossed in his work that he had barely noticed two youths haring around the tea shop, not until one of them knocked into his table. He caught his laptop just in time to save it from crashing to the floor, but the table was now soaked with tea. The lad who had done it didn't even say sorry. Best not to react, Jock decided. He didn't want any trouble.

"Here, let me clean that up." Angie rushed forward with a cloth. "You'll have to leave," she told the youths. But they took no notice.

A couple of the old ladies at the next table tutted and

shook their heads. One of them muttered something about manners and her friends nodded in agreement. Jock watched as the youths moved towards them. The one with a gold tooth lifted the lid off their teapot and spat into it. Both boys laughed hysterically.

One of the old ladies, a well-dressed woman with coiffured hair and high cheekbones, eyed the boy's skinny jeans.

"Is that what people are wearing these days?"

Gold Tooth's face turned ugly. "What did you say, you old hag?"

"Would you like to borrow my hearing aid?" she asked, with deliberate enunciation. Her cut-glass accent sliced through the air.

Angie darted a glance at Jock, as if she expected him to do something. But what could he do? Seconds passed and she was still looking at him with that hopeful expression in her eyes. In the end, it was her who spoke.

"Out!" she ordered the boys. "I told you to leave."

The boys were all wide-eyed innocence. "What have we done? We just wanted to see the May Queen. You know, before it's too late."

Dylan stepped forward. "OK, that's enough!"

Jock sucked in his breath. Why didn't Dylan just stay out of it? Who knew what these boys were on?

Gold Tooth looked at Dylan and scrunched up his face in distaste.

"You wanna take this outside?" Dylan asked.

"Not particularly." Gold Tooth did not quite meet his eye. They were now standing at an arm's length of each other.

Without warning, Gold Tooth swung his fist and hit Dylan squarely in the jaw. Jock winced as he fell back against the counter. Instead of getting up, Dylan grabbed Gold Tooth's leg out from under him and pulled him crashing down to the floor, upturning a table in the process. The old ladies shrieked as china cups and plates smashed to smithereens. Gold

Tooth's friend swooped down and grabbed a shard of broken china.

"Dylan!" Jock yelled.

Dylan ducked out of the way and the lout only succeeded in stabbing the counter. In the next instant, Dylan was up on his feet again. He grabbed the lad from behind and pinned him against the wall so that he couldn't move.

"Get off me, you freak!"

The lad struggled wildly, but Dylan held him fast.

Jock looked at the other youth to see what he would do.

At that very moment, a young woman floated out of the kitchen. People turned towards her, the way flowers reach for the sun. Everyone, including the troublemakers. This had to be Sapphire, the proprietress. Jock had seen her name over the door. She set a vase of tulips down on the counter and clapped her hands together with authority.

"OK, that's quite enough, boys. The police are on their way. I suggest you hop it before they get here. That includes you, Dylan. Though, you can give the lads a ten-minute start."

Something in her tone got through to the boys, making them slink towards the door. Gold Tooth swiped a blueberry muffin on his way out.

"Let him have it," Sapphire said. "He needs to save face."

"Talk about ungrateful," Dylan muttered, sitting down beside Jock to pull on his shoes, which he'd taken off for some reason Jock couldn't fathom.

Jock nodded mutely. He watched Sapphire as she brought the old ladies a fresh pot of tea and spoke to them in a calm, soothing voice he wished he could bottle. He saw her flit among the tables, smiling and reassuring everyone in turn. Her red dress whirled and shimmied as she moved and her golden curls danced around her face. Such poise, such elegance! She winked at him as she passed, and his heart tripped over itself. He averted his eyes, focusing instead on his computer, but it was her reflection he watched as she sashayed away and whatever else Dylan might have said was lost on him.

"Can I have the bill, please?" he asked Angie, once things had died down. She brought it over straight away, without stopping to serve half a dozen other people the way they did in London. She had even doodled a little teapot on the bottom of the receipt. He smiled then frowned as he saw the damage. Wow, these were London prices! Reluctantly, he produced his wallet and slipped his card onto the plate. She looked a little taken aback. For a horrible moment, he thought he had come so far into the country that everyone still paid in cash. He had.

"I'll just fetch the card machine, then." She sounded a little flustered. "I'm sure I saw it in the store room, just yesterday."

He could have kicked himself for not bringing any real money, but he had yet to see a cash machine in Fleckford and the bank seemed to be permanently closed.

"Hey, don't worry," said Sapphire, stepping forward. "This one's on the house." She treated him to the most wonderful, dazzling smile. "I'm sorry about the disturbance earlier. It's not usually so crazy in here."

"No, I'm sure," he managed. "Thanks."

"Make sure you come back tomorrow, won't you, darling?"

"Yes!" Wild horses wouldn't keep him away.

He went back to his room at the Dragon and climbed onto the bed. From there, he had a good view of the tea shop. It would be even better if weren't for the manky net curtains. He watched as one of the waitresses went back and forth with the mop. Someone must have spilt their tea, he guessed, from the way she was scowling. His phone rang abruptly, making him jump.

"Hello?"

It was his nephew, Robbie, who was house-sitting for him.

"Nan turned up this morning," he said. "She wouldn't believe me when I said you were away."

"Sorry."

"No bother. She cleaned the loo while she was here and she filled the fridge with food. She's a treasure, your mum."

"I know."

"So when are you coming home?"

"I don't know yet. I might stay a while."

Robbie clicked his tongue. "What's her name?"

"It's not like that."

"Yeah, right! So what shall I tell Nan? You can bet she'll be back."

"I don't care – just tell her I'm busy with my book."

"What's this one about? Is there anything interesting in it?"

"There are no goblins or elves, if that's what you're asking."

"I bet there's no blood or gore either."

"Probably not." His heart beat a little faster as Sapphire walked into view. He watched, rapt, as she poured tea for a customer. He grabbed his camera and took a few snaps. The pictures would be a bit out of focus, but better than nothing. He didn't think he had ever seen anyone quite so beautiful. Not in real life, at any rate.

"Jock, are you still there?"

"Yeah, the reception's awful. I'll give you a call later in the week, OK?"

"Right-ho."

"Bye then, and don't forget to feed the hamster."

"You've got a hamster?"

"What do you think you're sharing a room with?"

He set down the phone and watched as Sapphire tossed back her hair and laughed at something a customer had said. How he wished he were that customer! He had to see her again. He couldn't wait till morning. His hand flew to the nape of his neck. His scarf! He must have left it at the tea shop. Or perhaps his subconscious had done that for him. He jumped to his feet then sat down again. No, he wouldn't go now, while she was busy. He would wait until closing time. That way he would get her alone.

He watched until the last couple of customers drifted out the door, then Sapphire flipped the sign from 'open' to 'closed'. This was his cue. He hurried down the stairs and across the cobbles, pausing briefly to catch his breath. There was no bell, just a black door knocker in the shape of a twisted rope. He pulled it and waited.

She opened the door with the chain on.

"Hi?"

In his imagination, she had been more pleased to see him.

"Sorry to bother you, but I think I left my scarf. It's red tartan …"

Her eyes narrowed slightly. "Wait there. I'll have a look in lost property."

He watched through the gap in the door as she walked to the back of the shop, her hips wiggling as she moved. Did she do that on purpose, he wondered, or was it just the way she walked?

"Yes, that's it," he called, as she pulled his scarf from the cupboard.

"I don't suppose you'd take this one, too?" She held up a lurid purple one, with bright green spots on it.

He giggled. "I'd really like to see the rest of that outfit!"

A smile tugged at the corners of her mouth and she unchained the door to hand him the scarf.

"You have such soft hands," he said, as their fingers touched.

She drew back. "Thanks."

He racked his brain desperately for something else to say, something that would stop her from shutting the door. He felt such a powerful connection to her. She had to feel it too.

"Can I take your picture?" he asked.

"Pardon?"

"It's a hobby. Photography, that is."

She looked at him oddly. "Maybe another time. I'm just closing."

"Yes. Yes, of course."

"Good night, then."

He felt a twinge of panic. She was closing the door. He had to do something, say something.

"I've been watching you," he blurted out, "from my bedroom window."

Her mouth fell open and instantly, he knew he had said the wrong thing. "I'm sorry, I …"

"Look, I really do have to close now."

She couldn't bolt the door fast enough. What had seemed spontaneous and romantic in his head had come out sounding creepy and weird. Bollocks! What the hell had he done?

2

The village hall was surprisingly crowded as Jock queued for his ticket to *Vertigo*. He had seen it before, but there wasn't much else to do of an evening. The whole village seemed to go into lockdown after five.

"Just the one ticket?" the elderly seller asked, glancing behind him.

"Yes please."

He handed over a ten pound note.

She held it up to the light.

"Seems OK." She didn't sound completely satisfied.

"Let me see," said her equally elderly crony. He recognised them both from the tea shop. They were part of the group Dylan had referred to as the Fleckford Wives.

"There's a small tear," she said, examining it carefully. "Has it been through the washing machine?"

"No, I just got it from the cash point."

"The one in Castle Street?" she asked with suspicion.

"There's one in Castle Street? I walked all the way down to the garage."

"The one on Castle Street is no longer in operation," the first lady informed him, in a superior tone.

"Er … right." He wondered if all the customers had to pass this level of scrutiny or if it was just him.

"Hand!" she barked.

Reluctantly, he extended his right hand. She took a large rubber stamper and pressed down hard. He bit back an exclamation, but when he looked down, he saw it had barely left a mark. The stamper was bone dry.

"Come on, move along," she said abruptly. "There's a long queue forming behind you."

Jock did as he was told. He wasn't going to stop at the refreshment table, but the blue-haired lady caught his eye.

"Victoria sponge? It's homemade."

"Yes please."

He tried to remember the last time he had eaten cake at the cinema.

She served him an outrageously large slice, together with a milky cup of tea.

"How much is that?"

"No charge, dear." She gave him a wink. "It's nice to see a man eat! Enjoy the film!"

He thanked her and shuffled towards the main hall. The usher waved him through, oblivious to the lack of a stamp on his hand. He took a seat in the very front row. It was a bit close to the screen, but he couldn't stand having people sit in front of him, blocking his view. He perched his cake on his knee while he drank his tea, then switched over. The lights went down and the audience grew quiet in anticipation, then the screen flickered and … nothing.

Eventually, a timid-looking old lady came up to the front.

"I'm afraid tonight's screening has been cancelled due to technical difficulties."

"Boo!" shouted someone at the back.

"Happens every time!" complained the man sitting directly behind him.

In that case, why on earth did they all still turn up?

The old lady cleared her throat. "If you'd like to form an orderly queue, you can collect your refund at the ticket desk."

Jock followed the crowd out into the foyer. He couldn't be bothered to queue to get his money back. He was also keen to avoid the inevitable wrangle that was bound to take place when he was unable to provide proof of purchase, due to the invisible stamp on his hand. No, it wasn't worth the effort. It was a sunk cost, as his father would say. But it wasn't as simple as just walking out. Everyone was clamouring round the ticket desk so he couldn't get through. He wandered up the other way and found a side door. He pushed it open.

"What did you do that for?" demanded one of the villagers. "You've set off the frigging alarm!"

His cheeks burned fuchsia as he heard the commotion behind him.

"I'm sorry. I didn't know that was going to happen."

"Now someone will have to come and deactivate it."

"Sorry," he said again.

He tripped out into an alley lined with smelly dustbins. A cat prowled along the gutter, stalking its supper and loud, energetic music pulsated from the youth club opposite. A couple of teenagers looked up as he approached.

"Hey, can you buy us some cider? We'll give you the money."

He pretended he hadn't heard them. He didn't much care if they wanted to drink. He just didn't want to be involved.

"Oi! Are you deaf?"

A moment later, a missile narrowly missed his back. He glanced around. The little bastards were lobbing cans at him.

"Hey, are you alright?"

She was like an angel, standing in the doorway with a cloud of blonde hair curled around her face.

"I'm fine," he managed.

"Come on." She took him by the arm. "I know a shortcut."

The teenagers watched in disbelief as Sapphire led him away. He could hardly believe it himself. He glanced at her out of the side of his eye. She was wearing a thick, woolly scarf and bobble hat, which seemed a bit excessive for the time of year. They made her look warm and cosy.

"Not having the best day, are you?" she said, as she guided him up the steps to the high street.

"No."

"I bet you're wishing you never came here."

"I wouldn't say that."

Why was she even talking to him? After the way things had gone earlier, he hadn't expected a second chance.

"What are you really doing here? Angie told me you're a famous writer." Her eyes shone slightly as she said this, as though she thought he was someone special. He wouldn't have picked her for the bookish type, but it seemed he was wrong. "Isn't this an odd place to come to write a book?"

"I wanted to try somewhere completely new."

"Why?"

"I just … needed to get away."

"You're not going to write about me, are you?"

"Oh no. It's completely fictional."

"Oh." She looked a little disappointed.

"But you can have an advance copy, if you like. Then you can let me know what you think."

"I'd love to."

"So, I hear you're going to be the May Queen?"

She shrugged. Perhaps she was fed up of talking about it and dealing with people's questions. Or maybe she was nervous, though it was hard to imagine Sapphire being nervous about anything.

"So tell me, where can I get a cup of coffee around here?"

He glanced around the silent street. "Neil doesn't keep any at the Dragon. He says it's vile stuff."

"You'd have to go to McDonald's, unless …"

He looked at her expectantly.

"I could make you one?"

"I don't want to put you to any trouble."

"It's no trouble. I was going to have one myself."

"Thanks. That would be nice."

With a tingle of excitement, he followed her into the shop, but instead of going behind the counter, she walked towards the stairs that led up to the flat above.

"Watch out, the ceiling's a bit low."

Unable to believe his luck, he followed her up the narrow staircase.

3

The hum of the bees drove her crazy. All night they flew, in and out of her dreams, in and out of her head. Sapphire woke up swatting them away with her hands. But when she opened her eyes, she saw that there wasn't a single bee in the room. She sat up and her eye fell on the May Queen dress, which hung from a hook on her bedroom door, still cocooned in its wrapping. She felt a strange tingle in her tummy. Today was the day.

She pulled on her dressing gown and walked through to the kitchen. The evidence of last night was everywhere: coffee cup rings on her best table, cushions strewn about, an open packet of crisps allowed to spill all over the carpet. She picked up a dustpan and brush and started to sweep up the crumbs, when something stopped her. 'It doesn't matter,' said a voice inside her head. 'Not today.'

It wasn't raining, which was unusual for May Day. Everyone who came into the tea shop that morning commented on it.

"Shh! We mustn't talk about it!" Angie warned, as if a mere mention of the weather was enough to bring on a storm.

Sapphire busied herself at the counter. She hadn't planned

on working, but the prospect of sitting alone in the flat appealed less now than it had last night. She needed to keep her hands busy. She needed something to push out all the unwelcome thoughts zipping through her mind. She did not see Simon so much as feel his large shadow loom over her as he approached the counter.

"Camomile tea and a bran muffin please," he said, needlessly. He came in about the same time every day and always ordered the exact same thing. He held out his reusable flask for her to fill.

Her eyes flitted over his high-visibility cycling gear. "Where are you off to?"

"I'm going up into the mountains to fish." He patted his huge backpack. "Got everything I need in here: cooker, kettle, even a tent."

"Are you sure you'll be alright on your own?" Angie fretted.

Simon smiled. "I am, but you're welcome to come with me."

"I have to work," Angie told him. "Plus, I hate insects. You know I do."

"You don't know what you're missing out on." His eyes shone. "There's nothing quite like a night under the stars. On a clear night, you can see the glow of the Andromeda Galaxy. It's really quite remarkable."

"I'll have to take your word for it," Angie said. "I need my home comforts."

"I still say you should try it someday. You might find you like it." He picked up his cup and wrapped his muffin in a napkin. "Well, I'd better get going. Thanks for the tea."

Sapphire looked away as he leaned over the counter to give Angie a long, lingering kiss.

"I'll miss you!" Angie whispered. She waved wildly, as if he were a soldier going off to war.

"Have a safe trip!" Sapphire called after him.

"And you have a great May Day," he said. "I hope the weather holds off."

Angie bit her lip as he said this and for a moment Sapphire thought she was going to cross herself, but instead she picked up a piece of chalk and began scrawling the day's specials on the board.

"I'd like a pot of Earl Grey and an almond croissant please," said a man in a green raincoat, setting his rucksack down on the counter. Sapphire ignored him and tried to concentrate on writing a to-do list for Angie.

He raised his voice. "Hey! I'm talking to you!"

Still, she refused to look at him. Angie ignored him, too. Eventually, he would get bored and go away.

"You know, you really should go and get ready," Angie said. "Morgan and I can manage."

"Where *is* Morgan?"

"She's probably overslept. You know what she's like."

Sapphire nodded.

"Though I did think it was a bit strange that they didn't choose her to be one of your attendants," Angie added, in a low voice. "I mean, I'm really pleased for Bronwyn of course, but don't you think Morgan would have been the more obvious choice?"

"Not really," Sapphire said. "Bronwyn is smiley and enthusiastic, whilst Morgan has her own permanent rain cloud. I know who I'd choose."

Angie smiled. "You're right, of course you're right, Sapphire. And I'm sure Bronwyn will do a great job."

❄

"Heard you singing in the shower this morning. Beautiful falsetto!" Dylan called out, as Jock walked through the bar on his way out of the Dragon.

Neil the landlord smirked from behind his tea towel, but

Jock didn't care. He felt like doing cartwheels. He skipped across the road and burst into the tea shop, almost colliding with a homeless woman.

"Sorry," he muttered, trying not to screw up his nose in revulsion. He was surprised to find such a person so deep into the countryside, especially in a place as elegant as Sapphire's tea shop. Still, he didn't wonder about it for very long. He wanted to see Sapphire.

He glanced around, but the place was almost empty. He walked up to the counter and tried to see through the rainbow-coloured tassels that separated the kitchen from the shop, but the only person he could see was Angie, humming to herself as she worked.

She stepped out of the kitchen. "Can I help you?"

She must have eyes in the back of her head.

"Is Sapphire here?"

She gave him a knowing smile. Perhaps Sapphire had told her about last night, or perhaps she was just used to men asking after her. He didn't like that thought at all.

"No, I'm afraid she isn't. She's getting ready for the May Fair."

"Is that today?"

Sapphire hadn't mentioned it as they had snuggled together on her sofa.

"Didn't you notice the bunting outside?"

"No."

"I'm amazed you haven't been roped into helping! There's an army of old ladies out there, organising everyone."

"I seem to have got away with it."

"Well watch out or they'll have you blowing up balloons and weighing marrows."

This was his cue to smile, but he didn't feel like it. "When's the parade?"

"Noon."

He glanced at his phone. Two whole hours till he got to see Sapphire again. He didn't know how he would stand it.

He walked around the village, taking shots of the transformation taking place. A maypole had been erected in the square, and he watched as a group of teenagers grabbed the ribbons and skipped about. Their fun didn't last long, as they were soon swatted away by the Fleckford Wives, dressed in their best twinsets and tweed. Those old ladies seemed to be everywhere, marching around with clipboards and arranging flowers and oversized fruits and vegetables onto competition tables. He suspected the old men had taken refuge in their sheds, scared away like frightened snails.

By noon, the village was packed. Jock was curious to see what happened. He had never been to a May Day parade before. Not many villages had them these days. They were considered a bit of an anachronism by some and downright inappropriate by others. It had been hotly debated whether they should be allowed to continue at all, but there were many who had grown up with them and refused to let negative connotations blight the festivities.

Hundreds of people lined the route to the castle, waving union flags and Welsh dragons. Little girls clutched May Dolls fashioned out of wicker, and Morris dancers jingled as they walked. Angie stood in the doorway of the tea shop, her arms crossed tightly across her body.

"I've never seen so many people in the village," she said, staring at the sea of tourists as if they were an invading army.

"What happens at these things, anyway?" Jock asked.

"It's a bit like a cross between a carnival, a village fete and a harvest festival," Angie said. "But instead of a Carnival Queen, we have the May Queen. After the procession, there will be competition stalls up at the castle. Sapphire will have to judge the best fruit and veg."

"Sounds riveting!"

"Sh! Here comes the parade," she said, as the drumming began.

The majorettes marched in front, looking terribly solemn in their sparkling white costumes. They twirled their batons with more enthusiasm than skill, but the crowd cheered them on as though they were Olympic athletes, and the little girls glowed with pride.

Behind them came two children, carrying the weirdest doll he had ever seen. It was green from head to toe, with leaves coming out of its mouth.

"What the hell is that?"

"That's the Green Man."

"Why's he got leaves coming out of his mouth?"

"He always has leaves coming out of somewhere."

"Why?"

"I think it's supposed to be a symbol of rebirth."

He shuddered. "Kind of creepy, isn't it?"

"Shh! They'll hear you!"

Just then, the May Queen's float came into view and the crowd roared. Sapphire sat upon a throne decorated with fruits and flowers, looking like the world belonged to her. In her white dress and golden tiara, she was even more breathtaking than she had been the day before. She sat in between two attendants: one slight and attractive with reddish gold hair, the other big and broad as a man, with ears that stuck out at odd angles. The big girl looked completely out of place next to the two beauties, but the crowd seemed to love her.

Sapphire waved majestically. Her manner was more reserved than her attendants', who waved their arms like crazy and called out greetings to their friends. The big girl put her fingers to her lips and delivered an ear-splitting whistle. The crowd went wild. Looking around, he noticed several people with large ears and broad shoulders. Perhaps she was everyone's favourite cousin.

He moved forward a little, trying to find the best position

to photograph Sapphire. He didn't think she would be able to see him in the crowd, but she sought him out with her eyes and smiled a secret smile that was just for him. He felt his stomach flutter and he almost dropped his camera. He must be the luckiest man alive.

※

SAPPHIRE FELT a chill as the float drifted up Daffodil Lane. The parade was like a huge snowball, gathering people in its wake.

"Isn't this amazing?" said Bronwyn. Her ears flapped with excitement.

Sapphire forced herself to smile.

"Feeling a bit nervous?" her other attendant asked.

She brushed off the enquiry with a swift shake of her head and continued to look out at the crowd. After a while, the other two stopped trying to draw her into their conversation and spoke across her instead. Sapphire barely noticed. She had waited a long time for this day and now that it was here, she wasn't going to miss a single detail. She looked around, taking it all in. So this was how it felt. The crowd. The excitement. She felt a shadow fall over the float and she looked up at the sky, willing it not to rain for just a little longer. Then she looked back down the valley. From her unique vantage point, she could see all around, from the lambs in the field to the train waiting at the station, and the glittery blue water of the canal beyond. She could see everyone and everyone could see her. And there it was, the face in the crowd. The one in a million face that made her suck in her breath and hold it tight. She leapt down from the float, ignoring the helping hands held out to her by those nearest.

"Sapphire?" the call echoed through the throng.

Her bouquet fluttered to the ground as she pushed her way through the crowd.

4

Jock watched Sapphire run, like a bride fleeing her wedding. He hadn't seen that expression on anyone before. She had looked … spooked. He hesitated only for a moment, before he took off in pursuit. It wasn't like him to be so impulsive, but there was something about Sapphire that made him feel reckless.

People turned to stare, but she was incredibly fast. He could still make out her blonde head but the gap between them was widening. She seemed frantic, pushing and shoving, not caring who got in her way. Through the cobbled streets, he chased her, his camera swinging perilously from the strap round his neck. Past the square she went and over the railway bridge. The crowd had thinned out now and there were fewer people to block the way. But he couldn't tell which way she had gone. She could have followed the canal path through the tunnel, or else taken the other route towards the Black Mountains. There was no way of knowing.

"Bugger it, Sapphire! Where are you?"

He clutched his side and his breaths came out in long, panicky gasps. He had lost her. An invisible hand reached in and grabbed at his heart, squeezing it like a sponge. For a moment, he thought he would have a heart attack, but the pain was purely in his head. He forced himself to focus on his breathing and the symptoms eased enough for him to trudge back to Daffodil Lane.

He thought through the possible explanations, trying to work out what could have happened to make her run off like that. The festivities had moved on now and all that was left were the empty drinks cans in the street and the beat of drums in the distance. He couldn't believe the parade was still going. How could they carry on without the May Queen?

He trudged back to Sapphire's tea shop. The place was virtually empty, aside from one lone waitress who sat at an empty table, flipping though a copy of *Kerrang*.

"Has Sapphire come back?" he asked.

She looked startled. "Isn't she leading the procession?"

"She just ran off," Angie said from the doorway. She sank down in the nearest chair. "Oh God, I knew I should have talked her out of being May Queen. I had a bad feeling all along."

"Why are you getting so worked up?" asked the other waitress. "She probably just went to the loo!"

Angie smiled nervously. "Maybe Morgan's right. Maybe she did just go to the loo or something."

But he knew she was kidding herself. The procession had only got as far as the top of the road. If she had really needed the loo, or anything else for that matter, wouldn't she have come back here? Before anyone could speculate further, the phone rang. Angie dashed over to the counter and picked up the receiver.

"Hello?" She listened for a moment. "It's Verity," she told them.

"Who's Verity?"

"One of the ladies from the May Fair committee. They're all really worried. Everyone's looking but no one's seen her. Christ, where is she?"

Morgan looked back at her magazine.

"How can you read, at a time like this?" Angie's face was flushed with anger.

"Well, what should I be doing?"

Morgan scraped back her chair and took a step towards the door, when something stopped her in her tracks.

"Ahh!" She screamed as a brick came through the window, landing just where she had been sitting. For a second, there was total silence. Then all of the glass at the front of the shop shattered.

"Morgan! Are you alright?" Angie had to shout to make herself heard over the burglar alarm.

"I think so."

Carefully, Morgan shook the glass from her skirt. "Look at me! I'm shaking like a dog having a sh…"

"It's OK," Angie soothed. "You're OK."

Jock was shaking, too. He needed to get up, but his legs wouldn't work. He couldn't even get his mouth to close.

"Are you alright?" Angie asked him. "You're not hurt, are you?"

He managed a noise that must have passed for 'no' and she moved over to Morgan, who had far more business being upset.

"What was that?" fumed Morgan. "What the bloody hell!"

Jock sat with his head in his hands, waiting for his heart to stop hopping around in his chest. Angie pressed a switch that shut off the alarm, but he could still hear it, ringing in his ears.

She looked back at him. "Maybe you should go and have a look? Whoever it was might still be out there."

"I'm not sure that's a good idea."

What if there was still someone out there? What if they had more bricks?

Feeling like a gutless wonder, he darted for the counter.

His legs shook like crazy. He didn't know how much more he could take.

"I'm calling the police," said Angie.

"Good."

He buried his head in his lap, wishing for all this to be over. When he looked up again, Morgan was sitting beside him, examining the tips of her long, violet fingernails. If she had been a softer sort of girl, she probably would have cried but as it was, she was holding up better than he was, or at least she was able to give that impression.

"Hello?" a voice called. He peered over the counter. To his relief, it was a policeman. Angie strode over to meet him and they spoke in excited voices.

"This is Constable Wesley."

She brought him over. Jock struggled to his feet, doing his best to look normal.

"Is anybody hurt?" Wesley asked.

"Just a couple of cuts," Angie reported.

"So nothing serious?"

Morgan shook her head.

"It's not just the brick through the window," Jock said, finding his voice. "Sapphire … the May Queen's gone missing."

"What does it matter if she's the frigging May Queen?" Morgan asked, clearly affronted by his continued concern for Sapphire. Jock stared at her for a moment.

"She's too young to remember," Angie said.

"Remember what?"

"About the May Queen."

"May Queens," Jock said. "Oh come on, you must have heard?"

Morgan looked from one to the other, her snake earrings swinging from side to side. "What are you going on about?"

Jock took a deep breath. "Five years ago, a May Queen disappeared from a village called Whiteford. When the police investigated, they discovered that she wasn't the first May Queen to go missing. Over the last twenty years, at least three other May Queens had disappeared, from all around the British Isles. All on the day they were crowned."

He met Morgan's wide, unbelieving eyes.

"But the police solved that crime," Constable Wesley said quickly. "Peter Helston confessed."

"So this Peter Helston's in prison, then?"

"Peter Helston is dead," Jock said.

"But he did it?"

"Probably."

"Almost certainly," Constable Wesley agreed.

"All the same" – Jock looked down at his feet – "the case was never brought to trial. Helston died in prison before it came to court."

"You're scaring the poor girl," Wesley objected. "There was an enquiry and he was found guilty, so you can put your mind at rest."

"Then why did someone throw a brick through the window?" Morgan asked. "I mean, this is Sapphire's tea shop! And where the hell is Sapphire?"

"I think it's best if we close the shop," Wesley said. "Don't clean up just yet. My colleagues are on their way and they'll want to see it all just as it is."

"Shouldn't we be out looking for Sapphire?" asked Jock. "I mean, what if she's up in the mountains or something? She'll freeze!"

Wesley looked at him with studied patience. "If you wouldn't mind waiting here, my colleagues will want to talk to you. I know it feels like you're not doing much, but this is really the best way you can help for now. We need to build up a detailed picture of everything that's happened. It'll give us a better chance of finding her."

Jock nodded, but he couldn't help thinking how incredibly young Wesley looked. Did he really know what he was doing?

Angie made them all a cup of tea while they waited. Jock didn't normally take sugar, but when she added two lumps, he didn't object. The hot, familiar liquid soothed his stomach. He glanced at Morgan. She had gone back to reading her magazine, but she had been on the same page the whole time he had been drinking his tea. He wanted to say something comforting, but she was as prickly as a hedgehog. She would probably tell him to eff off.

The door opened to admit two men in dark suits. The elder of the two had an air of confidence about him that told Jock he was in charge. The other hid behind tinted sunglasses, despite the fact the sun wasn't out. Wesley scurried over to them. He probably didn't see a lot of action in his everyday work, Jock guessed. This must be a really big deal. After a moment, they walked towards him.

"This is DCI Stavely, and his colleague, DI Sweep," Wesley told him.

Stavely looked straight past him, his eyes sweeping the room. He was short-legged and stocky, with one hell of a moustache. Without warning, he zeroed in on Jock.

"You saw Miss Butterworth run off?"

Jock nodded.

Stavely leaned in closer, and Jock caught a whiff of menthol. "So what's your take on this? Why did she run off?"

"I really don't know. One minute she seemed fine, the next she was off."

"So what made you run off after her? I mean, everyone else stayed put. Why did you think something was wrong?"

"Well, she's a May Queen isn't she?"

Stavely continued to look at him, as if he expected him to say something more.

"It was the look on her face. It wasn't normal. It was like she'd seen the face of the killer."

"Do you think she expected you to follow her?"

"No, she was too busy running. She ... she looked like she was running for her life."

Stavely consulted his notebook. "And she lives here, in the upstairs flat?"

"Yes."

"By herself?"

"Yes."

"Do you have the keys?"

"No."

He looked at Angie.

"They must be here somewhere," she said. "She didn't take a handbag. They're probably in one of the kitchen drawers or something."

Stavely turned to his colleague with the sunglasses. "See if you can find those keys, Sweep. Her phone might be around, too." He turned back to Angie, his eyes skimming over her fluffy hair and cow-brown eyes. "Does she have any relatives, anyone she's close to?"

"Her life revolves around the tea shop. The staff and the customers, they're her world."

"Does she have any health problems?"

"God, no! She's as strong as an ox."

"Do you have any recent photos of her?"

"I have," Jock butted in. "I got some close-ups of her on the float."

"Great. Email them to me." Stavely handed him a card with his details.

"I'm just popping outside for a cigarette," Sweep called across the room. Stavely frowned his disapproval. Probably an ex-smoker, Jock guessed from the state of his teeth.

"Did you find those keys yet?" Stavely asked.

"No. They're not in the kitchen."

"They might be in the safe," Angie suggested.

"Do you know the combination?"

"It's seven, seven, seven, seven," Morgan called out. She was sitting at the counter, her legs dangling down aimlessly.

"Thanks."

"Now I understand why some of the customers were so weird about the May Fair," she said, dully.

"I don't think anyone's held one for about five years," Jock said. "But I suppose they thought enough time had passed."

"Not everyone thought so," said Angie. "Not by a long way."

Jock thought of the two teenage boys who had been causing trouble the day before. He was about to mention them, when he heard a high-pitched shriek. But it wasn't Morgan who screamed this time, it was Stavely's colleague, Sweep.

5

Jock watched as Stavely ran down Daffodil Lane towards the source of the commotion. He hesitated just a fraction of a second before going after him, but his fear for Sapphire spurred him on. She needed him and he needed to know what had happened. Tiny dots of blood splattered the cobbled streets. That blood hadn't been there half an hour ago, or if it had, he had missed it. He saw a group of people clustered in front of an old yew tree and braced himself.

It wasn't a pretty picture that drew the assembled crowd. A trio of lambs lay on their sides, their white wool splattered with blood. While everyone had been watching the parade, someone or something had broken into the sheep pen and mauled them to death. Some of the older sheep had been hurt, too, but the little lambs had borne the brunt of the assault. Those lambs would likely have ended up on the dinner tables of some of the villagers anyway, but to witness their grisly deaths was nonetheless unpleasant. Parents did their best to shield their children's eyes, but the young were wilful and curious and wanted to see what all the fuss was about.

Stavely strode to the front.

"What did this?"

"A dog, most likely," said a man in a dark blue bodywarmer, whom Jock took to be the farmer. "More than one, I'd say."

There was no sign of any dogs now, not dangerous ones at least. Several people had brought pets to the fair, but they all looked the tame, friendly variety. Not that that stopped people looking with suspicion from poodle to Labrador to see if any had blood dripping from its fangs.

Angie appeared at Jock's side. "Do you think this has anything to do with Sapphire?"

"I don't know." His heart hammered in his chest. "Let's not jump to conclusions."

DI Sweep emerged from the cover of an oak tree, behind which he had evidently been vomiting. Jock would have thought a detective of his grade would be desensitised to such scenes by now but Fleckford was the sort of place where nothing ever happened, until it did. Stavely looked at Sweep with derision and began talking rapidly, barking out instructions. He spoke so fast, he might as well have been speaking another language.

"What were these sheep doing here?"

"I brought them down for the fair," the farmer said, "for the kids to pet."

"Did you obtain a license from DEFRA?"

"I bring them to the summer fete every year. There's never been any trouble before."

Stavely looked back at the sheep pen. One of the larger sheep kept nuzzling the dead lambs. She bleated loudly at the farmer, as if she expected him to do something, but there was nothing he could do but remove the bodies.

"Leave them," Stavely said. "I'll have someone come down and take photographs."

"What about them?" the farmer said, referring to the crowd.

"You got a whistle?"

"Yes."

"Blow on it, then."

The farmer made a long, shrill noise and everyone looked up.

"Good," said Stavely. "Now I've got your attention, I'd like anybody who thinks they might have seen something to hang around for a minute so I can get your details. The rest of you, please move along."

Everyone looked at each other then began to move off. Jock glanced back, but there didn't appear to be anyone who wanted to talk to Stavely. It didn't seem possible that no one had seen anything. Perhaps they just didn't want to talk to the police.

He fell into step with Angie. "What the hell is going on?" he whispered. "Why would anyone do this?"

"I don't know. I really don't … Christ, look at the maypole!"

He gasped. The pole was bent in the middle and the ribbons torn and frayed. Hundreds of colourful fragments blew around in the wind.

"Mummy, I'm scared," a little girl said and her mother pulled her away.

"Someone didn't want us to celebrate May Day today," said the Mayor, twiddling her heavy chains. Jock avoided her gaze. He wished she would stop looking at him like a two-headed devil.

Angie pulled him away. "Come on, let's check on Morgan."

He nodded gratefully. The longer he stared, the closer he came to coming undone.

❄

THE TEA SHOP was eerily silent. Morgan stood alone in front of the broken window, looking out with a dazed expression.

"You go home, love," Angie said to her kindly. "You need an early night after the shock you've had. I'll call you if there's any news."

"Thanks."

Morgan slipped on her suede jacket. Jimmy Eat World blared from her earphones as she walked out the door.

Moments later, Sapphire's big-eared attendant appeared. Her smile was gone now, replaced with lips that had been chewed without remorse.

"Oh, Bronwyn!" Angie wrapped her arms around her and hugged her tight as she convulsed with sobs.

Jock stood back, embarrassed. Normally this would be his cue to leave, but if he left now, he might miss something.

While Angie was calming Bronwyn down, Stavely reappeared. His shoes smelt of sheep dung and he had mud on his trousers.

"If you don't mind, I'd like to ask you a few questions."

He produced a packet of Fishermen's Friend. He offered them around, but no one else wanted any, so he popped one in his own mouth and slipped them back in his pocket.

Bronwyn wiped her eyes with the back of her sleeve. "What did you want to ask me?"

"Well let's start with how well you know Sapphire."

"Well enough. I've worked for her for three years now."

"Do you consider her a friend?"

"We get along, but I don't really see her outside of work?"

Stavely ground his teeth and Jock wondered if he found it irritating, the way she made her answers sound like questions.

"I'm curious," said Stavely. "What made you carry on with the procession after Sapphire ran off? Weren't you worried?"

Bronwyn shook her head. "People were saying she had tummy trouble and we should cover for her. I never would have stayed on the float if I'd thought something bad had happened."

"I want you to think really carefully, Bronwyn. Did you see anything, or anyone who looked suspicious?"

"No."

"Think about it for a minute. Play the scene back in your head. Are you absolutely sure?"

She fell silent for a moment. "She was a little quiet, but she is sometimes. There was nothing out of the ordinary."

Stavely pursed his lips. "Well, if you remember anything, anything at all, please give me a ring. You've got my card."

Jock watched as he got up and walked towards the door. Just before he opened it, he turned back and addressed the room.

"Constable Wesley's down at the village hall organising a search party. It would be great if you could show him some support."

He didn't fix on anyone in particular. His comment seemed to be directed at everyone in the room, yet Jock felt like he was probably the intended target.

"Yes, of course."

He jumped to his feet. At last, something he could do.

❄

I walk among the search teams, brush shoulders with the locals as they hunt for their missing May Queen. I hug my secret to my chest. I like being here, among them, knowing what I know.

It's starting to grow dark as we move down the footpath towards the canal. The villagers are raucous and hot-headed, disinclined to listen. Despite Wesley's attempts to separate us into groups, there are still way too many of us. I get kneed in the back by a woman with a baby strapped to her chest. She smiles apologetically and I pretend to coo at the baby, but honestly, I can't understand why she's making such a martyr of herself. She ought to be sitting at home in front of the TV with half a bottle of wine in her belly, and that baby ought to be tucked up safe in bed.

I smother a laugh as someone stumbles over a mooring rope. The water down there is cold and bleak, just perfect for a drowning. We are getting close now and the feeling of adrenaline is building up inside me. I expect the police dogs to sniff it out right away. They stop right outside the lock keeper's cottage but then one of the handlers spots another trail and they are off, leading the dogs further and further away from the truth.

"Wrong way!" I want to shout after them.

Only one solitary figure lingers beside the canal path and I'm betting he has no idea of the significance. Someone should take pity on him, throw him a bone. But he won't get it from me. Because I'm not telling.

※

"They've found something!" someone yelled. "Down on the railway tracks!"

Jock watched in amazement as the entire party surged towards the railway. He stood in the doorway of a little cottage and waited for them to pass. It was only as the last of the group scurried off that the words reached his brain. Had they found the body?

"What is it?" he asked a woman at the back of the throng.

She narrowed her eyes, her bushy brows becoming one.

"Do I know you?"

He opened his mouth to reply but her friend butted in. "Whatever it was, it was small enough to fit in one of those evidence bags."

They hadn't found her then. That was all he needed to know. He looked up at the heavens. The promised rain had not materialised. Instead, the sky was splattered with stars, far more than he had ever seen in London. Part of him wanted to stay out all night. How could he possibly rest until he knew Sapphire was safe? But another part of him had already admitted defeat. His presence here wasn't adding anything.

He was cold and miserable, and sick of the way the locals kept staring at him. He might as well call it a night.

He turned back, trying to remember which way he had come. He had never had much sense of direction. He spotted a road sign up ahead, but it was in Welsh. There ought to have been an English equivalent, especially given that this was the English side of the border, but it had probably been stolen. He tried the GPS on his phone, but that was useless, too. He would have to go with his gut. He took the country lanes at a pace. He wasn't built to rush. He rarely even broke a sweat, but the panic was growing inside of him, billowing out like the endless darkness. He should never have left the group. There was no knowing who or what was out there.

Danger lurked around every corner and the twitching birds sent him hurtling along. The trees came alive, all of them moving, rustling. Nothing was silent. Nothing was still. Nothing was safe.

Sapphire's tea shop was still open when he finally reached the village. He peered in. Angie and Bronwyn were making drinks and sandwiches to fuel the search teams. Bronwyn's tears were all gone now, he noticed, as she carried a tray of pastries out of the kitchen. She looked strong and determined, managing a smile for the weary volunteers. Angie's eyes, by contrast, were red and raw, as if she had spent the entire time since he had last seen her peeling onions.

He helped himself to a paper cup of lemon squash.

"Any news?" he asked.

"No, nothing. They found a shoe down on the railway tracks but it turns out it belongs to a member of the search party."

"How did they manage to lose a shoe?"

"Some of them were carrying hip flasks. I think they got a bit tiddly."

"Ah."

He hung around, staring at the wall as he nibbled on a

slice of Battenberg. He wasn't particularly hungry, but he needed something to occupy his hands. He looked around as the last of the searchers came in and devoured the food like a plague of locusts. PC Wesley was amongst them. Jock watched as he accepted the cup of tea Angie pressed into his hands.

"What now?" she asked.

"That's it for the night. We'll resume the search in the morning."

"By then it will be too late." A tear rolled down her cheek. "The longer she's missing, the less likely it is she'll be found. Isn't that true?"

Wesley clasped his fingers together, as though he was afraid he might lose one.

"We're doing our best."

If only that were enough.

Jock felt a strange ache in his stomach as he left the tea shop. Probably, it was caused by eating too much cake, but the rest of his body ached, too. He walked across the cobbled street and saw that the lights were still on at the Dragon.

"Lock the door behind you," said Neil. "We're closed."

Jock did as he was told.

"You're welcome to have a drink, all the same." He poured himself a pint of ale.

"Thanks."

Jock was dog-tired but his body still buzzed with adrenaline.

"Been out on the search?" asked Dylan, the only other person at the bar.

He nodded.

"I hope they find her, but I don't like the chances."

"It's only been a few hours."

"Long enough for a May Queen."

Jock rubbed his eyes. "You think Peter Helston was innocent?"

"Anything's possible." Dylan looked at him with scrutiny. "You look like crap. Can I get you a pint?"

He attempted a smile. "I'm in a pub aren't I?"

"So what are you drinking?"

"Whatever you're having."

"OK. Two pints of Welshman's Ruin, please," Dylan said to Neil. "And a couple of shots of Venom."

Neil smiled a sadistic smile as he produced a bottle with no label from under the bar. Jock watched as he poured the dark liquid into two shot glasses then filled two pint glasses with beer: half larger, half brown ale. Good, he could drink ale. But now what was he doing? He watched as he took two more shot glasses and filled them with scotch, dumping one neatly in each pint.

"Here you go, lads."

Jock grimaced at the choice, but dutifully accepted his pint and shot.

"You're buying the next round," Dylan informed him, as they clinked shot glasses. He held his nose and downed it. Jock did his best to match him then took a big slug of his pint.

"Well?" Neil asked. "How is it?"

Jock shuddered.

"Tastes like dragon's piss." Dylan was laughing. He glanced wickedly at Jock. "We'll have another round."

"I haven't finished this one yet, and can't we just have a normal pint?"

"Not on your Nellie. We've started with the shots, so that's how we'll go on."

"Can we at least make them Sambucas?"

"Are you wimping out on me?"

"Yeah, I think I am."

Dylan shook his head, but he was probably bluffing. No one could drink a second round of that stuff. Not unless they had a second liver.

The Perfect Girl

❄

THE SUITCASE IS a dead weight as we wheel it along the canal path towards the boat. I almost jump out of my skin as a man approaches us, carrying a broom.

"Morning!"

He blocks our path.

"Morning," we chorus, neither one of us making eye contact.

"What you got in there? Must be heavy if it takes two of you to push it!"

"Books," I smile condescendingly. "Lots of old books."

"You look like you could use a hand."

"No, it's fine. We can manage."

"Really, it's no trouble."

To my horror, I realise the May Queen is moving, squirming about inside the suitcase. The idiot doesn't appear to have noticed, but the moment he does, it's all over. I fight the urge to shove him into the canal. But it's not in my nature to be careless. I've been so meticulous. I'm not about to slip up now.

He hovers at my side, not actually helping at all in any real sense. He just wants company, I suppose. Fleckford has turned into a village of gimps. I don't know where they've all come from. It's as if someone popped the lid off the sewer and they all bobbed up to the surface in a flood of human excrement: the May Day anarchists, the rubber-necking tourists and the worst of the lot, the journalists. They're just about everywhere, taking up so much room I can barely breathe.

Between us, we heave the suitcase onto the boat and our helper 'helps' further by untying our mooring ropes and flinging them back to us in a pale imitation of a cowboy. Why do people take it upon themselves to interfere like this? He's still watching as we pull away. Watching and waving, because he clearly has nothing better to do. I sit down on the suitcase, to keep it still as the boat starts up. The May Queen is wriggling inside. Must be time to knock her out again.

6

Jock awoke with a bad case of Welsh flu. The alcohol had put him into a heavy sleep, which he wouldn't otherwise have managed. But now he could feel it stripping away the lining of his stomach. He drank one pint of orange juice and one of liquid aspirin, then settled down in front of the toilet to disengage with his insides. He emerged weak and empty.

He traipsed downstairs, past Dylan, who was inexplicably *still* at the bar where he had left him.

"Man, you look like you've just given birth to a ferret!"

Jock grimaced. "How come you're so chipper?"

"I can take it, my friend. I can take it."

He glanced up at the TV, which was tuned to the BBC. "Have they found her?"

Dylan shook his head. "They haven't even drained the canal yet."

Jock swallowed the lump in his throat. "I'm sure it won't come to that."

"She's been missing for twenty-four hours. Trust me, something's happened."

He might have had more to say on the subject, but Jock

couldn't bear to hear it. He walked across the cobbles to the tea shop. The window was boarded up with wooden planks. They were like bandages, covering the gaping hole where the glass had been. Out here in the sticks, it would probably take days to repair and to add insult to injury, one of the letters had fallen off the sign, further contributing to the derelict appearance. You wouldn't even know the shop was open if it weren't for the words 'Open as Usual', written in large, spidery letters across the wood.

He felt compelled to go in, but once inside, he just stood in the middle of the shop and stared. It no longer felt quaint and kitsch. It wasn't just the shattered window. Something fundamental had changed in the atmosphere. It was no longer a cosy, English tea room. It was poignant and tragic; the home of the missing May Queen, a voyeur's paradise.

"Has there been any news?" he asked when he got to the front of the queue.

"No, nothing," Angie sniffed. "I don't know any more than you do."

"Sorry, I didn't mean to upset you."

She wiped her brow. "It's not you, Jock. It's all of these journalists badgering me with their bloody questions. They seem to think if they ask me enough times, I'll trip up and tell them something. Except I don't know what happened any more than they do. I wish I did."

"Are you sure you want to stay open? You must be under a lot of pressure."

"It's what Sapphire would want."

She glanced inadvertently at the cash register. Sapphire's disappearance was good for business, he guessed. Too bad she wasn't around to enjoy it.

"Sorry, Jock. What can I get you?"

"I'll just have a glass of orange juice, please." It was about all he could manage with a dicky tummy.

She pasted a smile onto her face and poured his juice.

"Here you go. Sorry about the wait."

He looked around for somewhere to sit. Every table seemed to be taken. He had just resolved to neck his juice and go, when he saw an elderly woman rise to her feet. The old man with her was putting his coat on. It looked like they were leaving. He moved towards their table and hovered at a polite distance, pretending to examine the pictures on the wall. Someone else wasn't quite as discreet.

"You off?" Dylan asked the woman.

"Yes, we …"

Before she could even finish her sentence, he parked himself in her seat. The woman puffed out her cheeks in distaste, but Dylan had no shame. He put his hands behind his head and leaned back in contentment.

"Alright, Jock?" he called out. "I thought it was you! What are you doing skulking in the corner?"

Jock mumbled something incomprehensible and wished the elderly couple would get a move on.

"Oh, waiting for a table, were you?"

How Dylan could decipher his mumble, Jock had no idea. He wasn't entirely sure what he had said himself.

"I was loitering by the table in the middle," Dylan went on loudly. "They said they were leaving, but they've been gas-bagging for the last five minutes. On and on and on, they go. Hey, are you going to sit down or what?"

"Just a sec."

He pretended to struggle with the toggles on his coat while the elderly man shuffled away on his Zimmer frame. Oh, to be like Dylan and not have to worry about social graces! How easy his life must be!

He sat down and drank his orange juice. A couple of minutes later, Morgan trudged over and dumped a pot of tea and a plate of teacakes in front of Dylan. She looked like she would have happily dumped them in his lap. Did she have something against Dylan, he wondered, or was she just feeling on edge after yesterday?

"Another cup for my good friend here," Dylan said brightly. "Go on, have a teacake, Jock. They're scrumptious."

"I'm fine, thanks," he protested, but Dylan plonked one on a plate for him anyway.

He took a bite. It was warm and buttery. Maybe it was just what he needed.

"I bet she's filthy," Dylan murmured, as Morgan slinked away. "You can see it in her eyes."

Jock reddened. "Keep your voice down, will you? She'll hear you!"

Dylan shrugged. "Not really my type, anyway. Bit too sullen."

A bit too young, Jock thought.

He took another bite of his teacake. "How did you get served so quickly anyway? The queue's practically out the door."

Dylan laughed. "Well, for a start, I never queue. It's against my religion." He touched the side of the teapot. "Shall I be mother?"

Without waiting for an answer, he splashed a little milk into each of their cups then poured the tea.

"Cheers!" He toasted Jock with his cup.

Jock didn't have the energy to argue. His mind had drifted back to the last few moments before he lost sight of Sapphire. How fast she had gone, running as if her life depended on it. His best hope was that she was still out there, hiding somewhere, until it was safe to return. He couldn't bear to think of any other possibility.

Dylan slurped his tea and wolfed down the rest of his teacakes. Once he had finished, he rose to his feet.

"You off?"

"Yeah, got to see a man about a dog. See you at the Dragon later?"

"Yeah, maybe."

Dylan's departure seemed a little abrupt until Angie came over with the bill. It was only then that Jock realised he hadn't left any money. Cheeky bugger! He would have to foot the bill himself.

"You and Dylan are getting along then?" She picked up the empty plates.

"I suppose so."

At least Dylan's shenanigans helped take his mind off Sapphire. He considered telling Angie what had happened, but he was too embarrassed. Best not make a fuss.

"You know him well?"

"Oh, everybody knows Dylan." There was a ghost of a smile.

"How come?"

"Well, for one thing, he's always in here."

"Doesn't he have a job?"

"Don't you?"

He rolled his eyes. "Haven't heard that one before."

"Sorry." She tucked a strand of her honey-blonde hair behind her ears. "Actually, he's on gardening leave."

"Why?"

"He had a very stressful job. Are you always this nosey?"

"Just got an enquiring mind."

"Ah, is that what it is?"

He poured himself the last cup of tea from the pot and glanced towards the kitchen, remembering how Sapphire had walked out the first time he had seen her. How beautiful she had looked. How perfect. He had a sudden revelation that his sickness wasn't just from the alcohol. He was suffering withdrawal symptoms. He was addicted to her and he had no idea if he was ever going to see her again. A fresh wave of nausea hit and he hunched over, waiting for it to pass.

Once the sickness had eased off a bit, he fished a pad and pen from his bag. If anything could take his mind off her, it was his writing. He didn't think he could bear to look at his laptop right now, but that was OK. Sometimes he liked to write freehand. It helped the creative juices flow. He wrote quickly, his mind forming words faster than he could scribble them down. He poured all his confusion and grief into the book, diverting it into the plight of his amateur sleuth, Audrey Winifred, as she grappled with her latest case.

"My, what pretty handwriting you have."

He turned to see DCI Stavely, the collar of his mac turned up against the wind.

"Thank you," he said evenly. "What can I do for you?"

"Do you mind if I ask you a few more questions?"

"No, go ahead." He tried to remain calm. If he were running the investigation, he would want to talk to him, too.

"What are you doing in Fleckford, Mr Skone?"

He swallowed. "Looking for inspiration." The panicky feeling had reached the pit of his stomach.

Stavely raised a bushy eyebrow. "That's a new one on me." He leaned closer, giving Jock an unnecessary close-up of the crow's feet around his eyes. "You're a mystery writer, aren't you? So tell me, Jock, who do you think did it?"

Jock didn't like the way he had worded the question. Not 'what happened?' but 'who did it?' How could he be so sure?

"In my books, it's always the last person you'd ever suspect. The one you'd never think could be a criminal. Either that, or the person who is so obviously bad, you rule them out straight away."

"Huh! If only it were that simple." Stavely attempted a smile, but it looked unnatural on his downward-slanted mouth. "A lot of people know something about this case and most of them think what they know is insignificant. My job is to get all the pieces and stick them together so I'm looking at the whole picture. So any time you want to share your piece, that's fine with me."

"I don't know anything."

He reached for the teapot. He didn't quite know how he managed to keep his hand steady.

"No, of course you don't. Do you love her, Jock?"

"Sapphire?" He couldn't keep the quiver from his voice. "We'd only just met."

Stavely tilted his head. "That doesn't really answer the question, though, does it? Did you love her? Even a little bit?"

Jock felt his cheeks tingle. His heart quickened and his brow filled with sweat. He had heard of women having hot flushes, but not men. He gave an emphatic shake of his head. "You can't love someone a little bit. Either you love them or you don't. I like Sapphire very much. I wanted to get to know her better, but it's too soon to be talking about love."

Stavely gave him a long, hard look. It was just a matter of time until they found his fingerprints in her flat.

7

"She's coming round."

The gentle voice jarred Sapphire's head. Gingerly, she opened her eyes. She was lying on a cold, hard floor, surrounded by women in posh dresses.

"What is this? A party?"

Her eyes shifted from left to right. The walls were painted a very dark shade of metallic green, the exact shade found in model aeroplane kits. There were no windows or lamps. The only source of illumination was a beam of light that shone from under the door at the top of a flight of stone steps.

"What is this?"

Silence.

It was as if they wanted her to remember. She closed her eyes and tried to replay the memory, but her mind was filled with strange images that didn't ring true. She willed herself not to panic, but she couldn't remember where she was or how she had got there. She tried to stand, but she couldn't get her balance. She grabbed someone's arm to steady herself but missed and sank back down to the floor. She was like a coin rattling around in a jar, unable to stop the perpetual motion.

She must have been drinking. What on earth had possessed her?

"Where am I?"

She was aware of a terrible smell, like extremely rotten eggs.

One of the women knelt down beside her. Her ice-blue eyes were filled with concern. "Shh! Don't try to speak. You must rest."

There was a certain rhythm to the way she spoke that suggested she wasn't British. German? Dutch? Scandinavian maybe. Her mangled mind couldn't work it out. She patted herself down, but she had no bag or pockets. She glanced about. "Can someone lend me a phone?"

"A phone?"

"Look, I really don't feel well. Could you call me a taxi?"

The other women exchanged glances, as if she had suggested they rob a bank.

"I want to go home."

"That's what we all want," said the woman with the ice-blue eyes.

Sapphire looked at each of them in turn, taking in the significance of their dress. One had flowers sewn into her hair and another had a rusty tiara. May Queens. They were all May Queens.

"What's going on?"

She felt as if she were hanging from the edge of a cliff. She needed to pull herself back up, but she didn't quite know how.

"Please!" whispered the foreigner. "You must keep quiet or there'll be trouble. For all of us."

The women, one of them just a schoolgirl, looked at her with mute sympathy.

"What is this place?" She lowered her voice. "What are we doing here?"

The young girl covered her mouth with her hand, as if to stop herself from speaking.

"What's wrong with you all?"

Her feet made contact with the ground, wobbling as she took a few tentative steps towards the stairs. She gripped the rail with both hands and pulled herself up onto the first step.

"Sapphire, don't!"

She looked down. How did they know her name? She didn't remember telling them. But then, she didn't remember a great deal. The last thing she recalled was talking to a customer. He had come back to the shop for a scarf he had left behind – deliberately, she suspected. The rest was a complete haze. She couldn't even remember shutting the door. Maybe she hadn't. Maybe he had done something to her.

Her memories might have been stuck, but her survival instincts were sound. She needed to do whatever it took to get out. Inch by inch, she climbed her way up until she reached the top step. She searched for a handle, but there wasn't one. She grabbed the bottom edge of the door frame and pulled, but it wouldn't budge. She tried pushing instead. The door was stuck fast.

"Come back down," one of the May Queens called out to her. "You can't get out that way."

"Then how?" She pounded on the door with her fists. "Help!" she shouted. "Help!"

"Shh!" the others hissed in unison. "They'll hear you!"

"Who'll hear me?"

"You don't know what will happen!"

"Then tell me!"

Her blue-eyed friend climbed the steps and put a hand on her shoulder.

"Hey! What are you doing?"

"We're just trying to keep you safe. You haven't learnt the rules yet. You don't know what you're getting into."

There was really only so long she could bang and kick the

door, anyway. She sank down onto the top step, giving into the pain of her aching head. She was dizzy and confused but most of all, she was frightened. She looked around the dusty cellar. There were no chairs or tables, not even a rug to lie on.

"What's going on? Just tell me. I can't stand it."

"My name is Ingrid," the woman said softly. "And I was a May Queen, just like you."

"What happened?" Sapphire felt her voice quiver. "How did we all end up here?"

"None of us remember exactly. But we were taken. We were all taken."

"By whom? Don't you know anything at all?"

"Shh!" Ingrid pressed her finger to her lips. "From now on, you must be as quiet as a ghost. It is very important. It's best not to attract attention."

"From whom?"

Ingrid looked up at the locked door with foreboding.

※

IF THE MOOD of the mob had been hopeful that first night, a sense of destructive pessimism followed. Trainloads of people arrived from London and Cardiff, swelling the search party numbers to unhelpful levels. Some, Jock suspected, just came to ogle the village where the latest May Queen had disappeared. And then there were the news crews, armed with their cameras and booms. Few ventured into the Dragon, though. The dimmed lights and threadbare stools weren't to many people's liking, nor was Neil's sour wit.

Jock and Dylan sat at the bar that night, eating microwaved shepherd's pies while Neil flicked through the TV channels.

"Stop! Stop!" Jock cried, as a picture of Sapphire flashed up on the screen. "Quick, put the sound up!"

"The May Queen is an ancient tradition which dates back

to Pagan times," an historian was explaining. "Traditionally, the May Queen led the May Day festivities, just as she does today, and legend has it that at the end of the day, she was sacrificed to the gods."

The presenter turned to the guest sitting opposite him in the studio. Jock sat up straight as he realised who it was.

"DCI Stavely, do you think the history of the May Queen tradition has any bearing on the disappearance of Sapphire Butterworth and indeed, on any of the other missing May Queens?"

Stavely looked directly into the camera. "Let me make one thing clear. We are treating Sapphire Butterworth's disappearance as an isolated incident. The Hampton Inquiry found Peter Helston guilty of the murder of the other missing May Queens and we haven't seen any new evidence to contradict those findings."

"But the bodies were never found, were they?"

"Helston died before he could lead us to them. But all the evidence still points to him as the so-called 'May Queen Killer'."

"You don't think there's a chance you got it wrong?"

"Given the facts of the case, it's highly unlikely." Stavely raised a hand to his temple. It was an unconscious movement, one he probably would have reconsidered if he could see his own reflection in the camera. He must have been wearing a little stage make-up, because the action of mopping his brow created a tell-tale streak across his forehead.

The presenter honed in on him. "So you think it's more likely we've got a copycat on our hands?"

Stavely looked him right in the eyes. "I wouldn't like to speculate at this point." He unclipped his microphone, signalling that the interview was over.

"Wow, he looked a bit hot under the collar, didn't he?" said Dylan. "His mistake for agreeing to appear on a programme like that. I expect it was his boss's idea. Bad ideas usually are."

Jock shovelled his last forkful of pie into his mouth. "What could she have seen out there in the crowd to make her run off like that?"

"Not what, but who?"

Jock nodded and positioned his knife and fork together on his empty plate.

"You going out on the search tonight?" Dylan asked.

"No." He didn't think it would do any good.

"Good. I'll get the beers in, then."

He accepted and told himself that it made up for the money Dylan owed him. As much as he appreciated Dylan's company, he didn't entirely trust him. He got the feeling he would sell his own granny for a pint, if the opportunity should arise.

Dylan necked his beer with impressive speed. "I heard they're going to feature Sapphire on Crimebusters. They're doing a re-enactment to see if they can jog people's memories."

"I hope it helps."

Jock twiddled his beer mat between his thumb and forefinger. He wondered who they would get to play him.

"*Run peth eto os gwelwch yn dda!*" Dylan said suddenly, raising his glass to Neil. Neil nodded and Dylan embarked upon what appeared to be quite a long-winded anecdote in Welsh. Neil laughed appreciatively, which was odd as Jock could have sworn he was English. He was about to ask for a translation when a group of strangers approached the bar. He couldn't tell if they were May Day protesters or rubberneckers, but he knew instinctively that the group was not local and apparently, not welcome.

※

Jock awoke the next morning with a kink in his neck and a mark on his face, where it had got smooshed into the window. He had watched Sapphire's place for ages before he fell asleep, unable to shake the idea that she might return under the cover of darkness when there was no one around to see. Unfortunately, his vigil proved fruitless. He had seen nothing more interesting than a youth relieving himself in the street.

He got out of bed and walked over to the small hand basin. He looked in the mirror above the sink and saw that his face had a grey tinge to it. It had been a couple of days since he had last shaved and his chin was coarse and bristly. He held a flannel under the hot tap, which started off warm and grew increasingly molten. He shoved his scorched hand under the cold tap until it started to go numb from the cold. Then he switched back to the hot. He hated shaving.

The tea shop was surprisingly busy that morning. He would have thought people would drift away, after what had happened, but it was like there was an invisible force field drawing them in, more and more of them as each day passed.

"Morning, Jock." Angie attempted a breezy smile.

"How are you doing?" he asked.

"I've been better but at least the shop keeps me busy."

He glanced out the window as a delivery van pulled up with barrels of beer for the Dragon – an impressive number of them for such a quiet pub.

"So what can I get you?"

She produced a pad and pen from her pocket.

"A pot of Yorkshire tea, please, and a slice of Battenberg."

She nodded and disappeared back into the kitchen.

He tried not to stare as a very tall man entered the shop, ducking his head to fit through the doorframe. He wasn't just tall, he was gigantic. Jock had never seen anyone quite as big.

"Hey, how's the view from up there?" a young lad called out.

The giant didn't bother to answer. He probably heard it all

the time. Jock watched out of the corner of his eye as he strode towards the kitchen.

"Angela!" he called, an expectant smile on his sunburned face.

Angie flung down her tea towel and ran into his arms.

"I'm taking my break," she called to Morgan, who was serving a table full of rowdy pensioners.

Morgan scowled in response. From the look on her face, you would think the tea shop and everyone in it had been put there just to annoy her.

He watched as Angie walked down the street, hand in hand with the giant, and had a strange urge to run after her and beg her not to go with him. Then he caught himself. He was being paranoid. And judgmental. Just because Sapphire was missing, didn't mean anyone else was in danger. Did it?

Morgan came over and plonked his tea and cake down in front of him. He attempted a smile but she seemed positively hostile, glaring at him when he asked for a spoon.

"Er, that's OK. I'll get it myself."

"Like hell, you will!"

He wasn't sure if this meant he shouldn't get it himself or he should. He had just about resigned himself to stirring his tea with his pen when she stomped back and pressed a spoon into his hand.

"Thanks." His voice came out in a squeak. He would have to leave her a generous tip. Maybe then he wouldn't annoy her so much.

"Alright, Jock?" A shoeless Dylan greeted him in the doorway of the gents.

"Alright." *Where were Dylan's shoes?* He had a feeling he shouldn't ask.

"It's ridiculous," Dylan grumbled. "You can't even take a slash without some smeghead pointing a camera at you."

He glared at the cameraman who was standing at the sink.

"Hey, I'm just washing my hands, mate."

"Yeah? Then why'd you bring your boom?"

"Why d'you think? To stop some chav from nicking it!" The cameraman stalked off, dragging the offending article behind him.

Jock walked over to the urinal. He was about to pee when he realised Dylan was still loitering.

"What?"

"Nothing." Dylan smirked. "You just strike me as the kind of man who wees sitting down."

"Thanks."

❋

THE CRIMEBUSTERS RE-ENACTMENT IS A SCREAM. *I watch it over and over again, revelling in every mistake. They've got some young actress, barely out of her teens, playing the part of a woman well into her thirties. Am I the only one who can see through the May Queen's lies? The papers are all reporting that she's in her twenties. It's a mistake I'm sure she would relish and I'm not about to correct them. If they can't get the facts right, how can they possibly expect to find her?*

8

The small ballet studio seemed much bigger when it was empty. Gertrude went to the barre and did a few warm-up exercises, admiring her new pink leg warmers in the mirror. They were ever so slightly sparkly and glimmered subtly with every move she made.

"Morning, girls!"

Madame Beringer breezed into the room and removed her long woollen coat.

"Morning," Gertrude answered enthusiastically. She grabbed her sister by the hand and dragged her up to the front. "Madame, this is my sister, Claire."

"Hello, Claire," Madame said, looking her up and down. "Welcome to the class. I hope you will enjoy ballet as much as Gertrude!"

She smiled from one girl to the other and Gertrude smiled back. There was something about the way Madame Beringer pronounced her name that made it sound quite beautiful and exotic.

Claire was tongue-tied. She stood awkwardly as Gertrude asked Madame if they could have some music while they waited for the rest of the class to arrive.

"Why, of course."

Madame obliged with a piece from *The Nutcracker* and Gertrude began to spin and whirl.

"Come on, Claire!" she beckoned her sister, who was still looking a bit shy. But as soon as Claire started to dance, the energy in the room altered.

"Oh my!" exclaimed Madame Beringer. Gertrude saw tears well up in the teacher's eyes. She didn't understand what was wrong and ran over to give her a hug, but Madame pushed her gently aside.

"Claire!" she exclaimed, peering down at the tiny girl in her brand new leotard. "Claire, you have been blessed with a great gift! Come, we must talk to your mother."

Gertrude watched as Madame called their mother in and excitedly told her that Claire had the potential to be a great dancer. There was talk of extra lessons and scholarships, and nobody mentioned Gertrude once. Nobody even looked at her.

"I taught Claire to dance like that," she chipped in, determined to get them to notice her.

"Well done, darling," her mother said, without even turning around. Claire, meanwhile, continued to pirouette around the room, oblivious to the sensation she was creating. Gertrude sat cross-legged in the most uncomfortable spot she could find on the wooden floor. Ballet had been her thing, her favourite thing, but now it was all Claire's.

She continued the lessons for a while, but her enjoyment was never the same as Madame Beringer cooed and exclaimed over her sister's incredible prowess. She loved ballet, probably always would, but she just couldn't bear it.

"I don't think I want to dance anymore," she told her mum on the way home from class a few weeks later.

"OK."

Gertrude felt a lump rise up in her throat. Her mother had accepted it without a word. All she had wanted was for her to reassure her, to tell her how good she was, that it would be a waste of her talent not to continue, but her mother didn't say anything of the sort. She was too preoccupied with Claire.

So Gertrude sat at home while Claire spent more and more time at the Ballet School.

"Maybe you would like to join the Brownies?" her mother suggested one night after she dropped Claire off for yet another lesson.

"Brownies?"

Gertrude ran up to her room and slammed the door in disgust. She tore down her posters of Darcey Bussell and the girls from *Fame*, and tossed them all in the bin, immediately regretting their loss. Then she threw herself down on her bed and sobbed her little heart out.

❄

MORGAN SAT by herself at the bar of the Dragon, chewing a strand of her long, brown hair. Jock considered tiptoeing past, but Neil saw him come in and asked if he wanted his usual.

"Yes please. Er ... Hi, Morgan."

"How do you know my name?"

"From the tea shop."

She looked blank.

"I was there when the brick came through the window."

"Oh, that was you?"

Either she was a really great actress or she really was that self-absorbed.

"I haven't seen you in here before," he commented.

She glanced up at the moth-eaten dartboard. "That's because it's minging."

Jock glanced at Neil, but in fairness, he didn't look particularly offended.

"It was my friend's idea to meet here but she's late. Actually, she's always late."

"I know the feeling."

"You're not from around here, are you?" she said. Her eyes looked a little bloodshot and glassy.

"No."

"So where are you from?"

She took a swig from her bottle, some kind of purple alcopop. Not her first, judging by the empties lined up along the bar.

"Notting Hill."

"Never fancied London myself. I hear the streets are paved with dog poo."

He didn't deny it. "Did they find out who chucked the brick through the window yet?"

"Not as such. PC Wesley thinks it was probably those May Day protesters. Some of them go in for dramatic stunts, don't they? Remember when they poured tomato ketchup all over the Houses of Parliament?"

He nodded. His mum had been livid.

"I bet they did the sheep pen, too. I saw one of them with a couple of whippets."

Jock frowned. "Would a whippet savage a lamb?"

"It would if you trained it to. Any dog could be dangerous in the wrong hands."

"Do you … do you think the May Day protesters took Sapphire?"

"No."

He looked at her closely. "How can you be so sure?"

"Well, what am I supposed to think? I mean, did you actually see anyone chasing her?"

"Now you mention it, no." *No one but me.*

"No, she staged this." Morgan flicked her hair back behind her ear. "Just like she staged the May Queen contest."

"What do you mean?"

She glanced quickly around the bar. "Don't tell anyone or I'll have to pay her back."

"What are you talking about?"

"She rigged it. Well, I don't know about the other contestants, but she paid me to drop out, right after they announced the finalists."

"She paid you?" He was incredulous, not just that Sapphire would pay Morgan off, but that Morgan would allow her to. Would she really turn down the chance to be May Queen for the day? Supposedly, she hadn't even known about the May Queen Killer. His curiosity was piqued.

"How much did she pay you?"

"A grand."

He whistled. "That's a lot!"

She nodded. "Especially as I would have done it for half." She took another swig of her drink. "She acted like she didn't give a toss, but she really wanted to be May Queen. You should have seen the way she pressed the money into my hand. She needed me to take it."

He picked up his pint and took a long swallow.

"And do you know who took my place?" Morgan asked, her tongue loosened by the drink.

He shook his head.

"Bronwyn. Sapphire's cook. I'm betting that was her doing, too. I mean, who'd pick Bronwyn for pity's sake? The girl has a face like a blob fish and a backside like a …"

"Yeah, I did think that was a bit odd. She seems popular, though."

"She was a charity choice and everyone loved it. You know, pick the ugly girl because we all feel sorry for her. Makes everyone feel all warm and fuzzy. But that's not why Sapphire did it. She just wanted to cut down the competition. There was no way they'd crown Bronwyn May Queen over her."

"Do you think Bronwyn had anything to do with it?"

"Hard to tell, but I heard she and Nerys had a whale of a time on the float."

"Nerys?"

"Sapphire's other attendant. I heard they were taking it in turns to sit on the throne. I don't know why the Mayor didn't just stop the parade."

"Well, nobody really knew what had happened."

Morgan sipped her drink. "I heard there was some rumour going around that Sapphire had a tummy bug. I don't know where it came from, but I suspect the committee. Those old biddies put a lot of work into organising the fair. They were hardly going to cancel." She took a big gulp of her drink. "God, Sapphire had better be coming back soon. Angie's never liked me. She's just looking for an excuse to get rid of me."

He thought of friendly, kind-hearted Angie and couldn't imagine her sacking anyone. He didn't envy her having to manage Morgan.

"Had you seriously never heard of the May Queen Killer?" He watched her closely.

"No, I don't watch the news."

"But you must have heard people talking?"

She shrugged. "I don't listen much."

That, he could believe.

"Babe! Are you ready to go?"

He turned to see another young woman who must have been Morgan's friend. Morgan hopped down from her barstool. "We're going on to Sonic."

He couldn't help wondering if she would even get into a club after drinking so many alcopops. She looked a bit unsteady on her feet.

"Hey, why don't you come with us?" her friend said, giving him an appraising look.

"Er, no thanks. I'm waiting for someone."

"Yeah, you're probably too old anyway," Morgan said, as she stumbled out the door.

He should have been insulted, but she was right. He had

never been into the clubbing scene. The one time he'd tried it, people had stared at him like he was their granddad. And he was only thirty, for Pete's sake. Still, a quiet drink was all he wanted. He decided to give Dylan ten more minutes. That was about how long it would take him to sink one last pint. But first, he needed a wiz.

He walked into the gents and unzipped his fly. He was just about to let loose when the door opened and a man approached. He heard an impressive gush of pee, in stark contrast to his own.

"Hello, Jock."

"Stavely."

Now this was weird. There was no way he was going to be able to pee now.

"So, anything you wanted to tell me?"

Jock couldn't be sure, since he refused to look up, but he thought Stavely was looking straight at him, in direct violation of the urinal code.

"Just a minute."

He willed himself to start weeing. All the while, Stavely's impressive torrent went on and on.

"Can't go?" Stavely asked, his own bladder finally relieved. "Well, why don't we talk about what's on your mind?"

Jock didn't want to talk to Stavely. He wanted to put himself away. But at that moment, his pee finally started. He wasn't going anywhere, not until he had finished watering the marigolds.

Stavely drummed his fingers against the wall. "So what was it you wanted to tell me?"

"I was with her the night before she disappeared," Jock blabbed. The words were out of his mouth before he even had time to think. "She invited me up for coffee, but I didn't stay the night. I didn't do or say anything to scare her. I certainly didn't kill her."

"I don't doubt it. Bet you feel better now you've got that off your chest, don't you?"

Jock nodded and pulled up his zip. He should probably mention what else he had discovered in Sapphire's flat that night, but they would find out soon enough if they took a good enough look. It wasn't for him to tell.

❄

Sapphire huddled with the other May Queens on the cold, hard floor. Only the closeness of their bodies brought any warmth. One snored like a warthog while the little one coughed incessantly in her sleep. It ought to have annoyed her, but she found those sounds strangely comforting.

She had strange, vivid dreams where she was May Queen, waving merrily to the crowd. But nobody waved back. They were all looking up at her with fear. Somewhere in the crowd was the May Queen Killer. She needed to hide, but she didn't even know what he or she looked like. It could be anyone.

"Follow the light," someone shouted at her and she was suddenly aware of a beam of light shining a path out of the parade. She jumped down from the float but it was a lot further than she had expected. She felt herself falling down, down, down until she jolted awake. She looked up and saw a beam of daylight as it filtered in through the gap under the cellar door. Her eyes were crusty from crying. She just wanted to go home.

"Morning," said Ingrid. "I hope you managed to get a little sleep?"

"A little."

"That's good. Here, you should drink this."

"Is that tea?"

"Yes. You should drink it while it's still warm."

She took the cup, draining the lukewarm liquid in a couple of mouthfuls. The tea was sweet and strong, with just a dash of milk, the way she liked it. She could have drunk a dozen cups, but one was all she was offered.

Sapphire looked down at the cup. It had the same distinctive leaf pattern as the ones she had in the tea shop.

"Is this one of mine?"

Ingrid shrugged. "I don't know."

"Can't you tell me anything?"

One of the other women stirred beside her. "We don't mean to be unhelpful," she said, sitting up. Her long, curly hair formed a frizzy mane around her shoulders.

"We just don't know much. They don't tell us anything."

"I'm sorry, what was your name again?" Sapphire asked.

"Fizz."

"What's that short for?"

"Elizabeth, obviously."

Under normal circumstances, she might have smiled.

"Take a moment to wake up," Ingrid said. "Fizz is going to lead us in some yoga in a minute. That's how we usually start the day."

"I'm not really into yoga," Sapphire confessed. She touched her throat. Her mouth was so dry that it hurt to speak.

"You should give it a go, all the same. It keeps us nimble and it relaxes the mind."

She stood at the back and watched as the others took their places. They moved in perfect unison, which made her wonder how many times they had done this. How long had these girls been here? She was afraid to ask.

A chill breeze rattled through the cellar, kicking up dust and the youngest girl, Harmony, coughed loudly. Sapphire looked around, but she couldn't see any water.

"There's nothing for the rest of you to drink?"

Fizz shook her head.

"I'm sorry. I didn't realise. I drank all the tea."

"It's OK," said Ingrid. "You needed it. You need to recover."

"Yes, but if I had known …"

"Don't fret," Fizz warned her. "There will be more. We just have to wait."

"How long?"

"I don't know. They might bring something later. If not, then tomorrow."

"God!"

She licked the dryness in her mouth and tried not to think about how thirsty she was. Her head throbbed intermittently, demanding more air, more water, but she was going to have to be patient. She didn't know how the others could stand it. She paced from one side of the room to the other. She had been ignoring the deep pressure in her bladder for a while, but it was becoming painful.

"Where are we supposed to pee?"

"Use the empty cup," Ingrid said. "They'll take it away when they collect the tray."

Sapphire shuddered but she wasn't sure how much longer she could hold it. With great indignity, she squatted over the dainty tea cup. She filled it right to the brim with dark, orange urine, a colour not unlike the tea that had originally been in it.

"What if the rest of you need to go?" She placed the cup by the steps.

"We'll use the tea tray," said Harmony.

"What if we need to … you know?"

"Have a guess."

"This is too much!"

She looked up at the ceiling. There were a few pipes, but none big enough to crawl through. There were no windows either and no significant cracks in the walls. As far as she could see, there was only one way in and one way out. Without tools or keys, it was impossible to get through a locked door.

"Tell me about the people who took us."

The others just looked away.

"You said they come down here?"

"Only to bring food and drink."

"So why don't we overpower them?"

Ingrid shook her head.

"Have you tried?"

The May Queens looked at each other. "There was another girl," said Ingrid. "She tried to escape."

"Well, what happened to her?"

"Don't ask me that. It's better you don't know."

More than anything, she desperately wanted to know. But there was a look in Ingrid's eyes, a look that begged her not to push it too far.

She sat down, defeated.

"What would you normally be doing now?" Ingrid asked a little later, as they huddled together on the floor.

"I'd be sitting down to breakfast."

Ingrid smiled. "What would you be having?"

She could feel their eyes upon her. "Maybe yoghurt, with fresh strawberries."

"Hmm …" Harmony licked her lips.

"Or eggs and beans on toast."

"God, I miss baked beans!"

"I miss eggs!"

She paused for dramatic effect. "Or even a slice of cake."

"Describe the cake," Fizz implored. The others listened eagerly, salivating at her every word.

"Well, my favourite is lemon drizzle cake. I make it myself. You take just the juiciest of lemons and—"

A loud, grating sound filled the air.

"What's that?" she whispered.

"That's the lift," Ingrid said grimly. "Someone's coming down."

9

The door opened slowly. Sapphire shielded her eyes as a torch shone down into the cellar. After so many hours in the half-light, the brightness burned.

Clunk.

Clunk.

Clunk went boots on the stone steps. The light grew brighter, the closer they came.

"Keep your eyes covered," Ingrid hissed. "Once you've seen their faces, they can never let you go."

Sapphire kept her hands over her face. The May Queen Killer was so close now. It was all she could do not to look. She could hear breathing, a little fast and heavy from the effort of the steps.

"Please let me go," she said, her voice shrill. "I haven't seen you. I can't tell anyone who you are."

The only reply was the sound of feet thudding back up the steps. The light grew dim as the footsteps retreated and she peeked through her fingers. The door opened and shut once more, leaving them to their darkness.

"Now what?"

"Now nothing," said Ingrid. "Just be thankful you were spared."

※

GERTRUDE SAT up sharply and threw off her covers. At first she thought a car had veered off the road, but when she pulled back the curtains, she saw that the outside lights were on. The loud buzzing noise was actually coming from the lawn mower. Swearing under her breath, she pulled on her dressing gown and stomped across the landing. The door to Claire's bedroom was wide open, a tangle of shoes and clothes spilling out into the hallway. Her sister lay face down on the bed, snoring contentedly. Nothing short of a civil war was likely to wake her.

Kicking a bright pink kitten heel out of the way, she trudged downstairs to find the back door swinging in the breeze. As she stepped outside, the lights came on in the house next door. Her cheeks burned at the thought that the neighbours were watching. She marched down the garden and leaned over her mother to switch off the mower.

"Are you mad?" her mother screamed, her face pale and anxious in the moonlight. "Can't you see I've got work to do?"

Gertrude thought quickly. "It's Claire," she lied. "She's got a fever. Do you know where the thermometer is?"

"It'll be in your father's study, where it always is."

Gertrude bit her lip. Her father had moved out years ago.

"I can't find it. Can't you help me for a minute? You can finish mowing later."

With an irritated sigh, her mother followed her back into the house. A couple of neighbours nosed over the garden fence, craning to see what was going on.

"Everything OK, love? Do you want some help?"

Her mother's head turned slightly in the direction of the

voices, but Gertrude looked straight ahead as she herded her mum back inside to bed.

❄

"WHAT'S THAT?" Jock asked, pressing his nose up against the glass.

"Fat Rascal," said Angie.

"I beg your pardon?"

"Fat Rascal. It's like a cross between a scone and a teacake."

Dylan smirked. "Sounds like it was made for you."

"Thanks, but I think I'll stick with my Battenberg."

Angie smiled. "You know what you like, don't you?"

Jock settled at the table by the newly repaired window and Dylan plonked himself down beside him. He never seemed to have anything better to do than hang around the tea shop – or the bar.

"You like this table, don't you?" Dylan said.

Jock shrugged. "I like looking out the window while I drink my tea."

"It's OK, as hobbies go. Of course, some people exercise."

Jock ignored him and took a bite of his cake. It was deliciously light and sweet. He felt guilty, enjoying such simple pleasures while Sapphire was still missing, but he had to get through the day somehow. He could go crazy thinking about her.

"You know, I would have thought this May Queen business would be right up your alley," Dylan said. "You write about mysteries for a living and now here's your chance to solve a real one."

"I'm not sure being a writer is much of a training for playing detective," Jock said, feeling a little defensive. "Not when there's a real life at stake."

"But you must have done some digging?"

He nodded. He had barely thought of anything else.

"So?"

"So I can't help thinking, why her? I mean, there were eight May Queens crowned on Saturday, three of them in this county, so why Sapphire?"

"Because she's blonde," Dylan said, without missing a beat. "I saw a couple of others interviewed on the local news. One was ginger and the other looked Indian, but the missing May Queens have always been blonde, haven't they?"

Dylan was right. Every single one of them had blonde hair and blue eyes.

"Why *is* that?"

"Because the first one was blonde," Dylan speculated. "The killer is trying to recreate their first time, over and over."

"How would you know?"

"I don't. I'm just trying to put myself in his shoes." He picked up his iPhone and began to play Angry Birds, signalling that the conversation was over.

"And what time do you call this?" Angie asked, as Morgan skulked in.

Morgan pulled a face. "I had a dentist appointment. Thought I told you?"

"No, you didn't."

"Uh oh, handbags at five paces," Dylan said loudly.

"Shh!"

Why did Dylan always have to poke his oar in?

"Then I must have told Bronwyn," said Morgan, determined she wasn't in the wrong.

"You don't work for Bronwyn."

"I don't work for you, either."

Angie blinked rapidly. For an awful moment, Jock thought she was going to cry. He busied himself with his laptop just in case.

"When is Sapphire coming back?" he heard Morgan whine.

"I really wish you'd stop asking me that."

"But you must know something! I thought she was your best friend?"

"I thought so, too," Angie said. "And frankly, I don't know what I'm going to do about the shop. I can't keep on authorising new stock."

He glanced up and saw that Bronwyn had come out of the kitchen. "We're all going to be out of a job, aren't we?"

"Not just yet. We can keep things ticking over for a few more weeks."

"And after that?"

"And after that, it will be out of our hands."

Jock stared at the screen in front of him. Come on, Sapphire. You have to come back now. He bent his head over his keyboard and bashed out a few hundred words. He looked up just in time to see Angie's boyfriend limbo under the door frame like some kind of superhuman.

Dylan looked up from his phone. "Alright, Simon? How was your trip?"

The giant nodded pleasantly. "Not bad. Not bad at all."

"Pity you had to come back to this."

Jock wasn't sure if he was talking about Sapphire or the fact that her tea shop had turned into a circus.

Simon nodded. "Do you mind if I sit with you? The place is chocka."

"Course."

Jock waited for an introduction, but Dylan went back to his Angry Birds with an air of studied concentration, so it fell upon him to introduce himself.

"Hi, I'm Jock."

"Yes, Angie told me about you."

"Told you or warned you?" Dylan asked.

Jock chose to ignore Dylan's remark.

"And you're Simon?"

"Thanks. I'd wondered."

Was that supposed to be a joke? If so, Simon was extremely deadpan.

"So ... er ... what do you do, Simon?"

"I teach environmental geography, amongst other things."

"Oh." He couldn't really think of anything to say to that – Good for you? I'm sorry? "What ... er ... what does that entail?"

This resulted in a long, drawn-out reply that made Jock wish he had never got out of bed that morning. Simon spoke in a slow, deliberate manner, enunciating each syllable as if it were his last. Every time he thought he had finished speaking, he started up again.

Jock glanced at the next table, where a group of people sat in ripped jeans and camouflage jackets.

"Someone should tell them May Day's over," Dylan said, a little too loudly.

Jock reddened, but to his relief, they didn't look up. Only one of them ordered anything, he noticed. The rest ate packed lunches they had brought with them. Some did so sneakily, by hiding their sandwiches in their laps, but one was quite brazen, as if he wanted to be challenged.

"Who do they think they are?" he whispered. He felt outraged on Sapphire's behalf. She would know how to deal with them.

"In a way, I can sympathise," Simon said.

"What?"

"I mean, of course there is a certain thug element that naturally attaches itself to these groups ..."

Jock nodded and stifled a yawn. He fought the urge to rest his head on the table and close his eyes.

"... But in their defence, I think these people have a genuine gripe with ..."

Jock glanced at Dylan, but he had got up from his chair and was pretending to examine some of the fifties memorabilia hanging on the wall.

"… in the face of the … er … ongoing global economic crisis … austerity measures …"

Jock tried not to watch as Dylan constructed a fake noose behind Simon's back and pretended to hang himself. He was being incredibly rude, even for Dylan, but that didn't stop the laughter that was welling up inside of him.

"… poor working conditions." Simon looked at Jock, as if he had asked him a question. Since Jock had no idea what the question was, he smiled awkwardly.

Simon looked round. "How about you, Dylan?"

"Sorry, just gotta point Percy at the porcelain," Dylan said and charged off towards the gents.

"Why isn't he wearing any shoes?" Jock asked, desperate to change the subject.

Simon shook his head. "Ah, Dylan and shoes. Now that's a complicated history."

Dylan returned a couple of minutes later, by which time Simon appeared to have run out of steam. Out of the corner of his eye, Jock was aware of Stavely approaching their table. He swallowed and loosened his collar. What did he want now?

Dylan looked up from his phone. "Oh yeah, Simon, the police came looking for you while you were away."

"What?" Simon turned from Dylan to Stavely, who was now standing in front of him.

"Simon Carter, I'd like you to come down to the station," Stavely said in a grim voice. His colleague Sweep appeared beside him.

"Why? What's going on?"

"We would like to question you in connection with the disappearance of Sapphire Butterworth."

Jock gasped. Why did they need to take him down the station? It had to be serious, didn't it?

Simon's nostrils flared with indignation. "I know my rights. If you want to talk to me, I demand a lawyer."

Stavely nodded. "We'll sort all that out down the station."

Simon opened his mouth and closed it again. For a moment, it seemed like he might resist, but then he looked towards the door, where Constable Wesley was standing, and he walked quietly out to the waiting Panda car. Without quite meaning to, Jock followed them to the door and watched them drive off.

"They think he's the May Queen Killer, don't they?"

He turned to see a shocked, frightened Angie behind him. She let out a strange, strangled sob and fled to the kitchen.

10

"Simon?" Dylan chuckled, as if it were all a great joke. "They think Simon is the May Queen Killer? Is that the best they can do?"

"It's not funny! Didn't you see how upset Angie was?"

"Yeah, well she has a tendency towards hysteria."

He glanced around the tea shop. Dozens of journalists sat tapping away on their handheld devices. Had anyone noticed Simon's arrest, he wondered, or were they all too engrossed in their own lives? Certainly, there didn't seem to be much of a buzz. If they were aware of what had happened, wouldn't they be tripping over themselves to question Angie?

After about ten minutes, she re-emerged from the kitchen, looking remarkably composed. Jock guessed she was aware that the walls had ears. She came over and stood by his table, pretending to look out at the street.

"Why did they arrest him?" she asked in a low voice. "He hasn't done anything wrong!"

"I'm not sure they *did* technically arrest him," Jock said. "From what I heard, they just wanted him to help them with their enquiries."

"Oh, we all know that's just a euphemism."

"Maybe they want to know if he saw anything suspicious while he was up in the mountains," Jock reasoned. He wasn't sure he believed it, but anything to comfort her.

She closed her eyes. "Stupid fishing trip. He didn't even catch any flipping fish!"

"Well, good luck to them interviewing him," Dylan said, as she went off to serve a customer. "I bet he talks even slower when he's nervous."

Jock shook his head. "I don't know how you can joke about it."

"Oh come on, it's never going to be Simon, is it?"

"Then what do they want with him?"

"Who knows? They've got to look like they're doing something, haven't they? Just be grateful it's him and not you."

❄

"What on earth have you done?"

Gertrude looked around the utility room in disbelief. Her mother had scrawled all over the walls, from the ceiling, right down to the floor. She must have climbed up on top of the machines to have reached so high. She was lucky she hadn't fallen and hurt herself.

"What does it even say?" She squinted at it all. But the writing was too shaky to decipher.

Her mother opened and closed the washing machine door, repeating the same phrase over and over again: "Are you mad? Are you mad? Are you mad?"

Gertrude placed a hand on her shoulder. "Come on. Let's get you a cup of tea."

Her mother spun round. "No! You're trying to poison me!"

"Mum, I can promise you I'm not."

Her mother's face filled with rage. "Don't you dare call me that! Only my daughters call me Mum."

"But it's me, Gertrude!"

"You can't fool me! I can always tell when you're not you. You get that devilish look in your eye."

Gertrude bit her lip, choking back the words she wanted to say. She knew her mother couldn't help it, but that didn't make it any easier.

She stepped out of the utility room and drew a long breath. She would check on her mother again in ten minutes. She walked into the kitchen and pulled a tub of ice cream from the freezer. Anything to calm her nerves.

"Sorry, I got talking to some of the parents after the lesson," Claire said when she got in from work. She had enjoyed a short but glittering career as a ballerina, but these days she taught lessons at a local dance studio. "How's Mum?" she asked, almost as an afterthought.

"See for yourself."

They peered into the living room. Their mother sat in her favourite armchair, calmly knitting a cardigan while she watched *Coronation Street*. She didn't even look at Claire. She was too engrossed in her programme.

"She looks happy enough."

"Yeah, she's nice and calm now. Might attempt to get some dinner into her."

"Good luck." Claire checked her mobile. "I need to get ready to go out. I'm meeting my friends in half an hour."

❄

"I'll put the kettle on, shall I?" said Fizz.

Sapphire opened her eyes and blinked. For a moment, she thought Fizz was serious. Then an unwelcome draft blew across the cellar and she realised it was just a joke. She closed her eyes again and attempted to go back to sleep, but all around her, the other May Queens were starting to stir and the warm pile of bodies she had been snuggling against pulled apart.

"Right, who's first in the shower?" Fizz called.

"You go ahead," Ingrid said, sounding tired.

Sapphire watched as Fizz mimed stepping into the shower and hummed as she lathered herself under the imaginary jet. "Oh crap, I'm going to be late for work," she cried, pretending to rub herself down. She tossed her imaginary towel on the floor and pretended to dress in an elaborate outfit.

"I am always cleaning up after you!" Harmony scolded her, stooping down to pick up the invisible towel from the floor.

"You must all have a lot of time on your hands," Sapphire said, shaking her head at their display.

Ingrid nodded. "And so do you now."

"Hey, I'm just going downstairs to the loo," Harmony said.

Politely, they all looked away and pretended not to listen.

"I can't go!"

"Sing Twinkle Twinkle." Ingrid told her. "Always works for me."

"Is there anything for breakfast?" Sapphire asked hopefully.

"'Fraid not," Ingrid said. "No one's been down."

"How about some champagne?" said Fizz. She made a show of wrestling with the cork, before spilling the imaginary liquid into each of their hands.

"Ah, the real reason for your name now becomes apparent," Sapphire said with a smile.

"Where's my champagne?" Harmony held out her hands.

"You're underage."

"Oh, go on! No one's gonna know!"

"Oh, alright then. But don't tell anyone, or I'll lose my licence."

"What'll we drink to?" Sapphire asked. She was a little tired of this charade, but at the same time, impressed by the lengths they were willing to go to.

"To friends," said Harmony. "May we never argue and never part."

※

JOCK COULDN'T MISS the cover of the *Fleckford Star*, splayed out on the bar at the Dragon.

'Is this the face of the real May Queen Killer?' the caption read. Underneath was a terrible picture of Simon, towering over the village like Godzilla.

"It's not just the Star," Dylan said. "It's in the national papers, too. Guess those journalists were on the ball after all. They're saying some terrible things about Simon, all of it lies, I'm sure."

Jock scanned the article.

"How well do you know him?"

"Well enough."

"And you trust him?"

"Simon? He's like a human tractor – slow and steady. He could bore for England."

"You're not a fan then?"

"Oh, no – he's sound. You won't meet a nicer fellow than Simon. Believe me, he's no killer."

They walked over the cobbles to the tea shop. There were other cafes dotted up and down the street, but they never even considered going anywhere else.

"Hello," Dylan said, as Bronwyn approached their table. "What are you doing above stairs?"

"Angie asked me to swap with her. She wasn't feeling up to serving customers today."

"I'm amazed she's come in at all," Jock said.

Bronwyn looked at him a little oddly, as if trying to work

out who he was. He had one of those faces that people instantly forgot.

"Well, that's Angie for you. Good Protestant work ethic," Dylan said.

Bronwyn tapped her foot. "So, what will it be, boys?"

"A pot of tea and a slice of Battenberg, please," Jock said.

Dylan patted his tummy. "Nothing for me, thanks. Got to think of my figure."

Jock rolled his eyes.

"Hmm, what blend is that?" Dylan asked when she returned with the tea.

"Just the normal Yorkshire," Bronwyn said, setting it down.

"Are you sure? It smells like heaven."

"Dylan, do you want a cup?" Jock asked.

"Well, if you insist."

Dylan poured some tea into Jock's cup and took a sip.

"I'll get another cup then."

He noticed an old lady staring into her tea cup. He had seen her before. She had struck him as a lively lady, the kind who refused to retire quietly. But there was no sparkle in her today. Her coiffured hair was less than immaculate and her face was bare of its usual make-up.

"That's Simon's mum," Bronwyn told him, as she handed him his cup.

No wonder she looked so wretched. He returned to his table and listened to Dylan rabbit on about Minecraft while he ate his cake. It was almost eleven and he hadn't even opened his laptop yet. Perhaps he should go somewhere a little quieter, where he could concentrate. He caught Bronwyn's eye. "Can I have the bill, please?"

Bronwyn nodded and scuttled off, but another ten minutes passed and she still hadn't brought it. Morgan was around, but he wasn't in the mood to deal with her. You never knew whether you were going to get friendly Morgan or moody

Morgan. He decided it would be easier to go up to the counter. Dylan trailed after him, caught up in the middle of a long anecdote about a Playboy bunny and a bullfrog.

Jock sniffed. "Can you smell that?"

Instead of answering, Dylan barged through the tassel curtain that led to the kitchen.

"I don't think we're supposed to go in there," Jock called after him.

He watched as Dylan grabbed a pair of oven gloves and pulled a tray out of the oven.

"Bloody Nora!" came Angie's voice. "I knew I should have left the baking to Bronwyn!"

"Can I have them?" Dylan asked. "I'm sure they'll be fine if I cut the tops off."

"Help yourself." Angie let out a strangled sob.

"What's up?"

"What do you think?" she hissed, her voice a little too loud. "He spent the night in a cell, Dylan, and they still won't let him go. How could they possibly think it was Simon? He wouldn't hurt a fly!"

"Well, they must think they've got something on him," Dylan said. "But whatever it is, it's not enough. Otherwise they would have charged him by now."

"Of course they haven't got anything on him!" she snapped. "He hasn't done anything! They're just picking on him because he's big and he doesn't have an alibi."

"No, it's more than that," Dylan said, a bit too loudly. "There must be some other evidence that's led them to this."

"Dylan!" Jock tried to warn him, but it was too late. Simon's mum was right next to Jock at the counter, trying to see into the kitchen.

"You think my Simon did it?" Her voice crackled a little as she spoke.

Dylan peered out of the kitchen. "No, that's not what I said."

Simon's mum shuffled towards him, wobbling precariously on her walking stick.

"Let me tell you something about Simon," she said. "It's not easy for him, being his size. All his life, he's had people point fingers at him, calling him a freak and now the police think they can pin this on him, too. Well, it isn't right!"

"Oh, Verity!"

Angie stepped through the curtains to soothe her but it all seemed too much for the old lady. She leaned heavily against the wall and then sank to the floor, her mouth quivering and her eyes half closed.

11

"She's breathing." said Dylan, kneeling down beside her. "But we need to get her to hospital. Come on, we'll take my car."

Jock cleared his throat. "I don't think you should be driving. Not after the skinful you had last night."

"What? I'm fine."

"No, he's right," Angie said. "You drive, Jock."

Jock reddened. "I can't. I haven't passed my test."

"Right then, ring 999."

Verity pulled herself up into a sitting position. "I'm fine. Really. Just help me up, will you?"

"So … Should I call an ambulance?" Jock asked, as he helped her into a chair.

"Don't be silly, dear. I told you, I'm fine." She dusted off her skirt as if nothing had happened and glared at Dylan. "You really think my Simon is guilty?"

"Of course not."

Jock believed him. From what he knew of Dylan, he wouldn't lie, not even to appease an old lady.

"Then why are they holding him so long?" She looked at

each of them in turn, as if expecting them to provide an answer.

A couple of journalists murmured conspiratorially.

"Let's take this into the kitchen," Angie said.

Verity grabbed Jock's arm to steady herself as they walked through. He squirmed with embarrassment, but he couldn't very well refuse.

The kitchen smelt of charcoal, mingled with chocolate chips. Angie indicated a chair in the corner for Verity, but she continued to cling to Jock, until he couldn't stand it another minute.

"I'm sorry," the words spilled from his mouth before he even knew what he was going to say. "I'm late for … an appointment. I really have to go."

Dylan shook his head as he pulled himself from Verity's grasp. Jock knew he was being a wimp, but he felt like he couldn't get enough air. He had to get outside.

❄

Why hadn't they replaced that stupid doorbell? Gertrude wondered, as she went to answer it. It made the most irritating noise. She wanted to punch it. She opened the door and immediately regretted it.

"Hello, Fiona Hinklebury, Department for Work and Pensions."

Fiona's ready-made smile probably came free with her sensible, navy blue suit.

"Yes, we've met before," Gertrude tried to smooth the worry lines from her forehead. "Should we be expecting you?"

"I made the appointment with your mother last week. Didn't she mention it?"

"No."

Fiona looked past Gertrude, into the immaculately clean hallway. "Is your mother in?"

Reluctantly, she led Fiona through to the lounge, where her mother was drinking tea in front of *Emmerdale*.

"Mum, this is Fiona—"

"Yes, yes, I know. Come on in. Can I get you a cup of tea?"

"Not for me, thanks." Fiona smiled pleasantly and perched her bony bottom on the sofa. "You don't mind if I ask you a few questions, Maureen? Just to see how you're doing."

Gertrude hovered in the doorway, trying to see her mother as Fiona must have seen her, sitting so calmly in her armchair, neatly dressed and washed. Where had Fiona been an hour ago, when she was screaming at the yoghurts in Tesco?

"What do you want to know?" she asked, taking a seat in between her mother and Fiona.

"Actually, I think I would like that cup of tea after all," Fiona said.

Her mum smiled at her. "Gertrude, would you be a dear?"

"Er ... yes, of course."

"She is a gem," she heard her mother say, as she left the room. "But she does insist on doing things for me and it's really not necessary. She should be out living her own life, don't you agree?"

Rage rippled inside Gertrude. She tapped her foot as the kettle boiled, the noise drowning out the conversation in the living room. What to do? What to do? She seized her phone and texted Claire:

'DWP are here. Mum acting normal. HELP!'

She kept glancing at the phone but Claire didn't text back. She was probably in the middle of a class, instructing a dozen or so tiny tots on how to point their toes. Just before the kettle reached boiling point, she took it off the heat and slopped the water into a cup. She didn't even use real tea leaves, just dunked a teabag into the mug and showed it some milk.

"Here," she set it down on the coffee table.

"Thank you. Do you have any sugar?"

She stalked back to the kitchen. While she rummaged around in the cupboard, her phone beeped:

'Show them the utility room!'

She smiled. Claire was good.

"So your mother's been telling me she's feeling much better," Fiona said when Gertrude returned with the sugar. "Perhaps it's time for her to take the first steps towards getting back to work?"

"No way! That's ridiculous!"

Gertrude ignored the hurt look on her mother's face. If the situation weren't so horrendous, she would have laughed.

"Wouldn't you like to re-enter the workplace yourself, Gertrude?" Fiona consulted her notes. "It says here you've—"

"Never worked," Gertrude said. "How can I when Mum needs a full-time carer?"

Fiona screwed up her forehead. "But if your mother is getting better…"

"She is not getting better," Gertrude said, through clenched teeth. "She's always had lucid days, but it never lasts. Then we're back to the same old pattern: cleaning the house for hours on end, refusing to eat or drink to the extent that I've had to take her to A&E and have you seen what she's done to the utility room? Come on, I'll show you."

"Well, I…"

Reluctantly, Fiona followed her across the hall. Gertrude pulled open the utility room door and her jaw dropped in shock. The walls were completely bare and the room whiffed of fresh paint. Golden magnolia, to be precise.

"When did you do this?" she gasped, turning to look at her mum, who had followed them.

"When you were out."

"But I never go out!"

"Oh, come on. Don't exaggerate."

"I'm not. You must have done it in the night! Where did you even get the paint?"

Her mother smiled, as if this were all completely normal. "I just wanted it to be a surprise, dear. It was getting so tatty in here."

"Where are the washing machine and dryer?"

"I just popped them outside. Don't worry, I'll put everything back once the walls are dry."

"But how? Those machines weigh a ton."

"Oh, they weren't that bad."

Gertrude shook her head. If the DWP needed evidence that her mother was bonkers, surely this was it.

"You see, there's no knowing what she might do from one moment to the next," she explained to Fiona in the corridor. "She might be right as rain one minute, but completely barking the next."

"Tell me, Gertrude," Fiona said, quietly. "Is your father still in the picture?"

Gertrude snorted. "He's not even in the country, as far as I know. It's just the three of us. Has been for a while."

"I see, well, thanks for the tea." She edged towards the door. "I'll be in touch about the next step."

"What next step?"

"The next step in getting you and your mother back to work." She attempted a friendly smile. "Don't look so worried, Gertrude. You'll both get plenty of help. We can assist you with everything from CV writing, to interview technique. We can even help you find something decent to wear, if you'd like." She cast an uncomfortable eye over her shapeless tent dress and worn, beige slippers. "I'm sure you'll be just fine!"

The moment she was out the door, Gertrude picked up her tea cup and hurled it at the wall. She watched with satisfaction as it smashed to pieces. She didn't even care when she cut her finger cleaning it up. In fact, it felt kind of good.

By the time Claire got home, she had everything under control. The floor was freshly swept and mopped and all evidence of the broken cup had been hidden in the outside bin. Shame it had been one of her father's cups, but hopefully Claire wouldn't miss it.

"Hello?" Claire called, as she pulled off her coat and shoes.

"In the kitchen," Gertrude called back. She was about to launch into a description of her encounter with Fiona Hinklebury, when she realised Claire had a friend in tow.

"Oh! Hi, Gaby."

"Hi, Gertrude. How are you?"

She smiled. Of all Claire's friends, Gaby was probably the nicest, even if her fashion sense was a little over the top.

"Fine thanks." She pulled off her marigolds.

"How's your mum? Claire said she was doing a bit better?"

"Not too bad at the moment. A bit up and down, you know how it is."

Gaby nodded. But she didn't really know. How could she?

"So tell me your news," Claire said, as she and Gaby settled at the kitchen table with steaming mugs of hot chocolate. Gertrude lingered nearby, pretending to busy herself with the dishwasher. She wanted to sit with them and join in their chit-chat, but she didn't quite know how.

Gaby's eyes gleamed. "I've been nominated for May Queen!" she squealed.

"May Queen?" Claire said, absently. "Aren't you a little old for that?"

Gaby laughed. "Who are you calling old? I'm a year younger than you!"

Claire smiled. "I know. I just thought, you know, it was for schoolgirls or something?"

"Well it's not. There's no age limit."

Gertrude caught the look on Claire's face. Her eyes narrowed and the smile froze on her lips. Claire wanted to be May Queen. She had just made up her mind. And what Claire wanted, Claire got.

Jock spent the afternoon in Fleckford Library. He had always loved libraries. There was something incredibly soothing about the combination of dust and mildew that hung in the air. He opened his laptop and read over what he had written the day before, but every time he started to get into the story, Sapphire would drift into his consciousness. It was no good. He put his work aside and started scrolling through old newspapers. He wanted to read everything he could get his hands on about Peter Helston, the so-called May Queen Killer. Several books had been written about him, detailing everything, from his apparently ordinary life as a family man and academic, to his arrest and subsequent confession. None of his friends or family had suspected him. No one had come forward to say they had always had their suspicions. Quite the opposite. Friend after friend had said how shocked they were. Many were convinced of his innocence – none more than his wife, Daphne.

After confessing to the murders, Peter had promised to reveal the burial place of the missing May Queens. But on the morning he was due to lead the police to their final resting place, he was found dead – hanged in his cell. The official story was that he had killed himself, but there were numerous conspiracy theorists who contended otherwise.

Jock was just about to take a break when he discovered a documentary, which had aired after the last May Queen had disappeared. It included emotional interviews with the May Queen's family and friends, some of which were really hard to watch. His eyes welled up as he watched an interview with Claire Scutter's older sister, Gertrude.

"My sister had big plans," she said, barely able to control the pain in her voice. "She was about to open a ballet school here in Whiteford. She wanted to teach a new generation of children how to dance. She also wanted to travel and maybe one day get married and start a family. The May Queen Killer took so much away from us, more than just Claire. Our lives will never be normal again."

Jock swallowed a lump. Gertrude's speech really resonated with him. If he didn't find Sapphire, he would never know what kind of future they might have had. And he would spend the rest of his life wondering.

"The library's closing in fifteen minutes," the librarian called out. She walked around the tables, picking up discarded books and placing them back on the shelves.

"Just a minute," Jock murmured, staring at the screen in front of him. He felt like an idiot for not realising it before. Here he was, investigating the May Queen disappearances and he had missed something bleeding obvious.

12

"You'll have to go to the National Archives in Kew," the librarian told him, after he had explained what he was looking for. "You can't get that information online."

"Kew?" Jock pulled a face. The last thing he fancied was a trek back to London.

He went outside and rang Robbie. Luckily, the library was at the top of a hill, which meant that he could get a signal.

"Listen, I need a favour. Can you pop down to the National Archives for me?"

"Right-ho." Robbie was a student, after all, so it wasn't like he had anything better to do. "Have you called your mum yet?"

Jock ran his tongue over the roof of his mouth. "I've been busy."

"She's really worried because you haven't updated your Facebook."

"That's because she's always bloody stalking me. I've had enough of it. I'm thirty, for Pete's sake."

"Hey, it's none of my business, but couldn't you send her a postcard? She can't very well reply to a postcard, can she?"

"Are you kidding? She can trace me from a postcard. She'd be on my doorstep within the hour. Just tell her I've been in touch, will you?"

"Right-ho."

※

"You heard they let Simon go?" Dylan asked in the Dragon later.

"No? When did this happen?"

"A couple of hours ago."

"So they didn't charge him with anything?"

"No. He's a free man. Told you he didn't do it."

"Then why did they hold him for so long?"

"No idea. Probably wandered down a rabbit hole."

Jock nodded thoughtfully, but he felt a little discomfort in his stomach. What if Simon was guilty, but the police just couldn't prove it?

※

"Where are you off to?" Gertrude asked. Claire was wearing a denim mini-skirt and a T-shirt covered in blue feathers. On Gertrude, that outfit would have looked ridiculous, but on Claire, it was stunning.

"They're having an old-school disco at the social club."

"But I thought we were going to watch Billy Elliot! I've already made the popcorn."

"Why don't we record it and watch it tomorrow?"

"Well, I suppose." She let out a sigh as the prospect of yet another long, boring evening stretched out ahead of her.

"Hey, why don't you come with us?" Gaby appeared at the top of the landing in frayed shorts and a neon T-shirt. "I mean, it'll probably be really naff, but still …"

"Yeah, why not?" Claire said.

"What about Mum?"

"Just give her her sleeping pill a bit early. It's only a couple of hours. Come on, you could use a night out."

"I suppose I could see if Brenda could pop in to check on her. She does owe me a favour."

"There you go, then."

She pretended to be cool about it, but deep down, she was elated. She ran up to her room and changed into the most flattering outfit she could find: black jeans and a sparkly top that had been sitting in her wardrobe since Christmas.

"You look nice," Claire said, as she returned downstairs. She sounded surprised.

"Thanks."

"Hey, why don't you wear my silver sandals? They'd go really well with that top."

"Really? Thanks." It wasn't like Claire to be so generous with her clothes. She opened the shoe cupboard and extracted the glittery sandals. They were half a size too small for her, but she didn't care. "Hey, is Brenda here yet?"

"Sitting in the living room, stuffing her face with popcorn."

"Shh! She'll hear you!"

"Well, are we going or what?"

"Let's go!"

A thrill of anticipation pulsed through Gertrude as they arrived at the club. It was nowhere special: just a poxy village social club. There wasn't even much of a queue. But loud music pumped from inside and bouncers stood at the door, vetting who could or couldn't go in.

"No trainers," they told the lad in front of them.

Gertrude glanced nervously at Claire's trainers, but she needn't have worried. Her sister didn't have any trouble getting in. She never did.

As soon as they went inside, Claire spotted someone she knew and that was it, she was off. Gertrude trailed after her for a while, when she spotted the bar. A drink. That was what she needed. A bit of Dutch courage would help her relax.

"What are you drinking?" the barman asked.

"Er …" For a moment, she was absolutely flummoxed. She couldn't think of the name of a single drink, except beer. And she hated beer.

"I'll have a pint of Bulmers," the man next to her told another bartender.

"I'll have a Bulmers," she repeated.

The other customer turned and looked at her. "A Bulmers girl!" he said, sounding pleased. "What's your name?"

"Gertrude," she shouted over the music.

"Never met a Gertrude before," he said, as their drinks were poured. "I'm Jeremy."

She stole a look at his face. He had kind, expressive eyes and an easy smile.

"Cheers!" he toasted her.

"Cheers!"

She took a swig. OK, she could do this. The song that had been playing ended, to be replaced with Michael Jackson's 'Thriller'.

"I love this song!" she shrieked.

"What?"

"I love this song!"

Jeremy smiled. "Me too."

It had been a long, long time since she had danced anywhere except her bedroom, but she couldn't help herself. As soon as she started to move, Jeremy gulped back his drink and started to move too.

"Hey, you're a great dancer," he whispered in her ear.

She smiled. "Thanks. You're not so bad yourself."

In fact, she suspected he had had lessons. As their confidence grew, the two of them began to whirl around the dance floor, outdoing each other with their outrageous moves. The song ended and an even better one came on in its place. She was having a ball and it had nothing to do with the alcohol.

Sometime later, the DJ tapped the mic.

"Ladies and gentlemen! Please can I have your attention?" he asked, pausing the music for a moment. "The judges are ready to announce the names of this year's May Queen and princesses."

Everyone clapped their hands and waited expectantly. She tried to spot Claire in the crowd, but she couldn't see her. She crossed her fingers and waited.

"This year's May princesses are Kathryn Piper and Gaby Helston."

Gertrude gave Gaby a thumbs up and sucked in her breath. "And the May Queen will be Claire Scutter."

She allowed herself a smile. Claire had done it again. Well, she was happy for her, at least she was for about half a minute.

They all watched as Claire ascended the stage, looking like Keira Knightley in her trendy clothes.

"Who's that?" Jeremy breathed.

"That's my sister."

She watched his mouth drop open. Any chance she had with him was now dead in the water. Claire probably wouldn't touch him with a barge poll, she was extremely picky. But that didn't matter. Gertrude didn't want any man who lusted over her sister, even if that was all of them.

If Gaby could be a good sport about Claire being crowned May Queen instead of her, then surely Gertrude should be a good sport, too. But somehow, it was all too much. Something inside her cracked. If only she had known then how little time she and Claire had left.

❄

THE RATS CAME out that night. They scampered out of the walls, dozens of them, with bright red moonbeams for eyes. Sapphire did not realise what was happening until they were inches from her face, dozens of pairs of eyes, glowing in the darkness.

"Ingrid!" she hissed. "Ingrid! Wake up!"

"Just cover your face with your hands," Ingrid murmured sleepily. "Honestly, you'll be fine."

"But they're everywhere!"

She held back a scream as a rat scampered over her, running down her back. She leapt to her feet and brushed herself down. They were all around her, pulling the room apart as they foraged for food that wasn't there. She edged towards the stairs, but as she did so, she slid on something soft.

"Ugh!"

She had trodden on one. She could still feel its coldness beneath her feet. She dived for the stairs, taking them two at a time until she reached the top. And there she huddled, waiting to see if they would follow.

After a while, she curled herself into a ball and tried to block out the eerie whistling and squeaking noises as the rodents took over the cellar. None of the other May Queens even stirred. They must be used to it, she thought. But not her. She would never get used to the freaky sensation of rats on her bare skin. She wondered with repulsion if they had been there the previous night, running over her as she slept. Her head jolted. She was too tired to stay awake, but too disturbed to give in to the sleep her body craved.

In the morning, all was quiet. She clambered back down the steps and wondered if she might have dreamt it, but then she saw their shiny, black droppings. The smell was fearsome. She slept for most of the morning, comforted by Ingrid's insistence that the rats only came out at night.

"So you met Bertie and his friends?" Harmony said when she woke up.

Sapphire looked at her blankly.

"That's right, she's named them all," Ingrid said. "She can pick them out by their different squeaks, can't you, Harmony?"

"Except there are more of them every night," Fizz said. "Those bastards breed like you wouldn't believe. Hey, do you want some breakfast?"

The rat talk should have put her off, but Sapphire was starving. Their filthy tea tray was gone, replaced with a fresh one containing a cup of tea and a hot cross bun.

"They came while I was asleep?"

Ingrid nodded.

She couldn't understand how she could have slept through it. She imagined them, looking in on them, watching her while she slept. It was an unnerving thought. She turned her attention to the tray, wondering how well it had been cleaned, but the bun smelt like heaven. It had been toasted, just the way she liked. The butter had melted and drizzled down the sides. Her mouth watered and her stomach ached. It wouldn't go very far. There couldn't be more than a couple of bites each, but still, such delicious bites. She lifted the bun to her lips and bit into it, immediately passing it to Ingrid because she couldn't trust herself to eat just her share. Then she reached for the cup and took a long, satisfying gulp. No one else seemed as eager as she was, although they had gone without for much longer. But then, she was used to full, wholesome meals and long, satisfying drinks whenever she wanted them. How was she supposed to adjust to a hell where food, drink and even light were scarce?

❄

JOCK PULLED his pillow over his head. He thought the loud, incessant banging was part of his dream, but as he opened his bleary eyes, he realised there was someone at the door.

"Who is it?"
"It's DCI Stavely. Open up!"

13

Jock unbolted the door, wishing fervently that he'd worn anything except the reindeer pyjamas his mother had thrust upon him last Christmas.

"What's going on?"

Stavely cast an eye around the room. "Jock. Are you missing?"

"What?"

"You know, gone from home. Absent. Absconded. Displaced."

"I'm sorry, I don't follow?"

"I asked if you were missing, Jock."

"Er ... no."

"Well, your mum seems to think you are. She made a police report yesterday morning."

"What?"

"Go on, get on the blower and deal with it."

"But I–"

"Are you scared of talking to your own mother, Jock?"

"No."

"Then I suggest you get on to it, pronto. I don't appreciate you wasting police time."

"Oh, for Pete's sake…" He pulled his phone from its charger and dialled his parents' number.

"Hello?"

"Hi, Dad, it's Jock."

"Just a minute, I'll get your mother."

"No, wait!"

But his father was already bellowing up the stairs. "Mavis! Jock's on the phone."

He could hear his mother's footsteps thundering down the stairs.

"Jock?" She sounded breathless. "What's happened? Are you alright?"

Jock frowned at the phone. "I'm fine, Mum. I can't believe you called the police!"

"But you weren't answering your phone. What was I supposed to think?"

"Didn't Robbie tell you I'd spoken to him?"

"Yes, but it's not the same!"

He could picture her lower lip trembling. At the same time, she would be examining herself in the hall mirror to check she hadn't smudged her mascara.

"I have to go now. Will you please tell the police I'm not missing?"

"But you haven't even told me–"

"Bye, Mum."

"Wow, you're cold!"

Stavely helped himself to a ginger snap from Jock's nightstand. His eye went to the kettle and the pea-green tea caddy beside it. He was probably hoping Jock was going to offer to make tea, but he didn't. The last thing he wanted was to give Stavely a reason to hang around.

"You don't know my mum. You give her an inch and she'll take a mile."

"Sounds like just about every woman I've ever known." Stavely swallowed the biscuit whole. "Now, while I'm here, I wanted to talk to you about your relationship with Sapphire Butterworth."

"We didn't really have one." He did up an errant button. "I mean, we barely got started."

"But she did invite you up to her flat, didn't she?"

"Yes."

"Do you think it's odd that she would do that when she barely knew you?"

"Like I told you, we had a connection. What are you getting at?"

"No offence, but you're a pretty ordinary-looking bloke, wouldn't you agree? More Shane MacGowan than George Clooney."

"That's a matter of opinion."

"You don't think it seems a bit desperate? I mean, you weren't the first customer to take a shine to her, you know. In fact, one poor sod tried to give her his rattling cage of a BMW. Not that she accepted."

"But I didn't even ask her out. It just happened. She just … liked me."

"So that's all there was to it?"

"Yes."

"We'll see."

❄

Angie was just on her way out when Jock arrived at the tea shop.

"Are you open?" He gazed inside.

"Actually, you're a little early, but go on in. Bronwyn's in the kitchen. I've just got a couple of errands to run before it gets busy."

He went in and stood at the counter.

"Hi, Bronwyn!"

Bronwyn peered at him. She wore a white chef's hat that

only served to accentuate her large ears. "Can I help you?"

"Sorry, I'm a bit early."

"Right." She looked at him uncertainly.

"Do you mind if I ask you a couple of questions?"

She glanced behind him into the empty shop.

"Angie will be back any minute."

"It's about the May Queen Contest. I wondered what made you take part, given the history of the May Queen Killer and all."

"Oh, well, that wasn't really my idea. One of the customers nominated me. I was quite surprised, really. I would never have thought of entering."

He didn't argue. "Do you know who it was?"

She looked at him with wide eyes, as if she wasn't sure if she should say.

"Please? I really want to help find Sapphire."

"If you must know, the police already asked me this and I told them. It was Simon."

She glanced towards the door once more and he realised she was looking out for Angie.

"Don't worry, I won't say you told me. I'm not trying to get anyone into trouble. I just want to find her."

Bronwyn nodded. "Me too."

A little later, he saw Simon sitting at the counter, reading the paper. He wouldn't have expected to see him back in the tea shop so soon, given how it was still heaving with journalists. But maybe he wanted to show them all he had nothing to hide.

"Hi, Simon. Er … how are you?"

"Much better now I've had a shower."

"I can't believe they held you for so long." He hoped his voice didn't sound as squeaky as it did in his head.

"Well, at least I know who my friends are now. Some people talked some awful rot about me while I was away."

Jock reddened. "I'm sorry to hear that."

Simon looked at him closely, as if trying to decide if he was one of those people.

"Have you seen Dylan?"

"No. I think he's still in bed."

"Well, do me a favour, will you, and tell him I'm looking for him."

"OK."

That sounded ominous. Maybe he had heard about the incident with his mum.

Simon's face softened as Angie came over and served him a large slice of carrot cake.

"Eat up! There's more where that came from."

He smiled and stabbed the cake with his fork, and Jock got a waft of cinnamon and nutmeg.

"I'm a very lucky man."

Jock nodded. "So I see."

He ran into Bronwyn again on his way out. She was carrying a crate of milk cartons.

"Do you want a hand with those?"

She snorted.

"Right. Maybe not then. Er … there was something else, actually."

"Yes?" She looked impatient. The cartons were probably heavy.

"Do you know the name of Sapphire's other attendant, the one who was on the float with you?"

"Nerys. Nerys Andrews."

"Any idea where I can find her?"

"Yeah, she works at Hot Paints."

He looked at her blankly.

"It's a DIY shop in Castle Street."

"Thanks, Bronwyn. You're a treasure!"

❄

CASTLE STREET WAS right at the top of the hill. The shop should have been easy enough to find, but the brown lettering did not stand out well on the equally brown building. If it weren't for the display of wood chippings in the window, he might have walked right past it.

The shop was quiet, apart from a couple of middle-aged men arguing over whether to buy a rotary hammer or a hammer drill. They turned to look at him.

"What do you think?" one of them asked.

Jock swallowed. DIY was like a foreign language to him – one he had no intention of learning. "Depends what you need it for?" he bluffed.

The men waited for him to elaborate, but he was out of ideas.

"Gotta go and look at screws," he said, spotting a display in the aisle.

"Good luck, son." The crustier of the two men patted him on the shoulder.

Jock shrank away. In London, if someone you didn't know touched you, that would be grounds for a fight or at the very least, a lawsuit. But around here, he had no idea of the rules. They just seemed to make things up as they went along.

He walked over to the nails and screws. He was mesmerised by the sheer quantity of them. Why were there so many? He had never bought a nail or a screw in his life and he wanted to keep it that way. He walked up to the cash desk, where Nerys sat with a pencil in her mouth. He wouldn't have recognised her in her red lumberjack shirt had she not been wearing a name badge. She looked up from her crossword.

"Can I help you?"

He wondered if she could tell, just by looking at him, that he was a DIY phoney.

"Er, hi. Nerys, isn't it?"

"Are you a journalist?"

"No, I'm a … friend of Sapphire's."

"I suppose you've come to ask me some questions?"

He nodded.

"Well, go on, then, but make it original. I'm getting sick of telling the same story over and over again."

"Do you have any idea where she might be?"

She shook her head, causing a strand of her hair to fall out of its plait. "Barely met the girl."

"Did she offer you money to drop out of the contest?"

She narrowed her almond eyes. "Who told you that?"

He reddened. "Put it this way, you wouldn't be the only one."

"No, I assumed that much."

"So she did pay you off then?"

"She tried, but I reported her to the May Fair committee. They told me they'd look into it but that was a load of old codswallop."

"So nothing happened?"

"Course not! It was a fix from the start. I mean, Sapphire donates the tea and cakes for most of the village functions, so of course they were going to choose her. I should have taken her bloody money. At least then I'd be a grand better off."

Another grand? Sapphire must have wanted to be May Queen really badly.

"Well, thanks for talking to me."

"That's OK. Made a change from staring at the wall."

He turned to leave.

"Hold on a mo …"

"Yes?"

"I would be remiss if I did not mention that the wood chippings are reduced to seventy-nine ninety-nine for the rest of the month."

"Good to know."

❄

THE LAST TIME Gertrude saw Claire was when her dress was delivered, the day before the May Fair.

"Aren't you going to try it on?"

"I'm sure it's fine," Claire said. "They took all my measurements."

"Don't you think you should make sure?"

Claire shrugged and slipped the dress on over her jeans. She looked incredible, but instead of feeling happy for her, Gertrude felt angry. Why did Claire get all the good genes: the wide blue eyes, the luscious blonde hair, the long, shapely legs?

"How do I look?"

She turned this way and that in the mirror, fretting about her non-existent fat bottom.

"Bloody perfect."

Gertrude stuffed a handful of Smarties into her mouth. She wondered what it would be like to look like Claire, even for a day. She bet people would treat her differently. In fact, she knew they would.

While Claire went out with her friends that night, Gertrude stayed in her room. *Dirty Dancing* was on TV, but she couldn't concentrate. The more she stewed over it, the angrier she became. Rage rode her. She grabbed a pair of scissors and burst into Claire's appallingly messy bedroom. The beautiful, white May Queen dress hung from the wardrobe, like an island in a sea of chaos. She held up the scissors, ready to cut, but she couldn't bring herself to do it. Instead, she pulled off her jeans and jumper and slipped the dress over her head. She could just about squeeze it over her hips. There was no way it was going to zip up, but that didn't matter. Standing there in front of the full-length mirror, she looked like a May Queen.

"Why her and not me?"

She looked mournfully at her reflection and tried to picture a slimmer, more confident version of herself, but she couldn't do it. Life had sucked her so far down its giant sinkhole that it seemed impossible she would ever climb out.

She should have slashed that dress. She should have burnt it. Because maybe then Claire wouldn't have gone to the May Fair, but Gertrude's jealousy prevented her from going to watch her sister being crowned that day. It also prevented her from saying goodbye.

❄

As had become his habit, Jock stopped for a drink at the Dragon with Dylan before going to bed that night.

"Alright?" they greeted each other simultaneously, neither of them feeling the need to reply.

"So, how's the novel coming?"

"Fine. But to be honest, I spend half my time searching for Sapphire."

Dylan looked at him oddly.

"Virtually, I mean."

"Oh. How's that going?"

"Not great. The more I discover, the more I need to know."

"Like what?"

"Well, for example, do you think it's relevant that Fleckford is only thirty miles from Whiteford, where the last May Queen went missing?"

"Could be."

"It seems odd to me. All the other May Queens disappeared from quite far-flung locations, as if the killer was on a prolonged tour of the British Isles, but Whiteford and Fleckford are quite close together. It breaks the pattern, doesn't it?"

"What do you think that means?"

"I don't know, maybe Peter Helston was guilty like the police said and this time it's a copycat."

Dylan scratched his chin. "It might mean that the May Queen Killer is still in the same area as he – or she – was five years ago. He probably lives around here or has something that ties him to the area, like family or a job." He took a sip of his pint. "Do you know if Peter Helston's family still live around here?"

"Why?"

"They're on the suspect list, aren't they?"

"Are they?"

"Of course they are because Sapphire's disappearance adds credence to their claim that Peter was innocent. According to them, the May Queen Killer is still out there and always has been. It's not much of a motive, I'll grant you, but if I were working on the case, I'd want to eliminate them."

Jock nodded. "I suppose it wouldn't hurt to talk to them, if only to rule them out."

14

Gertrude did not realise anything was amiss until the day after May Day. It wasn't unusual for Claire to sleep past noon on weekends, so she wasn't worried when she failed to turn up for lunch. She had said something about staying at a friend's house, so she texted her to ask when she would be back and got on with making the egg sandwiches.

Their mother was in the garden, singing tunelessly as she hung out the washing in the pouring rain. The wet sheets billowed in the wind as she struggled to peg them to the line. Her flimsy blouse was soaked through and her slippered feet were covered in mud, but Gertrude had already tried and failed to bring her inside.

When her mum eventually came in, Gertrude wrapped a towel around her and tried to get her to eat, but instead she proceeded to tackle the ironing. She did not seem to notice that the iron did not heat up. Even the fact that Gertrude had cut the cord did not give the game away. Gertrude ate lunch alone at the table while looking out the window for Claire. Her mother didn't take so much as a bite out of her sandwich, so she ate that, too.

"Mum, do you know where Claire is?"

"It's spring time, isn't it? She'll be in the daffodils."

"What are you talking about? I'm going to ring round her friends and see where she's got to."

She rang a couple of Claire's friends before she got to Gaby.

"She didn't come home?" Gaby's voice was a little shaky.

"No."

"Oh God! Then where the hell is she?"

A cold fork jabbed through Gertrude's heart. Claire wasn't just late. She was missing. She might have been jealous of Claire, desperately jealous at times, but she still loved her. She was her significant other, the second half of her. There had been no men in her life, no best friend. It was Claire she talked to about things: the absence of their father and managing their mother. What would she do without her? How could she possibly carry on?

❉

JOCK SAT on the number 67 bus with his TomTom poised on his lap. He'd bought it rather optimistically, when he'd begun learning to drive and was reluctant to give it up, despite the fact he now owned an iPhone. The bus wound its way round the country lanes, stopping forever at each stop. At this rate, it would take him years to reach his destination. Still, the countryside was breathtaking, with tiny thatched cottages set against a backdrop of lush green grass, clouds of sheep and the palest of blue skies. The canal ran alongside the bus for most of the trip, bending and dipping with the road. He was so busy looking out the window that he missed his stop and had to walk back, traipsing the hems of his trousers in the puddles.

Pepper Hill was a quaint little village, small but suburban, with neat little lawns. All the hedges were trimmed to the required height and the houses were painted in dull, tasteful colours. He didn't have much trouble finding the Pink Flamingo Gallery. There was a large wooden sculpture of a flamingo in the window. Actually, it was more peach than pink, but he wasn't about to quibble.

He pushed the door open and went inside. A quick glance up and down the long, narrow room confirmed that he was the only customer. He stopped in front of a large, abstract painting of an avocado sheltering under an umbrella and pretended to admire it.

"Morning." An older lady walked towards him. "I must apologise – I don't actually know much about the paintings. My daughter's just popped out. She should be back in a jiff." She gave him a crinkly smile. "I know you, don't I?"

"Do you?"

"You're J.K. Jeffries, aren't you?"

"Wow! It's not often I'm recognised."

"Well I saw you on the book show a couple of months ago. The Mother's Day special. I thought it was lovely how you work so closely with your mum. Gabriella will be thrilled you dropped in. I'm Daphne, by the way."

"Yes, I know."

The smile froze on her lips. "Yes, well I suppose people recognise me, too." She started to shuffle towards the back of the shop.

"No, wait. I really wanted to talk to you." He addressed this last sentence to her back. She stood rigid in the middle of the gallery. "I realise this is a bit awkward, but I'm a ... friend of Sapphire Butterworth's, the May Queen who's gone missing."

When she turned to look at him, there was pain in her eyes. "Would you like a glass of lemonade, dear?"

"No, I'm fine, thank you."

"Well, I hope you don't mind if I have one. I'm terribly thirsty all of a sudden."

She poured herself a long glass and drank it in large gulps. "I'm sorry to hear about your friend, but it just goes to show what I've been telling the police all along. Peter was framed. I don't know how, or who by, I just know that he didn't have it in him. The real May Queen Killer has been hiding away, biding his time and as soon as they brought back the May Fairs, he struck again. I predicted this would happen, but no one would listen." She eased herself into the desk chair. "Of course, I feel awful for that poor girl, but for me this is a vindication. People have stopped staring at me like I'm a leper. Oh, they still stare, but they're starting to believe that maybe Peter was innocent after all. If only he were still around to see it."

"So why do you think he confessed?" He hoped he wasn't overstepping the mark.

"They broke him," Daphne said. "I don't know what happened to him in that police interview, but something did. They drove him crazy. He wasn't the same man after they had finished with him. They made him confess to such terrible things and in such detail that they must have been feeding him the lines. Meanwhile, the real killer was lying low, waiting until there was a fresh crop of May Queens to harvest."

He was about to ask for more details when a young woman walked in. This, he guessed, was Gabriella. She was voluptuous, with glossy black hair, pulled back in a tight Croydon facelift. Her over-plucked eyebrows were knitted tightly together as she approached.

"Mum, what's going on? I thought we said we weren't going to talk to any more journalists."

"Oh, I'm not a journalist." Jock straightened his collar. "My name's Jock Skone. I'm a friend of Sapphire Butterworth's."

Gabriella arched an eyebrow. "The girl that disappeared?"

"That's right."

"Well, I don't know what Mum's told you, but we don't know anything about her or any of the other May Queens."

"Gabriella, there's no need to be rude."

"I'm not being rude, Mum. I'm sure he's just on his way." She glanced at his TomTom. "Where did you park, anyway? I didn't see a car."

"I came by bus."

"But we're a good mile off the bus route!"

"I know. I left my Porsche in London."

"Did you now?"

She was dying to know if he really had a Porsche, he could tell.

He trudged back to the bus stop, mulling over what Daphne had told him. The bus shelter was one of those supremely uncomfortable ones, with no seat to sit on as such, just a ledge that made it near impossible to perch. As the ground was wet and muddy, he could hardly sit on the floor. Jock scowled. He was cold, damp and tired. And he hated standing.

He didn't look up as the pink Seat Ibiza pulled up in front of him, not until Gabriella leaned out of the tinted window.

"Can I give you a lift? Not as fancy as a Porsche, but still …"

"It's probably a bit out of your way," he said. "I'm staying in Fleckford."

"Fleckford? Well, there won't be another bus going in that direction till this afternoon."

"Oh!"

"I tell you what, why don't you come into town with me and get some lunch? I can drop you back in time for the bus."

He hesitated for a moment. What was she up to? But it was wet and he was hungry. The prospect of a warm car and food sounded pretty good.

"Well, OK then. Just as long as I'm paying." After all, he didn't want to feel completely emasculated.

Gabriella grinned. "You'll get no arguments from me."

She leaned across to open the passenger door for him.

There wasn't much talk on the way to the restaurant. Gabriella turned up her music and it was all he could do not to cover his ears. He hadn't been subjected to much rap before and he wasn't sure he liked it.

"Here we are!"

She pulled up in front of a fancy-looking Italian restaurant. He took in the ostentatious building and hoped he wasn't going to regret his offer of buying lunch. And yet once they were settled at a table in the middle of the bustling restaurant, they were soon talking and laughing like old friends. She was quite nice, actually. Not quite the spitfire he had taken her for.

"So you really want to help clear Dad's name?" she asked, as they nibbled on steaming hot slices of garlic bread.

"I want to find Sapphire and to do that, I need to know the truth."

She nodded. "That's all I've ever wanted. Ever since Claire disappeared."

"Claire Scutter? You knew her?"

"She was a friend." She unfolded her napkin. "And I admit, I was a little bit envious when she was crowned May Queen, but I was happy for her, too. I said we should go out and celebrate after the May Fair."

"So what happened?"

"So we went out: me, Claire and a few other friends. It was a really great night but I was done in by about twelve. I wanted to go home, but Claire wanted to stay out longer. She was getting a lot of attention in her May Queen dress and I suppose she just wanted to enjoy it. She was supposed to be staying over at my house, so I told her I'd leave the back door unlocked for her."

The waitress arrived with their food and skilfully balanced the dishes on the impossibly tiny table.

"It wasn't until the morning that I realised Claire wasn't there, but I just assumed she'd gone home instead of staying over. I dropped her a text, but she'd had a late night, so I wasn't worried when she didn't reply. I thought she'd be sleeping. But later, her sister called and asked why she wasn't answering her phone. That's when I got scared."

Jock swallowed a forkful of lasagne. "What was her sister's name?"

"Gertrude. I didn't know her very well. She was a bit shy and mousy."

He brought up a picture on his phone.

"Is this her?"

She laughed. "No way! Gertrude was really …" she looked again. "Wait a minute, maybe. Maybe it could be. If she dyed her hair blonde and put on a little make-up and got in shape."

She stared at the picture for a long time. "This is Sapphire, isn't it – the girl who's gone missing?"

"Yes."

"And you think she and Gertrude are the same person?"

15

Jock scratched his head. "I don't know. It's just a hunch. Why don't you go on?"

Gabriella bit her lip. "Well, I'd rung just about everyone, but no luck. Then we had the police round, asking questions. I didn't even realise what it was all leading up to. They arrested my parents and took them down the station, and while we were there, they had people searching the house. As far as I knew, Claire hadn't been in the house that night, but the police said they'd found evidence that she had. I thought it must be some kind of mistake. She'd been round to drop off her stuff before we went out, so I thought that was what they were picking up on, but they were adamant. Claire had been in our house that night and now she was missing. Mum was released within a few hours, looking all grey and haggard. We stayed at the police station, waiting for news. But then they charged Dad with murder and what was worse, they said he'd confessed to three other murders, too. You can't imagine what that feels like. My stomach was going round and round like a washing machine. I thought I was going to be sick and then Mum just slumped back in her chair. She'd had a minor heart attack, though how a heart attack can be minor I'll never understand."

Jock looked at her with compassion.

"Your mum said your dad was innocent. She said he never should have been put in prison."

"Yes."

"Do you believe that, too?"

She hesitated for a fraction of a second. "I think he was innocent, but I'd like to know for sure."

"What was he like, your dad?"

Gabriella leaned on her elbows. "He was just like anyone's dad. He worked hard, liked a round of golf and a pint of beer. He was a very principled man. He had an opinion on everything. His friends called him an armchair conservative, but I never saw anything in him to make me suspect he was evil. And yet …"

"And yet?"

"The evidence was pretty damning. The police seemed so certain that Claire was in our house that night. And in spite of all the pressure, why would Dad confess? I just don't understand what they could possibly have said to him to make him. You couldn't 'make' my dad do anything. He knew his own mind. So why on earth did he say he killed those girls? It just doesn't make any sense."

He would have liked to press her further and ask about her father's death, but he didn't want to push his luck. So they both turned their attention to their food and ate in companionable silence.

"Your friend, Sapphire, what do you think happened to her?" Gabriella asked, as they finished their meal.

"I'm hoping she ran away."

"Is that what you really think?"

"No. If she really is Gertrude then it's more likely she jumped into the canal."

Gabriella frowned. "Did she seem suicidal?"

"No. But what do I know?"

"I hope you get your answers," she said, dabbing her chin with her napkin. "Just like I hope we get ours."

He nodded. They were both part of one big, complex mess.

"You let me know if you have any more questions," she said, as she dropped him back at the bus stop. "I mean it. I want to help, and let me know what you find out. I really have to know what happened, no matter what. It's killing me. Mum too."

He scribbled down his number for her and climbed out of the car.

"Don't forget your TomTom!"

"Thanks."

He had a good mind to drop it in the nearest puddle.

On the bus home, he drew a pencil line through Gabriella and Daphne Helston's names in his notebook. He wished he could scratch them off his list entirely. They couldn't have done it, either of them. They were both so nice and normal.

❆

JOCK STOPPED at the tea shop on his way back. He found Dylan sitting by the window, sketching. He set down his bag.

"I didn't know you drew?"

"Oh, I don't. These are just doodles."

He leaned over Dylan's shoulder. Simon was instantly recognisable as the Green Man from the May Day parade, all trussed up in feathers and tied to a broken Maypole. He was surrounded by journalists with pads and pens and tiny villagers with pitchforks. Angie and Morgan were down in the muddy sheep pen, pulling one another's hair. He had greatly exaggerated the size of Angie's boobs, and Morgan's skirt was hitched up so high it was almost indecent. Artistic license, he supposed. He flipped the page and found an impressive likeness of himself, cowering inside a huge tea cup, about to be tipped into Stavely's mouth.

"This is what you think of me?"

"It doesn't mean squat. Like I said, they're just doodles."

Jock looked closer. There was a monkey that looked remarkably like DI Sweep, hanging off the bristles of Stavely's moustache. He was all arms and legs with a sharp, serrated nose. He might have laughed if his own likeness weren't so uncanny.

"Did you talk to Simon? He was looking for you yesterday. He didn't look particularly happy."

"Oh, he's fine. Simon's a good egg."

"So you keep saying."

"Hey, look what the cat dragged in."

He turned to see Stavely and Sweep standing in the doorway.

"What are they doing here?"

"They're still trying to find Sapphire," Dylan reminded him. "Even if arresting Simon was about as advisable as doing a U-turn on the M1."

Angie glared like he had never seen a woman glare before, her lips narrowed to a point. Even Morgan looked impressed. Still, Stavely had a skin as thick as a mole's.

"We'd like to ask you a few more questions," he told Angie without as much as a hello. "When you've got a minute."

"Just as long as you don't arrest me," she said pointedly.

"We had to go on the information we had," Stavely told her.

She raised an eyebrow.

"Look, we all want the same thing, don't we? To find Sapphire."

"Yes." She looked weary.

They sat down at a nearby table. Jock tried to act like he wasn't eavesdropping, but every inch of him strained to listen.

"So tell me," said Stavely. "How long have you known Sapphire?"

"About three years," Angie replied.

"How did you meet?"

"I bumped into her when she was moving into this place – literally bumped into her. I had a load of shopping and she was carrying a large table lamp. We didn't see each other until it was too late. The lamp got smashed, but she just laughed her head off."

"And when did you start working for her?"

"The very next day."

"She gave you a job, just like that?"

"Well, I dropped in later with some flowers from my garden as a housewarming present. You know, I felt guilty about the lamp. We got chatting and she mentioned that she needed staff. Well, it just seemed like fate. I was working at a really crummy cafe, barely making minimum wage. I was pretty desperate to leave but I didn't get on with the owner and I was worried about what I was going to do about a reference."

"Did she even interview you?"

"She said she had a good feeling about me. She could just tell I was the right person for the job."

"She sounds most unorthodox." Stavely frowned his disapproval.

Sweep smiled slightly. "She sounds pretty cool."

"Yes. Yes she is."

"So you and Sapphire were friends outside of work?"

"Absolutely."

"Did she have any other friends?"

"Lots."

"Anyone special?"

"Not really." She glanced over at Jock and he did his best to look uninterested.

"Did she have any concerns about the May Fair? Did she say anything to you about it?"

"No, but then she knew I didn't like the idea. All those missing girls. The legend. I thought it was morbid, but there was no talking her out of it. Once she'd made up her mind, that was it. Sapphire follows her gut. That's just her."

"Do you think she knew something was going to happen?"

"Not at the time I didn't."

"But now?"

"With hindsight? Yes. Yes, I do."

❉

"There's a parcel for you upstairs, Jock," Neil said when they arrived back at the Dragon.

Jock frowned. "I'm not expecting anything."

"Well it's upstairs in the hallway, all the same."

Neil wasn't kidding. There was a huge box blocking the door to his room. He checked the address label and groaned.

"What is it?" Dylan asked.

"It's from my mum. She's tracked me down. She's like a bloodhound, that woman."

He unlocked his door and hauled the box inside. Dylan followed. Jock took some scissors from the nightstand and slashed the tape holding it all together.

Dylan dived in. "Dundee cake. Hmm! ... It smells homemade."

"I don't even like Dundee cake." Jock set it aside. He delved further and found a couple of shirts and a pack of underwear.

"Nice Y-fronts!" Dylan hooted.

There were also a couple of thermal vests, a packet of tea, several boxes of custard, a jam roly poly and a tin of spotted dick.

"She just can't help herself."

"Your mum sounds like a great lady." Dylan eyed all the swag.

"She's formidable. A force of nature. She'll kill me with kindness, one way or another."

"It's not a bad way to go." Dylan pulled out a jar of lemon sherbets.

Jock's mother had also enclosed a letter, which he read briefly then tossed in the bin.

"Are you going to eat that?" Dylan was eying up the Dundee cake.

"Take it. Take all of it. I don't want it."

"You can keep the Y-fronts," Dylan said, packing the rest back into the box.

"No, it's all or nothing. Now, if you don't mind, I've got some work to do. Make sure you shut the door on your way out."

❊

THE PUNCH LANDED in the middle of DCI Stavely's face, giving him a bloody nose.

"I'm sorry," Gertrude gasped. "I didn't mean to."

"I know, I know. It was the shock."

He produced a hanky and did his best to mop up the blood, but it clung stubbornly to his moustache, turning it from brown to red. The other policeman sat down with her and tried to explain what had happened, but Gertrude felt like her ears were full of sand and she could only take in a fraction of what he said:

"Peter Helston confessed … Body not yet recovered … There may be others … Terribly sorry for your loss."

Mum sat unmoving in her chair. She was pale and expressionless. But she heard every word – probably grasped it better than Gertrude did. She clicked her fingers in front of her, impatient for a reaction.

"Mum?"

"Why isn't she moving?" Stavely peered at her in concern.

"Mum!" Gertrude hurled a cushion at her, but it made no impact. She went for another, but helping hands stopped her.

"Mum!" she screamed, her throat on fire. "Mum!"

Her mother didn't move. She was still breathing, still blinking, but her mind wasn't there. She was gone.

"I hate you, Mum!" Gertrude fell back onto the sofa, exhausted.

Not even that got a response – not even the slightest twitch of an eyebrow. She couldn't believe this was happening. It was just too much. Her mum should have been the one to punch DCI Stavely, the one to slip her arm around Gertrude's shoulders and tell her they still had each other.

"Is there a friend or neighbour you'd like us to call?" Stavely asked, the blood still streaking down his shirt.

"No."

She was on her own and this would probably be it from now on. She thought of killing herself. Of course she did.

❆

Sapphire drummed her fingers on the floor as Ingrid wove her hair into hundreds of tiny plaits. She had nothing to tie the ends with, so once woven, they slowly uncoiled.

"How long have you been here?" she asked, shifting her weight from one side to the other. Her bum was numb from sitting on the cold, stone floor and no amount of shifting made it any more comfortable.

"A long, long time."

"You don't know how long?"

"I've lost count." She plaited more vigorously.

"She's been here the longest," Fizz said.

"Can you tell me a bit about Sweden?" she asked, changing the subject. "What's it like? I've never been there."

Ingrid thought for a moment. "Well, the capital is of course, Stockholm. At least, I think it is?" She glanced at Fizz for confirmation.

"Don't you know?"

"I should. It's just my memory …"

"They whacked her over the head pretty hard," Fizz said. "She has trouble remembering things, things she ought to know."

Sapphire nodded. "I think that's what they did to me, too."

She thought she remembered feeling a hard knock to the back of her head, but she wasn't sure if it was an actual memory or just her mind trying to fill in the blanks. Maybe it was better not to remember. It was probably less painful that way.

"Well, anyway, it's a big, bustling city," Ingrid went on. "I hardly ever went there. My family are from the countryside. A beautiful area, with lakes and trees."

"Did you celebrate May Day in Sweden?"

"Yes. We didn't have a May Queen but we used to light a bonfire. My Nan said it was to ward off evil spirits, but Dad would just roll his eyes. We'd eat a picnic of salted herring and meatballs, and if we were feeling brave, we'd dip our toes into the water."

"I had Swedish meatballs at Ikea once," chimed in Harmony.

"Why did you come to England, Ingrid?"

"I had the wanderlust, you know? I wanted to see the world. I was offered a scholarship at Liverpool University and I thought I'd be mad to pass it up, but now I wish I'd never left home."

"What are you drawing?" Fizz asked, looking down at the lines Sapphire had traced in the dirt.

"My shop. I've got a lovely little tea shop."

Ingrid smiled. "Maybe we can all visit it one day, when we get out of here."

Sapphire swallowed. "That would be nice."

Her eyes misted over as she thought of her little flat above the shop. She had only lived there for a few years, but it felt like much longer. She had chosen every stick of furniture and painted every wall. She had worked so hard to make it warm and cosy, and now she might never see it again.

"Hey, I know a song that might cheer us all up. Would you like to hear it?" Ingrid asked.

Sapphire nodded, though she wasn't really in the mood. Ingrid began to sing a tune she had never heard before. She had a beautiful, high-pitched voice and she sang perfectly in key. The others soon joined in. Fizz wasn't too bad, but Harmony was completely tone deaf, despite her name.

"Pipe down everyone!" Fizz hissed all of a sudden. "Can't you hear that?"

They all fell silent, their ears attuned to the sound of the lift creaking its way down the elevator shaft. A moment later, the door opened and someone stepped inside.

"Achoo!"

Sapphire hadn't meant to look, but the sneeze caught her attention. She saw her only for an instant, but that instant was enough.

"Claire!"

All at once, the world around her turned black and fuzzy. Her body was paralysed with shock, but before she could utter another word, Claire was gone.

16

Sapphire closed her eyes. She could remember how it felt, the adoration of the crowd, the applause, the excitement, as the float set off up the hill towards the castle. And then she had seen that one-in-a-million face in the crowd. Claire was not dressed in her May Queen dress as she had always pictured her. She was wearing a black hooded top and no make-up, but Sapphire had recognised her all the same. She would recognise her anywhere.

It was the ultimate game of hide and seek. She struggled to keep her in her sights as she wove in and out of the crowds, past the railway bridge and down, down, down to the canal. For a moment, she thought she had lost her, but then she saw her again, at the window of the little cottage that sat on the bank of the canal. The lock keeper's cottage, the locals called it. Despite its name, there hadn't been a lock keeper there for many years. Most people passed the old house without giving it a second thought.

She burst in without knocking, not caring as the door slammed behind her.

"Claire! It's really you!"

She grabbed her sister, finally held her in her arms. Claire did not resist, but she did not respond either. It was several minutes before Sapphire was ready to let go, several minutes before she noticed that her sister had not returned the hug.

"Let me look at you!"

She stepped back and took in her sister's hollow eyes and empty expression.

"What have they done to you? Whatever it is, it's over now. You're free Claire. We're–" but she never got to finish that sentence. She hadn't sensed the third person in the room with them, but perhaps she should have, from the way Claire's eyes kept shifting to the right. The heavy weight came down on her before she had time to react. This was not to be a happy reunion.

"Claire!" She now called into the darkness, but there was no reply. She turned, desperately to the others.

"That was Claire! That was my sister!"

Ingrid, Fizz and Harmony all looked at her.

"She's your sister?" Fizz said.

"What? Don't you believe me?"

Harmony licked her lips. "It's just, you're so nice and friendly and–"

"Don't you … like her?"

It was an added shock. Being Claire's sister had always been like a passport to acceptance. There was something in the look people gave her, something akin to respect. Everybody wanted to know Claire, to be her friend. For a very long time, being Claire's sister had been the only thing she was proud of, and then Claire had been taken. A tear trickled down her cheek.

Ingrid came and sat beside her. "I'm sorry. We didn't mean to make you cry."

"It's just all so overwhelming. One minute she's dead and the next she's alive. But why won't she talk to me? The least she could do is explain what's going on."

Ingrid shook her head. "Claire's not like the rest of us,"

she said, as Sapphire blotted her eyes on the hem of her dress. "Don't you get it? She sold us out. They let her live up there with them while the rest of us are trapped down here in this godforsaken cellar."

"But why?"

"They picked her off, treated her a bit differently, probably offered her extra food or an easier time of it. Whatever it was, she's their slave now. She's more like one of them than one of us."

"It's true," said Fizz. "She's been brainwashed."

Sapphire shook her head. "There's no such thing."

"You'll see for yourself. Just remember she can't be trusted."

"She's my sister!"

"I'm afraid that doesn't mean as much as it used to," said Ingrid. "We're your family now."

Fizz rolled her eyes. "Could you be any cornier?"

"I thought it was more creepy," Harmony said.

"But I don't understand. Why did you do it, Sapphire?" Ingrid asked. "Why did you choose to become a May Queen, knowing what had happened to Claire?"

"But that's just it!" Sapphire said. "I didn't know what had happened to Claire. Not really. I was told Peter Helston had confessed. But he never stood trial and part of me continued to wonder if the killer was still out there. I suppose, deep down, I just knew."

By taking the May Queen's throne, she had hoped to lure the May Queen Killer. But she had never expected her sister to show up in his place. She remembered running through the crowds after Claire, frantic, desperate to catch her. All she could think of was that they were going to be together again. And they could have been. Why had she done this to her? How could she?

Ingrid started to sing again, her beautiful voice lifting them all up out of the cellar. Sapphire lay back and listened. It

The Perfect Girl

seemed so unfair. She couldn't believe she was so close to Claire and yet locked away, on the other side of a cellar door. It was the worst possible kind of torture. She thought she had hit rock bottom when she was told Claire was dead, but this was far worse. She needed to know what was going on and she needed to know soon or she would go mad, she really would.

The lift started to rumble again. The May Queens looked at each other.

"She's coming back to talk to me."

"It might not be Claire," Ingrid warned. "You must be careful, Sapphire."

"I just want to see for myself that she's still alive!"

"She is. We've all seen her."

"Then why has she done this to me? How could she do this to her own sister?"

"Come away from the door!" Ingrid begged.

But Sapphire could not hold herself back. "Claire!" she cried, as the door swung open. She looked at the mournful creature who had Claire's eyes and nose, but not her confidence or her smile.

Claire looked at her strangely, as though they had never met before. "Bring me the old tray and I'll give you a new one."

Sapphire did as she was told, but when she handed Claire the tray, she deliberately brushed her hand with her own. Claire's fingers were freezing cold and she had gnarly nails that needed attention. Still, it was definitely her. And Sapphire craved her closeness more than ever.

"You're looking at me as if you don't know me. It's me, Gertrude."

Claire looked at her without emotion. She held out a tray with a cup of tea on it, but Sapphire refused to take it.

"What are we doing here? Why can't we go home?"

Claire pulled away from her, but Sapphire refused to let go.

"Don't leave me here. Let me come with you!"

"That's not possible."

Claire's voice sounded so unlike her, so cold and robotic.

"Who are you?" Sapphire asked. The sister she remembered could be self-centred at times, but this new Claire lacked all emotion. "What have they done to you?"

"I have to go now." Claire started back up the steps. Sapphire clung to her legs, but she lacked the energy to hold her back.

"Wait, please don't go yet! Please – I just want to talk to you!"

Claire did not stop. Whatever they had done to her, it had worked.

"Claire!"

The door thundered closed and she heard it lock. She picked up the tray her sister had left and hurled it as hard as she could. Its contents smashed against the door before clattering noisily down the steps.

❇

JOCK REPLAYED the documentary for what seemed like the millionth time. It was hard to imagine that the shy, dowdy Gertrude was actually his Sapphire. Yet there was a certain something, a likeness in her manner, that told him he was right. She didn't even look the same – her hair, her clothes, her weight, even the way she held herself. If this really was Sapphire then it wasn't just her name she had changed since Claire had gone missing, but he still needed proof. He had already checked for birth certificates and found there were no Sapphire Butterworths recorded in the UK around the time she was born, but she could have been born abroad. He had found the records for a Gertrude Scutter, however, born in Cardiff in 1985. That would make her a few years older than she had led him to believe, but as Gertrude was not a popular name for his generation, there was a strong likelihood that this was her.

The librarian tutted as his mobile phone vibrated loudly in his pocket. He stepped outside to take the phone call.

"Jock, it's Robbie."

"I know. Your name comes up on the display."

"Listen, I went down to the archives and there was no record of anyone changing their name to Sapphire Butterworth."

"Oh."

"You sound disappointed."

"It was just a theory."

"Well, the librarian fellow there said people don't usually bother."

"Don't bother?"

"With making it official. Apparently, you don't have to. You just decide to change your name and that's it done. I might change mine to Big Hairy–"

"OK, Robbie. I'm hanging up now. Thanks for your help."

Great! If there were no official documents, how was he supposed to get proof?

His phone beeped again and he smiled as he read Dylan's text:

'Beer and music in the park. NO TIME TO WASTE!'

It wasn't a hard decision. He had been in the library all afternoon. A cold beer would go down very nicely.

❄

JOCK HAD NOT VENTURED into Fleckford Park before, despite its central location. The grass was freshly mown and fragrant, the sun having dried off yesterday's rain, and there was a brass band belting out Beatles hits to a small, appreciative audience. He found Dylan snuggled under a blanket, a straw hat on his head and a pair of dark glasses hiding his drunkenness from the respectable people all around.

Jock nudged him with his foot. "What happened to you?"

"There were giving away free beer!" he lamented. "It was outrageous. In broad daylight. And none of these good people seemed interested, so I felt obliged to help."

"Wait, who's giving away beer? I can't see anyone."

"That's because I took it all," Dylan said. "No one else would touch it. They all wanted cider. So it was all on me."

"You drank it all?"

"I did what I could. The rest is in my rucksack."

Jock unzipped Dylan's bag and pulled out a Bishops Finger. "I'm doing this for your own good, so you won't end up drinking any more."

"You're a good man, Jock."

"I know I am."

He let Dylan sleep it off while he drank his beer and listened to the music. It was growing dark by the time the band stopped playing and the older folks packed up their picnic baskets and folding chairs and carried them back to their cars.

He prodded Dylan. "Come on, wake up. People are tripping over you."

Dylan opened his eyes. "Are we at Glastonbury?"

"No, we're in the park. Come on, show's over. Time to go."

He hauled Dylan to his feet and pulled one arm over his shoulder.

"Damn, you're heavy! Come on, you've got to walk. I can't lift you."

Dylan lolled against him. "My legs are on backwards," he slurred.

"Need a hand?" asked Simon, appearing at his side.

"Yes please," Jock said. Given his current predicament, he

didn't have much choice. There was no way he could get Dylan home by himself.

"Drunk as a skunk, isn't he?" commented Verity, walking along beside them. She was much steadier than Dylan, despite her walking stick.

Jock was getting a bit sick of it. Dylan was always bloody drunk. Why couldn't he just enjoy a pint like everyone else? Why did he always have to go overboard?

❄

FIONA HINKLEBURY STOOD on the doorstep. Her shoes were polished to a shine and matched her handbag: a sensible, navy blue affair, large enough to house all the various leaflets she liked to produce.

"Hello," she said with her fixed smile. "Can I come in?"

Gertrude fought back a fountain of anger and took her by the arm. "Please step this way. My mother is in the living room. Perhaps you'd like to discuss her job opportunities with her?"

She led Fiona through to the living room.

"Hello, Mrs Scutter. How are …?" she froze, her position mimicking Gertrude's mother's. "Maureen? Are you …?"

"No, she's not dead. She's catatonic. But why don't you go ahead and ask her a few questions? I'm sure she'll be excited to hear about her job prospects."

Somehow she could hear Claire's voice inside her, telling her what to say. Claire would really shove it in her face.

"Well, Gertrude, I really don't think it's appropriate for me to—"

"No, it isn't, is it? Just like it wasn't appropriate the last time."

As Fiona backed towards the door, she bumped into the piano, sending sheet music flying all over the room.

"Oh my goodness!"

She bent down to gather it all up, grasping at the papers as they blew about in the wind.

"Don't worry, Mum'll pick them up," Gertrude goaded her. She knew she was being a bitch. She just couldn't help herself. Years of rage bubbled to the surface.

Fiona gave up trying to pick up the papers. She looked close to tears. "I can see you've got a lot on your plate right now. I'll let myself out."

"You do that. I'll get Mum to give you a call in the week."

She watched from the window as Fiona climbed back into her sensible Vauxhall Astra and drove off, almost hitting the neighbour's wall. Then she slumped down beside her mother, who stared, unseeing, at the *Coronation Street* omnibus.

"So, what did I miss?"

Her mother heard every word she said, she was sure of it. Her face remained indifferent but Gertrude knew she was listening. Her mother was still in there somewhere. She was just temporarily missing, like lost baggage.

Her mother's GP, Doctor Benson, called round later that day.

"And how are you today, Maureen?" She addressed her mother directly. Gertrude waited to see if her mother would answer but, of course she didn't.

"When's she going to snap out of it?"

The doctor shook her head. "I really don't know what to tell you. It could be days, weeks or even months. Schizophrenia is a serious brain disorder, Gertrude."

She nodded impatiently. "Yes, I know. She's had it for years. But she's never been like this before. It's like she's just … frozen."

"I think the time has come to consider putting your mother into residential care. A bed has just become available in a local unit. Now, I know this must be very hard for you, Gertrude, but I don't think it's possible for you to look after her on your own at the moment, especially in light of the trauma you've just suffered."

The doctor looked at her as if she expected her to argue, but instead Gertrude felt a life force rising within her. Was it possible? After all these years, was she finally being released? She wanted to jump out of her chair and dance around the room, but instead she said, "Do you think it's for the best?"

Doctor Benson looked at her kindly. "I know you've been caring for your mother for a long time, but you have to consider yourself as well as her. I think it might be time."

Gertrude couldn't remember the last time she had considered herself. She couldn't remember the last time she had been allowed to consider herself. She wondered if, as the doctor had suggested, she would feel a pang of regret, but in truth she could barely even look at her mother anymore, at what she had become.

17

"Has there been any progress?"
"I'm afraid not, Gertrude."
"I see."

She dug her nails into the ample flesh of her thigh and hated herself for her own selfish thoughts. A good daughter would be upset that her mother wasn't improving, but she was not a good daughter. Not any more, because if her mother got better, then she would feel compelled to fly home to be with her. As it was … She put down the phone and poured herself a large glass of Corsican wine, which she carried out onto the balcony. The sun bronzed her shoulders as she watched people splash about in the pool below and the smell of garlic and oysters wafted up from the hotel grill.

She leaned back in her deck chair, her eyes beginning to close when she heard a knock at the door. She jumped up to answer it, expecting room service, but instead she found herself looking at the friendly faces of the girls staying in the room opposite.

"Hi, Gertrude. Do you want to come into town with us later? We're going to the Luna club."

"Er, tonight?" She was about to make an excuse, then she

stopped herself. Why the hell not? She was a free agent now. It wasn't like she had anyone else to worry about. So she smiled and nodded her head.

"I'd love to."

"Great. We'll knock for you at seven. We might grab a bite to eat first at the grill if that suits you?"

"Sounds great."

And so that was how she spent the rest of her holiday. She danced all night and slept in as late as she wanted. After a few weeks, she got herself a part-time job, waitressing at a pavement cafe where most of the clientele were English. The cafe owner, Sondra, rented her a room that was considerably cheaper than the hotel she had been staying in. Her schoolgirl French, although stilted to begin with, grew increasingly fluent and she was surprised how much she enjoyed herself, despite the pressing weight of her grief. The sun radiated warmth through her body and cleared up her blotchy skin. She took risks with her appearance, trying out a little make-up and dying her hair platinum blonde. Her appetite naturally reduced and she began to feel that she was finally her own person, quite separate from her crazy mother and her tragic sister. After everything she had been through, things were finally starting to look up.

❄

Someone was vacuuming the stairs as Jock left the Dragon the next morning. Neil must have finally hired a cleaner. About time, too. He bet those carpets hadn't seen a Hoover in years. They still stank of tobacco, despite almost a decade's smoking ban.

"Morning," said Angie, as he walked into the tea shop. "What can I get you?"

"I was meant to be on my way to the library, but my stomach had other ideas."

"What do you think your stomach would like?"

"Crumpets. Bring me all the crumpets."

"Very well, but we may need to reinforce the table." Her eyes twinkled. "No Battenberg this morning?"

He smiled. "Maybe later, for dessert."

"And your usual pot of Yorkshire?"

"Yes, please."

He ate his crumpets while he worked. He barely even noticed them as his fingers flew over the keys. He always seemed to write his novels in fast bursts and this one was no exception.

Just as he was wiping the crumbs from his mouth, Simon stormed in. Perhaps 'stormed' was too strong a word, given that he held the door open for another customer, but he had a face like thunder all the same. He seemed intimidating with his chin set like that, but maybe that was just down to the size of him.

"I thought you were working this morning?" Angie murmured, greeting him at the door.

"There were TV cameras outside the college. The head didn't want the students being harassed so she told me to take some holiday."

His eyes glistened slightly and for a moment, Jock wondered if he was going to cry. He turned quickly back to his computer, not wanting to get involved.

"Oh, poor love," he heard Angie say. "Take a seat, pet, and I'll bring you some camomile tea."

"And a wholemeal muffin, if you don't mind."

Simon slumped down at the empty table next to Jock's. He glanced up just in time to see Angie kiss the shiny spot on top of his head.

"How am I supposed to take time off?" He turned to Jock. "I really don't know how you do it. I can't imagine sitting around here all day."

Jock set his jaw. He was about to reply that he actually

worked very hard when he realised Simon was ribbing him. He had forgotten about his strange sense of humour. So subtle, you almost missed it.

"Now here's someone who could run a masterclass in pissing time away," Jock said, as Dylan walked in. "Alright?" he greeted him. "What's up?"

"Nothing. I just came over here to fart."

"Lovely."

He watched as Dylan pulled the lining out of one pocket and then the other. "You wouldn't lend me a tenner, would you? I'm a bit short this week."

"I wouldn't lend him money," Simon said in an undertone.

Jock opened his wallet and peeled off a ten pound note.

"Thanks, Jock! You're a lifesaver!"

"Well, you know what they say about a fool and his money," Simon said, as Dylan headed to the counter. "Don't expect to get that back any time soon."

"It's no big deal." Jock tried not to mind. After all, what was a measly tenner between friends?

"So what's this book of yours about, anyway?" Simon asked.

"I write murder mysteries."

"Sounds grim."

"Oh no, they're quite light-hearted usually." He glanced down at the words he had just written. "I suppose this one's a bit grittier than my usual stuff. Something about being here, at this time…"

He cast an eye around the tea shop. There was little wonder really. How could he be flippant about murder when he'd been plunged into the midst of the May Queen murders?

"Why did you choose Fleckford?"

"I don't know really. I'd decided to travel around the country and set a book at each place I stay."

"Have you actually seen anything of the area? As far as I

can gather, you've spent the whole time in here, typing away on your laptop and eating cake."

Jock reddened. "I've been to the library! And Pepper Hill."

Simon gazed out the window. "The Black Mountains are quite spectacular. You can walk all day and not meet another soul. It feels like you have the entire mountain to yourself."

"A bit too solitary for me."

In fact, the idea of climbing up a mountain almost made him choke on his tea.

"I'd be happy to take you up there. Looks like I've got time on my hands."

"I really don't …"

Simon leaned closer. His eyes seemed to bore right into him. "Have you ever seen a red kite in its natural habitat?"

"No."

"Nor have I, but I'd certainly like to."

"You could try pony trekking," interrupted Angie, setting Simon's tea down in front of him. Jock let out his breath as Simon's attention switched to Angie.

"There are some lovely rides over the Brecon Beacons."

"I'm not much of a rider."

"What about the abbey?" Simon asked. "It's really quite remarkable. It's the final resting place of King Llewellyn, you know."

"Maybe I'll take a look," he stifled a yawn. He wasn't sure abbeys were really his bag either, but Simon had a point. He owed it to his readers to give them a proper flavour of the area. Maybe he could incorporate the abbey into his murder scene. The acoustics would be ideal for a high-pitched scream.

A little later, Simon excused himself to go and talk to Angie at the counter. Jock was glad. He wanted to speak to Dylan and he still wasn't sure what to make of Simon.

"I think I've found something," he confided, "about Sapphire."

"Tell me," Dylan said.

"You're going to think it's stupid."

"Knowing you, it probably is."

"Just listen, will you? I've looked at the documentary footage, along with the newspaper articles and anything else I can get my hands on. It looks to me like Sapphire is actually the sister of Claire Scutter, the last May Queen to go missing. You don't believe me, do you?"

Dylan's face was unreadable. "I didn't say that. I just need to see some proof, that's all."

"I haven't been able to find any proof. It just … looks that way." He took a long sip of his tea and waited for Dylan to say something.

He didn't.

"So what do you think? Should I take this to DCI Stavely?"

Dylan narrowed his eyes. He actually looked kind of angry, though Jock had no idea why. "Absolutely not."

"Why not?"

Dylan rolled his eyes. "Because he'll just sit on it, like the complete dipstick he is."

Jock frowned. "I know the police must get a lot of leads, but I might actually have something here …"

Dylan shook his head. "Don't you get it, Jock? Stavely was the detective in charge of Claire Scutter's investigation. And you heard him in that interview. This case is not linked to the others. He was emphatic. Do you really think he's going to do a U-turn?"

"But don't you think he'll want to know the truth?"

"Not necessarily, no. He might be more concerned about covering his own arse."

"Wow! You have a really cynical view of the police, don't you?"

Dylan laughed darkly. "I think I have a right to."

"What's that supposed to mean?"

But Dylan just shook his head and pulled out his iPhone.

The conversation was over.

❄

CLAIRE BROUGHT food and drink down to the cellar every day, but there was never enough to go around and rarely any conversation to go with it. More often than not, she managed to slip in while they were sleeping and leave before they awoke. Then one morning, just before dawn, Sapphire heard the key turn in the lock and saw the door open. She thought about rushing forward and shoving her sister to the ground, but then she caught sight of the large dog behind her and decided against it.

"Claire?" she called, quietly enough so as not to wake the others.

Claire froze in the doorway.

"I'm not supposed to talk to you."

"Just for a minute. I haven't seen you in so long!"

"What is it, Gertrude?"

She winced at the name, but she couldn't mind now. "I've been wondering. When you came to the May Fair, why didn't you escape? I mean, why didn't you just run off into the crowd?"

Claire raised her face to look at her. "It wasn't that simple. You don't understand."

"Explain it to me. Please …"

Claire drew a sharp breath. "They could have killed me five years ago and yet I'm still here."

"You call this a life?"

"I'm living and breathing, aren't I?"

"Wait!"

Claire was backing towards the door and Sapphire hadn't said half of what she wanted to say.

"We need some things," she said, desperately. "It's so cold down here. Could you get us some blankets? And a bucket?"

"I'll ask, but I can't promise anything."

The door locked behind her.

❄

Jock stood on platform 1, waiting for his train. His editor, Hilary, was in the area and wanted to see him. When she had asked about the best place to meet, he had suggested the cafe opposite the abbey. That way, he could pop in after, thereby killing two birds with one stone. It shouldn't take too long to soak up the atmosphere of the place or at least enough to impress his readers, but he had to be careful that he didn't let anyone talk him into taking a tour. He lived in mortal fear of guided tours. They bored the pants off him in much the same way as football matches and classical concerts.

He shifted his weight from one leg to the other. He would have liked to sit down, but a group of youths occupied the only bench on the platform. They were passing round a plastic bottle of drink and smoking something that smelt sweet and sickly. One of them poured some of the drink into a dish for the dog and they all laughed raucously as she lapped it up.

A train arrived and a young boy got off, trailing his bag along the ground behind him. Jock watched as he wandered up and down the station, stopping to look at various notices. The youths noticed, too. One of them stuck out a foot to trip him, but the boy just walked around him. The loudest one took off his baseball cap and Jock recognised him as Gold Tooth, the kid Dylan had fought with that day at Sapphire's.

"Hey, what's your name?" Gold Tooth called out to the young boy.

Don't answer, thought Jock. Better to pretend you haven't heard.

The boy pushed his glasses up his nose. "I'm Anthony."

"Too long. I'll call you Ant."

"It's just Anthony."

Gold Tooth got up and walked towards him. He was a few inches taller than Anthony and he pulled himself up to his full height.

"Are you stupid?"

"Actually, I'm in the top set for all my subjects," Anthony informed him. "Except PE."

The teenagers on the bench sniggered.

"Are you giving me attitude? He took another step towards him, causing him to step backwards, towards the edge of the platform.

Jock swallowed. One more step and Anthony would fall off the edge. Anthony glanced around to see how close he was and his glasses slipped again. Before he could catch them, they had fallen down onto the train tracks.

"Go and get them!"

"What?"

"You heard me. Go and get them."

Anthony glanced desperately around, looking for a responsible grown up but there was nobody but Jock. It was down to him, and he was paralysed with indecision. If he yelled for help, someone might come, but the teenage boys might turn on him instead and who knew what they might do. He zoomed in on the rusty, metal train track and shuddered. He started walking, heading purposefully towards the exit. Maybe there would be someone out there who could help.

He didn't intend to look at Anthony or Gold Tooth, didn't want them to know he was aware of their stand-off, but somehow, Anthony got to him. His young, vulnerable eyes screamed at him for mercy. He couldn't just walk by. Heart pumping like crazy, he strode purposely towards the two boys.

"Have either of you got change for a twenty?"

His voice came out louder than he had meant it to. He sounded more confident than he felt.

Gold Tooth spun around at the mention of money. "I have." Leaving Anthony alone, he followed Jock towards the ticket machines. Jock had no idea what he was going to do next. He hadn't thought that far ahead.

Gold Tooth leant towards him. "Hand it over!" His knife glinted in the sunlight.

18

"Are you deaf? Hand it over, Fatso!"

"I haven't got it on me."

"Don't bullshit me!"

"I'm not! If you'll just let me …"

Gold Tooth held the knife inches from his left eye.

"I'm going to count to three. One, two …"

"Three."

A large shadow fell across them and suddenly, Gold Tooth was on the ground. The knife clattered to the floor beside him and a large foot kicked it hard, sending it all the way over the side of the platform and onto the railway tracks.

"Go and get it!" he boomed.

"It's the May Queen Killer!" one of the teenagers shrieked, recognising Simon's face. Despite his fear, Jock felt a twinge of satisfaction as the entire group legged it out of the station.

"Thanks, Simon!"

"No, thank you."

Simon turned to Anthony. "Now, are you going to tell me what the hell you're doing here?"

Anthony looked down at his feet. "I was worried about you, Dad."

Dad?

"What about your mum? She must be worried sick."

Jock shook his head. "If you didn't know he was coming, how did you know he was here?"

"He texted me as he was coming into the station."

Simon pulled his phone out of his pocket and dialled. The voice on the other end was so loud, the phone seemed unnecessary.

"No, no I did not know he was coming! No, it was a complete surprise. Kym. Kym! Yes, yes, of course …"

"Here, she wants to speak to you," he said to Anthony, without sympathy.

Anthony took the phone and nodded, even though the person on the other end couldn't see. There were a lot of 'but's and 'why can't I's and finally, a barely audible, "Sorry, Mum."

"She says I'm to catch the first train back tomorrow. Can't I stay for half term?"

Simon's face softened. "I'll speak to her when she's had a chance to cool down, but I'm not promising anything, Anthony. What you did was really irresponsible."

❋

Jock's editor, Hilary, stood as he walked into the cafe and shook his hand a little too firmly. She had the look of an old English sheepdog, with a long fringe that swept across her eyes.

"I'm concerned, Jock," she said, foregoing the usual pleasantries. "This book is nothing … nothing like anything you've written before. Your readers have come to expect a certain style, a certain pace. And this isn't it."

"I just think it's time to shake things up a bit."

He didn't quite know how to explain it. How could he go back to writing cosy, suburban mysteries when Sapphire's disappearance had thrown a shadow over his every waking hour? There was no going back. He was going dark and gritty and psychological. And he liked it.

Hilary flipped through the manuscript again. "It's just not like you."

"But it is! This book is more me, more real than anything I've ever written before."

"It's certainly very … raw. I have to ask, Jock, are you feeling OK?"

"I'm fine."

"Your mother rang me yesterday …"

"She has no business ringing you. I represent myself now and that's how it's going to be from now on."

"What about if I were to give you the number of a really great agent I know? Someone who represents several of the top authors in your genre?"

"Not interested. I don't need anyone else telling me what to do."

"I'm sure he wouldn't do that, Jock. Don't you want someone to help make your life a bit easier?"

He folded his arms. "I appreciate the suggestion, but I can manage."

She smiled wryly. "It's clear you've made up your mind." She gave him one more quizzical look, as if assessing his sanity. "Well, I must confess, Jock, I'm intrigued to see how this new direction of yours pans out."

※

THE BAR WAS empty when Jock arrived at the Dragon that evening.

"Dylan not in tonight?" he asked Neil, who was watching the women's rugby on TV.

"What am I, his keeper?"

Jock shrugged. "Just asking."

The smell of pine hung in the air as he trudged up the stairs to his room. He heard Dylan's voice, loud and accusatory, coming from the landing:

"You've been in my room!"

Another voice, this time female: "I was just cleaning!"

"Well, don't!"

He quickened his step, curious to see what was going on. Dylan had the look of a petulant toddler.

"Alright?" He looked from Dylan to the cleaning lady.

"No!" Dylan snapped. "She's messed everything up!"

And with that, he stormed up to his room and slammed the door.

Jock offered the cleaning lady an embarrassed smile and let himself into his own room, which now stank of bleach. His bed had been made and the dirty socks and underpants he had left in a heap on the floor were now folded in a neat pile on his pillow. He would have to change that pillowcase before he went to bed. He wondered if he should go and check on Dylan, but something told him to leave him alone. If Dylan was in a paddy, it was probably best to steer clear.

❄

CLAIRE POUNCES on me the minute I arrive. From the look in her eyes, you'd think it was years since my last visit.

"Where have you been?" she cries. "I thought something had happened to you." Tears collect in her eyes.

"I'm fine," I assure her, settling myself at the table. "Put the kettle on, will you?"

"Of course."

"Make sure you wash the cups thoroughly. I don't want to catch anything."

While she makes the tea, I open a packet of digestives and spread them out on a plate. Claire's eyes light up. I suppose this is a bit of a treat for her.

"Well? How is she settling in?"

"Just as expected."

I attempt eye contact, but there is too much hair hanging over her face. I eye her lank tresses with distaste. If I didn't know she was a natural blonde, I would never have believed it.

"Has she said anything?"

"She's still really confused."

"Good. The less she remembers the better."

"When are you coming again?"

"I'll come when I can." I refuse to put a timescale on it. Claire can be so needy. She reminds me of a little puppy I had as a kid. He used to cling to my ankle every time I tried to leave the house. Granddad cured him of that with the butt of his rifle.

She wraps her arms around herself and her veins bulge like snakes. There is no heating in the warehouse, no way of keeping warm. I could give her a better jumper, but I don't want her too comfortable.

"Have you spent much time with her?"

"I just bring her food and drink like you said."

"And you take care to lock up after yourself?"

"Always."

"Because if she gets out …"

"I know, I know. I'm very careful."

Strangely, I believe her.

I watch in disgust as she takes a second biscuit, cramming it into her mouth before she has swallowed the first. She reaches for a third, but I slap her hand back.

"Now, greedy. Make sure you save some for our guest."

The whole time I'm talking, her eyes flicker back and forth between the floor and the plate and I'm sure she's just plotting to eat the rest of those biscuits. Just in case, I wrap up the remainder and pop them back in my bag.

She looks stricken. "What about Gertrude?"

"Here." I place one solitary biscuit back on the plate. I'll leave it to her discretion what she does with it, but I'd be surprised if it ever finds its way down to the cellar.

19

Jock switched on the news while he was getting dressed the next morning. It paid to know what kind of world he was about to step out into. For a moment, he couldn't place the woman on the screen, but then he remembered. It was Gabriella's mother, Daphne Helston, looking solemn but respectable in her dark green trouser suit.

"I think this is a vindication," she was saying, "for us and for Peter. Peter is gone and yet May Queens are still going missing. Doesn't this tell you something?"

The interviewer adjusted his tie. "But the police have repeatedly said that Sapphire Butterworth's disappearance is not connected to the other missing May Queens. They're looking for someone else."

"What if they're wrong?" Daphne asked. "There haven't been any May Queens for five years, so the killer's had to wait that long. Someone that patient would be meticulous, someone who plans every last detail, someone who rarely makes mistakes. That's the real reason they've never been caught. They planned to frame Peter and they did it well. It bought them a lot of time, but now they are ready to kill again."

"Well, thank you for speaking to us today, Daphne," the interviewer said, cutting her off. "It's been interesting to get your perspective."

Daphne ran a hand through her soft, white hair. "Just a minute, there's something else I want to say." She looked straight at the camera, her eyes large and indignant. "I have a personal message for the May Queen Killer."

The camera zoomed in closer, so that her crinkly face filled the screen. "I want you to know that you don't scare me. Not anymore. You're taken lives and ruined others. Enough is enough. Show yourself, coward! Turn yourself in."

Wow! That was a bit intense, Jock thought, as he tied his laces. Daphne seemed so sure that her husband wasn't the May Queen Killer that it almost didn't matter if he was or not. No matter what proof he or anyone else uncovered against him, he doubted she would ever believe it.

❄

Sapphire closed her eyes, but she couldn't rest. She rolled over and knocked on the wall, hoping that Claire would hear and come down.

"We must be quiet," Ingrid reminded her. "We don't want to draw attention to ourselves. We just want to be left alone."

"But what good is it to be quiet if we die of thirst? If Claire comes down she can get us some water."

"We could do with more blankets," Fizz said, doing star jumps to keep warm. "Two between four isn't much use."

"It's better than nothing, isn't it?"

"Just be careful," Ingrid said. "We don't want anyone else to come down."

"Why don't they come down? What's it all for if they don't even come and see us?"

"But they will," Ingrid said, rubbing her temples. "And then you'll wish they hadn't."

"What do they do? Tell me!"

"It's better you don't know."

Sapphire clenched her fists in frustration. "But don't you understand that my mind is conjuring up all kinds of horrors? It can't possibly be worse than what I'm imagining."

Ingrid looked at her hard. "Can't it?"

"Anyone want a beer?" Fizz pretended to open a can and slug back its contents. A few minutes later, she was staggering round the room.

"Knock it off," Sapphire said. She really wasn't in the mood for Fizz's antics, but Fizz stayed in character, pretending to pee up the wall.

"Does she never get tired of playing the fool?"

"Never," Ingrid said. "I, on the other hand, feel very tired."

They snuggled side by side for warmth.

"I wish I had a duvet," Sapphire grumbled.

"I'd settle for a real glass of wine."

"Did someone say wine?" Fizz blundered over with her imaginary bottle, deliberately stepping on their toes.

"God, you're annoying!" Sapphire snapped.

"No, I'm not!"

"Yes, you are," agreed Ingrid. "You're all bloody annoying."

Sapphire nodded. "When we get out of here, I hope I never see any of you again."

Harmony looked shocked. "You don't mean that!"

"Of course I do. You'll be glad to see the back of me, too."

"No, I won't!" Harmony looked like she was going to cry and Sapphire immediately felt guilty.

"OK, you can come round for tea."

Harmony brightened up. "Can I bring Kiki?"

"Who's Kiki?"

"My dog. I wish I had my phone. I could show you some pictures of her."

"If you had your phone, we wouldn't be sitting around here talking about dogs."

She closed her eyes and prayed for sleep, then there was a soft knock at the door.

"I'll go," Sapphire said. She walked up to the top of the steps and waited.

"I just wanted to let you know it was me," Claire said when the door opened. She seemed almost shy. "Here, I thought you could have this for a bit." She held out a kettle. "Careful, it's full of water. I think I saw a socket under the stairs. There's only the one tea bag, I'm afraid. You'll have to reuse it but at least it will keep you warm."

Sapphire took it. "Thanks, Claire, I …"

"I have to go." She looked nervously around the room. "I'll be back to get it in the morning."

Night fell slowly. It was always dim in the cellar, but Sapphire's eyes had adjusted. She could make out forms and faces in the darkness and had got used to feeling her way around by reaching out with her hands. Her preferred place to sleep at night was at the top of the stairs, away from most of the rats, but that night her energy levels were so low that the stairs might as well have been Everest. She lay down with the others and closed her eyes, but it wasn't long before she heard the whistling and squeaking that signalled the rats' arrival. She braced herself, her hands firmly pressed over her face.

"Play dead," whispered Ingrid, "and they won't bother you."

Rat after rat poured out of the walls.

"I understand that they're hungry, but do they really have to piss everywhere?" Fizz moaned. "I've never known an animal to wee so much."

"It must be a territorial thing," said Ingrid. "Now hush up. I need my beauty sleep."

Sapphire lay awake, listening. She tried not to mind as the rats scampered by, preoccupied with their scavenging. She heard Fizz snoring softly and wondered how she could find such peace. A rat brushed her foot and she held her breath, waiting for it to move. Its razor-sharp teeth pierced her skin.

"Get it off me!" she shrieked, but the creature just hung on tighter. It was the one she had stepped on previously, she was certain of it. She grabbed her shoe and attacked it with the pointy heel, stabbing it three or four times before she was satisfied it was dead.

Ingrid touched her arm. "Are you hurt?"

"It bloody kills!"

It was more the shock than anything else. She lay down again and was trying to sleep when she felt another rat rub against her ankle. A second set of teeth clamped down on her skin. She jumped up and shook it off, but the evil thing had already taken its bite.

"What the hell?"

"It's the blood," Ingrid said. "They get a taste for it, especially when there's not much else to eat."

As if to prove her point, she felt more fur against her leg. She attacked the little blighter, whacking it repeatedly before it could bite.

"You've got to wash that wound," Ingrid said, "or they're going to keep going for you."

Carefully, Sapphire poured the last of the precious kettle water over her leg. It seemed such a waste, but she didn't have much choice. If she didn't clean off the blood, those filthy rats were going to keep biting her. She ripped off a piece of her petticoat and used it as a bandage, tying it tightly around the wound. When she re-joined the group, she sat with her leg tucked underneath her, a shoe in each hand. It was a long, exhausting night, but when the sunlight eventually came in, she had a pile of battered rat corpses in front of her. In the harsh light of day, they looked so small and helpless, despite their pointy teeth, and she felt uncomfortable in the knowledge that she had killed them all. With a quick glance at the still-sleeping Harmony, she scooped them up and dropped them all onto the tea tray. Hopefully Claire would take them away when she came down.

❄

M*OST PEOPLE GO* through life afraid: afraid to go out after dark, afraid of anyone who seems a bit different or out of control. But I don't have to be afraid. I can go out whenever I like, because I'm the one they fear and nobody even knows it. Most killers are careless and stupid. They are too lazy to plan ahead and ensure everything is properly executed. They are impatient, unable to wait for their next crime, their next kill. But not me. I've waited years. The fantasy is always better than the reality anyway. I'd rather get it right.

I arrive at the warehouse and tuck my boat round the back, where it is unlikely to be noticed by passing traffic. I remove the plank that hides the entrance, taking care to put it back when I'm inside. It wouldn't do for Claire to find out how I get in and out. My lantern lights up the room well enough for me to see. A little too well, actually. I could do without the endearing sight of two brown rats grooming one another. I shine it into the lift, checking carefully to ensure it's empty. If I am caught, it will be because of this lift. It's haunted, I'm convinced of it. It's downright creepy, the way it seems to think for itself. I will not allow myself to get spooked by it. Absolutely not. But if I get trapped in there, I'm betting Claire wouldn't have the gumption to call anybody, not even to save herself. I've trained her too well.

I travel down to the lower ground floor so I can have a quick peep in the cellar before I see Claire. I don't go in, just inch the door open and peer through. Sapphire is just waking up. She has her back to me, so I can watch her without her being aware of it as she attempts to stand on her head. It seems to have become a ritual of hers, that and the endless singing. She is nothing like Claire, nothing like what I've come to expect. After so many days, she is still wildly unpredictable. If I were to go in *there right now, I don't know whether she would attack me or beg for her life. I've allowed barely enough rations to keep her alive and yet she's not as worn down as I would expect. It's as if she has an extra energy source I don't know about. I wanted another Claire. I'm beginning to think this one's more trouble than she's worth.*

❄

"How was the abbey?" Dylan asked over tea at Sapphire's the next morning.

Jock shrugged. "About the same as a cathedral. What's the difference anyway?"

"An abbey is a monk's house," Anthony butted in. "A cathedral's more like a church. The main one in the diocese."

"Why are you using words like 'diocese' at your age?" Dylan asked with distaste. "Don't you know how to set traps and light fireworks?"

Anthony looked perplexed. He pulled out his phone and selected a game.

"Whatcha playing?" Dylan asked.

"Chess."

"Why on earth would you want to do that?"

"Because it's hard."

"Like a challenge, do you?"

"Maybe."

"Have you ever tried this?" He showed him what he was playing on his own phone.

"Angry Birds? That's for kids."

"It is not!" snorted Verity from the next table. She held up her phone to show that she was playing, too.

Dylan smirked. "See?"

Jock's phone vibrated abruptly and he lifted it to his ear without thinking.

"Hello?"

"Oh! Thank God!"

"Mum."

He glanced around the room, looking for an excuse. "Mum, I've got to go. I'm in a meeting. Yes, yes. I'll ring you later. Bye."

"You told a lie," Anthony said.

"Not a lie, a fib."

"What's the difference?"

"A fib is harmless."

Anthony met his eyes but Jock out-stared him. Eventually, Anthony got bored.

"My mum's got blonder hair than you," he told Angie, as she walked by.

"I expect she uses hair dye."

"I bet she's got more shoes than you. How many pairs have you got?"

"Forty-eight."

"What, you know that, without even counting?"

"Yup."

His eyes narrowed. "You're lying."

"Am I?"

He folded his arms. "My mum can eat more ice cream than you."

Angie smiled. "I'll give her that one."

"OK."

"OK."

Satisfied, he looked around for someone else to pester.

❄

JOCK HOLED up in the library for the day. His meeting with Hilary had given him a renewed enthusiasm for his book, in spite of the way she had reacted. He couldn't wait to get it finished. It felt so amazing to write something the way he wanted, without having to tone down his language and bury the real him. The clock moved without his noticing, the minutes running into hours. By the time he plodded back down the hill towards the Dragon, his body was stiff and aching, but his mind was free.

He trudged up to his room. There was something lying on the stairs: a shirt. It looked like one of Dylan's. He bent down to pick it up. It was covered in blood – lots of it, all down the front. He quickened his pace.

"Dylan?"

He climbed the steps that led to Dylan's attic bedroom. The door was ajar, but no sound came from inside.

"Dylan, are you alright?"

He pushed the door open. Dylan lay slumped on the floor in the middle of the carpet. The room reeked of alcohol, the source of which appeared to be a combination of Dylan's breath and the empty glass that lay beside him.

"Dylan?"

Dylan let out a loud grunt, but did not wake up from his stupor. On closer inspection, Jock saw that the blood had come from his nose, but had since dried. He wondered if the nosebleed was the product of a bar brawl.

He was tempted to leave him there, but Dylan was in such a state, he felt compelled to do something, so he pulled him into a sitting position. Experience had taught him that this was the best thing to do with the drunk. He picked up the empty glass and walked over to the sink to fill it with water. On his way back, he stumbled over one of Dylan's boots and as he did so, he nudged the computer. The screensaver vanished, giving way to a frozen image. It was a still of Sapphire, waving to the crowd from her May Queen float.

Jock's eyes darted to the left. On the wall next to the computer was a map of Britain. The map was dotted with pins, each pointing out to pictures of missing May Queens. His eyes travelled the length of the wall. The names of all the missing May Queens were up there with notes about their backgrounds, jobs and other attributes. He backed towards the door. If Dylan was investigating the May Queen abductions then why hadn't he told him? Quietly as he could, he pulled the curtains open to let in a little more light. He darted a glance at Dylan, but he was still sleeping heavily. Taking his phone from his pocket, he raised it to the wall and photographed each section as close up as he could.

Once he was sure he had got it all, he closed the curtains again and hurried back to his own room, where he locked the door behind him. He plugged his phone in and synced the pictures with his laptop. It would be easier to view them on a larger screen. He felt a deep feeling of unease in the pit of his stomach. What wasn't Dylan telling him?

20

Dylan staggered into the tea shop, clutching his stomach like a woman in labour.

"What happened to you?" Jock asked.

He had a face like a bruised banana. His eyes were red and bloodshot and his nose was purple and swollen.

"I think somebody slipped a hangover in my drink."

He sat down gingerly as if he thought bits would come off him.

"That bad?"

"It's my stomach," Dylan moaned. "Right now, I can't trust my arse with a fart."

Jock inched his chair away a little.

"You look as rough as the bottom of a bird cage," Angie said, her arms folded.

"Rougher," Dylan said.

"Right, I'm making you a cup of my special tea."

"Oh no! I'm feeling better already!"

But there was no arguing with Angie. He turned his head to look at Jock. "Stop blinking, will you? You're giving me a headache."

Jock watched him carefully. He looked rather pathetic, lying back against the edge of his seat.

Angie returned with an extremely pungent brew. "Now drink this down."

"What's in that?" Jock asked, covering his nose with his hand.

"Ah, you know. Eye of newt, wart of toad."

"All I need is a little hair of the dog!"

"Just get it down your neck. Go on. Not a word out of you till you do."

Dylan did as he was told.

"What happened?" Jock asked. "I thought you were immune to hangovers."

Dylan laid a hand on his shoulder. "None of us are immune, my friend. We are all but soldiers in the fight against sobriety."

"You go home to bed now," Angie said when he had drunk the last of the vile concoction. "Go on with you and don't come back till there's a splash of colour in those cheeks."

"You're a hard woman!" Dylan muttered.

"Well, you've no one but yourself to blame."

Jock watched as he stomped out the door. Whatever was going on with Dylan, it would have to wait.

"Where's Simon today?" he asked.

"He's off visiting the Museum of Agriculture with Anthony."

Poor Anthony.

"He's still off work, then?"

"It's half term this week, so he's hoping things will have died down by the time he goes back."

"It's not fair."

"Too right it isn't! The things they've written about him in the papers. They've just decided he's guilty, even though they don't know the first thing about him."

"Maybe he should sue."

"That's what I keep telling him, but he's not interested. He just wants it all to go away."

It would probably never go away, Jock thought. If the police didn't know that Sapphire might be Gertrude, they might not be looking in the right places. He thought again about how Dylan had reacted when he suggested telling Stavely. What if he was wrong? Or worse still, what if there was a reason he didn't want the police involved?

Simon came in a bit later. Anthony trotted at his side, firing questions at him.

"What were the police cells like? Were they all dark and dingy?"

"I think you're getting confused with dungeons," came Simon's reply.

"Did you have to sleep on the floor?"

"Yes, but only because they couldn't find a mattress big enough for me."

"Did you have to share the cell with criminals?"

"No."

"So, you didn't see any criminals?"

"Afraid not."

"Oh."

"I saw lots of police officers, though."

"Did any of them have guns?"

"No."

"Tasers?"

"Not that I saw."

"Truncheons?"

"I don't think so."

"Was there any police brutality?"

"What, in Fleckford?"

"You never know."

"Have you been reading my Amnesty leaflets again?"

"I was bored." Anthony fell silent for about a nanosecond and Simon took the opportunity to catch his breath.

"Daaaad?"

"Yes?"

"Is it true they live on doughnuts?"

"The police? No, they all eat responsibly sourced fish, meat and organic vegetables."

Anthony pulled a face. "Maybe I'll be a criminal."

"Over my dead body."

"Oh, I'll just do postal fraud or something like that."

"I thought you wanted to be a train driver?"

"God, Dad! That was years ago. Can I have some money for the jukebox?"

"If it will shut you up for a few minutes, then by all means."

He produced a handful of change and emptied it into his son's outstretched hands.

"Thanks, Dad."

"Just spend it wisely. No Justin Bieber. You understand?"

He shook his head as Anthony walked off to spend his ill-gotten gains. "I try to be a good role model for my son and all he wants to know about are bloody criminals."

"I suppose they're quite exciting at his age," Jock said.

"What, having people think your old man is a serial killer? Hey, you don't think I'm a serial killer, do you?"

"Of course not!"

"The thing is," he went on, lowering his voice, "some of the things the police told me were deeply unsettling. I mean I've lived in this area for a while now, so I was here when the last May Queen went missing, but I've moved a few times over the years and it turns out that I also lived within twenty miles of one of the other May Queens when she was taken. I had no idea but you can see how the police thought that was suspicious. If I were a more paranoid sort of person, I'd think somebody was trying to set me up."

"That is a bit of a coincidence," Jock agreed, wondering

why he was telling him all this. Maybe he wanted someone to know. Just in case.

"Do you know the reason they let me go?" he asked. "The real reason?"

Jock shook his head.

"My ex-wife gave me an alibi for Claire Scutter's disappearance. Think about it, Jock. After everything they've said about Sapphire's case not being linked with the others!"

"Wow!" Jock said. "That *is* interesting! I'm amazed your ex was able to give you an alibi. I mean, it was over five years ago, wasn't it?"

"Yeah, well it turns out it happened on the night of Kym's sister's wedding. And since I was one of the groomsmen, there are plenty of witnesses to back me up."

"That is a pretty good alibi," he agreed. "Er, tell me, do you think Dylan's … alright?"

Simon raised an eyebrow. "Dylan's a selfish git!"

"But do you think he's alright in the head?"

He looked perplexed.

"You know, not a psycho or anything?"

He broke into laughter. "Jock, if you're about to suggest that Dylan's the May Queen Killer, I'm going to have to stop you right there!"

"How can you be so sure?"

"Oh, come on! That idiot couldn't organise a piss up in a brewery."

"No, he probably couldn't," Jock agreed. "Not unless it was a party of one."

"Why are you asking anyway? I thought he was your mate."

"He's just a bit … odd sometimes. I don't quite know how to take him."

"Well take it from me – Dylan's OK. Slightly crackers, but aren't we all?"

"I suppose so." He fumbled in his pockets for his phone,

which had started to vibrate. "Er, is it just me or has that song been played three times in a row now?"

"Anthony!"

Jock's phone got louder the longer it took to locate it.

"You've got reception!" Angie said with the kind of awe normally reserved for someone who had won the lottery.

Jock glanced at the display.

"Hi Robbie," he said, holding it to his ear. "Everything alright? I hope Hampton's not keeping you up at night."

"Hampton?"

"My hamster."

"Oh, I call him Gangsta."

"Nice, but it's a her actually."

"Right, well …"

"Something wrong?"

"It's just … Nan. She's always over here, cleaning the place and bringing me food. I know she's just trying to help, but she's really cramping my style. I mean, I had a woman over yesterday. A real, living, breathing woman, and Nan just wouldn't take the hint and leave."

Jock bit his lip. "You have to tell her to stop. She doesn't take any notice of hints."

"But she's my Nan!"

"I know, I know …"

Damn her. He wouldn't let her run his life anymore, so she was interfering with Robbie's.

All day, he struggled to concentrate. He had told Hilary he would get her the rest of the chapters by the end of the month, but it was going to be tight and he couldn't afford to fail. He didn't want anyone to think he couldn't do it without his mum to guide him, and there were plenty of writers just dying to take his place on the bookshelves. The main thing he had going for him, above talent, if he was honest, was the ability to spew 'em out. That was what she had taught him.

He stayed at the library until it closed and then headed back to the Dragon.

"Jock!" Dylan said jovially, as he pushed through the doors. "Alright?"

Jock nodded. "You're looking a lot better than you were earlier."

"Angie's potion worked magic. Must be witchcraft or something."

"Or maybe it's because you started drinking again?"

"You want a pint?"

"We need to talk first."

"Sounds a bit girly," Dylan said. "Are you breaking up with me?"

Jock bit his lip. "I want to know what you know about Sapphire."

"Well ..." Dylan slurred his words slightly. "That depends on how long you've got."

"Just tell me!"

"She ran off because of someone – someone who was more important to her than her role as May Queen."

"Dylan! Careful!"

The drink slid from his hand, shattering against the bar and sending fragments of glass everywhere.

"Ow!"

"Are you alright?"

"I'm fine. I just need a paper towel."

Neil wrenched his eyes from the TV. "What happened?"

"Spilled my drink." Dylan made a show of lapping up the beer that was running down the bar.

"Watch it! There's glass in that!" Jock warned.

"Perhaps you've had enough," Neil frowned, surveying the mess.

"Don't be daft! I know my limits."

"I think we all do." Neil handed him some paper towels. "Some people think they're invincible."

Jock wasn't sure if this comment was addressed to him or if he was just speaking to himself. "The police make the worst drunks," Neil muttered, as he walked round to clean up the mess.

Jock blinked. "You're a policeman?" he asked Dylan.

"Thought I'd said."

21

Jock stared at Dylan in awe. "You said you were on gardening leave. You never said what from. I just assumed you were a civil servant or something."

"Never assume." Dylan stared longingly at the beer taps.

"So what happened? Why are you on leave?"

Dylan yawned. "It's a long, boring story. I wanted to make detective, but my boss was holding me back because he was worried I would take his job. He's a very insecure man, you understand. Actually, I *was* after his job and I told him so on many occasions, but that's beside the point."

"So what *is* the point?"

"I used a bit of a shortcut to help him solve a case and he found out. He could have let it go, but since he didn't like me, he had me put on gardening leave. They all acted like they were doing me a favour by not sacking me, but gardening leave is like being in a state of purgatory between employment and unemployment. I was pretty pissed off, as you can imagine, so I used the opportunity to show them what I'm made of."

"Which is?"

"Let's see, I took up drinking and gambling. I stay up all night and I slag off my boss to anyone who'll listen."

"And you grew that crazy hair!"

"Oh no, I already had that."

"So how's it all working out for you?"

"Not bad as it happens. The obvious thing for them to do would be to sack me, but instead they offered me a pay-off. I refused to take it. So they offered me more. Occurs to me I should hold out and see what they're really prepared to pay. Meanwhile, I'm doing a pretty terrific job of screwing up my life and taking as many people as possible down with me." He smiled broadly. "That's where you come in."

"Nice."

"Well, what can I say? Misery loves company, and a man has to have a hobby."

"Can't you just take up pottery?"

"Not with these hands."

He lifted one to demonstrate. He had the jitters.

"Yikes! You should really get that seen to."

Dylan drew breath and Jock could see he was about to launch into one of his monologues, so he cut in. "Why didn't you say you were investigating Sapphire's disappearance? I saw your wall."

"Wait a mo. How do you know what's on my wall?"

Jock reddened. "I found you on the floor, stone-cold drunk."

"You didn't move anything, did you?"

"No, I–"

"Thank Christ. Cos I had all my stuff mapped out on the floor the other day and that stupid cleaning lady put it in a heap on my bed. Took me ages to put it right."

"That's why you were so pissed off with her?"

"What did you think?"

"I dunno. I thought you were a raving crack hound."

"That's nice, coming from a nosey parker like yourself."

"I told you, I was checking up on you because you were drunk *and* covered in blood I might add."

"Yeah, well I got into a bit of a tussle with some heavies. They took Shirley, the bastards!"

Jock blinked. "Who's Shirley?"

He couldn't picture Dylan with a cat or a dog. For some reason, a big, furry tarantula came to mind. Just the kind of pet Dylan would own.

Dylan looked at him with disdain. "Don't you listen to anything I say? Shirley is my car. She's been repossessed. Those bloody yokels have no heart."

"Did you know you dripped blood all the way up to your room? Good thing Neil got that cleaner in. She got it all off. You'd never even know it was there."

"Amazing woman."

"Quite. Do you think she's the May Queen Killer?"

"Yeah. She's probably hiding them all in the cleaning cupboard."

Dylan looked across the bar at Neil. "Can I please have one more pint?"

"No."

"Just one for the road?"

"What do I look like? An idiot?"

"No, you look like Neil from The Young Ones. Is that who you were named after?"

"Get lost."

"Alright, alright! Come on, Jock, let's go up to my room. I'll show you what I've been working on."

Dylan's room still stank of alcohol. It was like a perfume, permeating the air. His beige carpet was just the same as Jock's, but it looked older: smokier, dirtier, more lived-on.

Jock sat down by the computer.

"Want a drink?" asked Dylan.

"Er, no, that's OK."

Dylan opened his wardrobe. Instead of clothes, it contained drinks and snacks.

"You've got a mini bar! That's so …"

"Cool, isn't it?"

"I was going to say 'excessive'. Where do you keep your clothes?"

Dylan shrugged. "Who cares about clothes?"

While Dylan poured himself a drink, Jock started to read some of the Post-it notes grouped around the computer. He had photographed most of them before, but there were new ones, which drew his interest.

"Who's CS?"

Dylan didn't answer, but Jock saw his reflection in the computer screen as he grabbed something that looked large and heavy. He jumped to his feet and whirled round. Dylan was clutching a machete.

"Oh my God!"

Dylan took a step towards him, a bit unsteady from the alcohol.

"Put it down! Before you hurt someone!"

"Before I hurt you, you mean?"

Dylan's face went from jocular to menacing. His mouth twitched oddly.

"Dylan?"

"I don't like people going through my stuff."

"I didn't!"

He inched back, but there was nowhere to go. He was pinned in between the computer table and the window. The window was wide open, the ugly net curtains billowing in the wind. If he could just reach the ledge, he ought to be able to jump. He was on the first floor, so it would be a bit of a drop, but what else could he do? He grabbed the windowsill and pulled himself up.

"Jock!" Dylan was on him within minutes, dragging him back down.

Jock struggled for breath, won and screamed as loud as his lungs would let him.

"Jock, for God's sake don't jump! It was a bloody joke, you idiot!"

"A joke?" For a moment, Jock wasn't sure if he believed him, but as he watched, Dylan fell against the computer table, letting the weapon drop to the floor. "Jesus, you scream like a girl!" Dylan was laughing so hard, there were tears streaming down his face.

Jock sat in stony silence, the cold air blowing against his back.

"I can't believe how gullible you are! This machete is made of plastic, can't you see that? I had it left over from Halloween."

Jock leant forward and touched it. Dylan was right. Close up, it didn't even look that realistic. "You are one sick son of a–"

"Now don't you start on my mother. I wanted to show you something, remember?"

"Forget it!"

"You want to find Sapphire, don't you?"

Jock stopped in the doorway. "Have you really found something or are you just wasting my time?"

"I think you'll be interested in this," Dylan promised. "And I'll tell you what, I'll order us a pizza. How's that?"

Jock cocked his head. He ought to tell Dylan to go to hell, he really should. But then he would never hear what he had to say.

"Pepperoni alright for you?"

Jock let out a sigh. "Yeah, alright."

He caught his breath as Dylan phoned in their order. Just minutes ago, he had thought Dylan was going to kill him and now he had agreed to have dinner with him. What was wrong with him? He really knew how to pick 'em.

"So come on then, what was it you were going to show me?" he asked when Dylan got off the phone.

Dylan came over to the computer and made a few clicks. A video came up. It was in black and white, and looked a bit grainy.

"What is this?"

"I've been examining CCTV footage from the route of the May Day parade. This particular clip is from the tea shop, taken just before the parade started."

"How did you get it?"

"It's amazing what people will give you if you ask. Now I could be barking up the wrong tree here, but it looks to me like this lady …" He zoomed in on a scruffy-looking woman. "This lady bears a strong resemblance to the archive pictures of Claire Scutter. Obviously she's aged a bit and she looks a lot less attractive, but she has the right features – same eyes, same nose, same cleft in the chin."

"But Claire's dead, isn't she?"

"Only if Peter Helston was telling the truth. If not …"

"Wow!" Jock said. "Bloody wow!"

Dylan allowed himself a smile. "From what we've been hearing, Sapphire saw something or someone to make her run off from the parade. I wanted to see who or what that could be. Judging from the time these pictures were taken, she was upstairs getting ready, so she might not have had any forewarning that Claire – if this is Claire – was coming. Probably, she saw her for the first time when she was up on that float. People assume it was the May Queen Killer she saw, but for that to happen, she'd have to know who it was. I think it's more likely she saw Claire."

"So if I'm right and Sapphire is in fact Gertrude Scutter, then she must have thought her sister had come back from the dead," Jock said. "No wonder she ran after her!"

"Now the question is, where did they run to?"

"You know, if we want to confirm that this is really Claire, we could send a copy to Gabriella Helston," Jock suggested. "She was Claire's friend."

"Good idea, except she'd be biased, wouldn't she?"

"How do you mean?"

"Her father was accused of killing Claire, so of course she wants her to be alive and well, doesn't she?"

"I suppose, but she also wants to know the truth, or at least that's what she told me."

"Can you think of anyone more neutral?"

"No."

"Gabriella it is, then. Hey, I think our pizza's here."

❄

"What I don't get," Sapphire said to Ingrid, "is why Claire brought me here, if she didn't want to spend any time with me."

"She was just doing as she was told. That's all she does these days."

"But that's just not like her. The real Claire must be in there somewhere, fighting to get out. Do you think they told her if she lured me here they'd let her go?"

"Claire does not want to go," Ingrid said. "Can't you see that? Being here has changed her. It's changed all of us in one way or another, but it's changed her the most. She wasn't strong enough to deal with this. She couldn't cope."

"Not strong? She's the strongest person I know!"

"The Claire I know is very different to the one you describe. She took one look at us all, in all our filth and squalor, and she crumbled. They broke her, Sapphire. She became their servant — anything to be allowed to live upstairs and not down here with the rest of us. She won't even look at us most of the time. She doesn't want to be one of us. That's why she won't help us. She's afraid they'll chuck her down here and there will be nothing to distinguish her anymore. If, just once, she would leave that door unlocked, we might stand a chance, but she won't. She's too scared of losing her privileged position."

Sapphire shook her head. Ingrid had got it wrong. She must have.

"But why do they keep her up there? Why not keep us all together? It doesn't make sense."

"They are toying with us," said Ingrid, "messing with our minds. By separating us from Claire, they create division. That's what they want."

"They'll let us go eventually," Harmony said, snuggling up beside Sapphire.

"You really think so?"

Harmony nodded. "My dad will come up with the ransom, no matter how much it is."

"Ransom? There are no ransoms!" Sapphire told her. "People think you're dead, Harmony. They probably think I am too by now."

Harmony looked up at her, aghast. "But if there's no ransom, then why are we here?"

Sapphire bit her tongue, wishing she hadn't said anything. She had let her anger get the better of her when she should have let Harmony hang on to what hope she had.

"I get the feeling they want to collect us. We're just ornaments, possessions. That's why they leave us down in the cellar, gathering dust."

"But we're people!" Harmony exploded. "They can't just keep us!" She was silent for a moment. "They're going to keep doing it, aren't they? Why should we be the last?"

Sapphire nodded. "I expect they will."

Poor, deluded girl. One thing she knew for sure: if there had been a ransom, there was no way her own father would pay it.

22

Gertrude gazed out at the cool turquoise waters and admired the stunning pink cliffs beyond. She smiled as she breathed in the heady aroma of eucalyptus and juniper berries. Even after several months on the island, she still thought Corsica was the most beautiful place in the world.

She hadn't picked it entirely at random. She had come here because this was where her dad was – or, at least, where she thought he was. She didn't have an address for him, just the occasional postcard, postmarked Ajaccio, Corsica.

Assuming he was still a chef, she had tried every holiday resort on the island, starting with the capital and working outwards. She had tried every restaurant, every cafe, but no one could tell her anything. She began to suspect that her father had left or, worse still, that he just didn't want to be found. Whatever the case, she refused to dwell on it, just as she refused to dwell on her dead sister, or her sick mother. She was finally starting to live life the way she wanted and she wasn't going to let anyone ruin it for her.

One Monday morning, she was cleaning down tables at Sondra's and watching idly as a group of old men played pétanque on the green opposite. The café was quiet that morning, aside from a few customers drinking coffee and eating croissants. Later, plates of cured meats and cheeses would come out, with bread and fig jam, accompanied by carafes of rosé. There would be lively discussions, conducted in a jumble of English and French, with a little Italian and Corsican thrown in. Everyone would be loud and passionate. Everyone would be having fun.

A man in a Hawaiian shirt sat down at an empty table and spread his newspaper out in front of him. Gertrude strolled over.

"Bonjour. What can I get you?" she asked in her broken French.

He looked up from his paper.

"Gertrude?"

"Dad!"

She dropped to her knees and hugged him as she had when she was a little girl. "Oh, Dad, I've got something awful to tell you …"

Tears rolled from her cheeks and down his shirt.

"I know," he said stiffly. "The police told me about Claire."

His eyes darted about, as if looking for the exit.

"You knew? Then why didn't you come home? The … the memorial service … We had to hold it without you."

Her father ran a hand through his thinning hair. "I don't really do memorials, Gertrude, love. That's not how I want to remember her."

"Then why didn't you come back for me?"

"You were better off with your mother."

She felt her heart erupt through her cheeks. "Better off? Mum's not in her right mind. She doesn't even know her own name."

"She's still a better parent than I'll ever be." He looked pained. "Your mum loves you, Gertrude."

"And you don't?"

The words hung in the air between them. They sat in silence for a moment and then her father got up and left. His feet scorched the pavement as he walked away. Gertrude could almost see the sparks.

※

"Fancy a spin on the fruit machines?"

Jock shrugged. He had no idea how to play, but Dylan had it covered. He watched as he hit what looked like a random sequence of buttons and there was a loud cha-ching as the money spurted out. Dylan held out his hand to catch it, but several coins shot out regardless and rolled under tables and chairs.

"I bet that's how Neil claws it back," Dylan muttered, dropping to his hands and knees to pick up his winnings.

Jock dropped down beside him, retrieving a handful of coins.

"Thanks." Dylan produced a plastic bag from his pocket.

"Wow! How much do you think you've won?"

Dylan felt the weight of the coins in the bag. "About twenty quid."

"Shall we go and sit down now?" Jock asked. "Quit while you're ahead?"

Dylan picked up his pint from the table and took a swig. "I never quit." He fed some of the money back into the slot.

"I can't watch," Jock said, but he couldn't look away as Dylan pressed another sequence of buttons and the machine spat out more loot.

"Wow! This is amazing. I always assumed these machines were rigged."

"Nah, it's easy!"

Neil looked up from the bar, an unreadable expression on

his face. He was probably worried about how much money Dylan was winning.

"I think it's empty," Dylan said, as the machine stopped spewing coins.

"Oh well, you had a good run." Jock was glad to sit down.

"Don't look now but here comes trouble."

Stavely and Sweep walked up to the bar. Stavely cleared his throat but Neil did not look up from the packet of crisps he was eating. For a long, embarrassing moment, Jock thought he wasn't going to serve them, but then he swallowed his last crisp, flattened out the packet and folded it into an origami swan.

"Do you think we should show them the video of Claire?" Jock asked in a low voice.

"Over my dead body," Dylan said. "Besides, if they're any good, they should have already worked it out."

"But if they don't know about Gertrude …"

"Then they're not much good at their jobs, are they?"

"Well …"

Jock watched as Stavely and Sweep continued to stand at the bar, clutching their drinks. "What are they doing here?" he whispered. "I've never seen them in here before, apart from that time Stavely came in to use the loo."

"I never see anyone in here," Dylan said. "It's a miracle this place stays open. Come on, let me show you a new app I found. It notifies you every time the Queen goes to the loo."

"Why the hell would I want to know that?"

"OK. Do you want to watch a polar bear get drunk?"

"That's sick. They're endangered animals."

"You've been spending too much time with Simon."

"Yeah, well he's a better influence than you."

"But can Simon show you actual pictures of bears pooing in the woods? That's what I call real wildlife photography."

"Again, why would I want to see that?" He glanced over at Stavely and Sweep again. They seemed deep in conversation.

He tried to ignore them, but their presence bothered him, made him feel paranoid.

"Note Stavely's got a scotch, but Sweep's just got a poxy tonic water," Dylan said.

"Perhaps he's driving?"

"Nah! Stavely ordered for him. He's being an arse. He did it to me once to see if I'd stand up to him and ask for a proper drink."

"And did you?"

"Of course I bloody did but Sweep's too much of a gimp to challenge him hence he's stuck with the toilet water."

"So Stavely's your old boss?"

"No, Sweep is. I wish I'd had Stavely. Better an arse than a gimp." He peered into the bottom of his empty glass. "Get another round in, will you? I need to shake hands with the vicar."

It wasn't technically his round, but he went anyway.

"Interesting company you keep," said Stavely, as Neil poured the drinks. Jock didn't really know how to respond.

"A good lad, Dylan. I wish we could have kept him on the team."

"So what happened?" Jock tried not to look too interested.

"You know it's impossible to sack anyone these days."

"I mean, what did he do that made you want to sack him?"

Stavely poured a little spring water into his scotch and swirled it around the glass. Then he took a large swig, leaving tiny droplets in his bushy moustache. "Dylan had the makings of a decent detective," he said. "But he thinks the law doesn't apply to him and that's a dangerous thing. You can't arrest people based on intuition, no matter how brilliant you are. You have to have evidence to back it up. You can't go around forcing people to confess."

Jock nodded. He could picture Dylan as a maverick.

"Who'd be a detective, anyway?" Stavely went on.

"It sounds like a pretty exciting job."

Stavely's eyebrows knitted together. "A missing person's case is the ultimate puzzle," he said. "It gnaws away at your insides. And if you don't solve it, it will haunt you for the rest of your life."

Jock nodded. He was already under the spell. He ached to tell him what he and Dylan had discovered, but if he did, Dylan would never speak to him again and for some reason, that mattered.

He paid for his round and carried the drinks back to the table. As he handed Dylan his pint, he was aware of a leggy woman in tight jeans.

"Cheers!" he and Dylan said in unison, clinking glasses.

The woman raised her hand and slapped Dylan across the face.

"Hey!"

But before he could react, she turned to Jock and slapped him, too.

Jock stared after her. "What the hell was that?"

He could see Stavely and Sweep laughing their arses off at the bar.

"Ah, that would be my girlfriend, Efa." Dylan rubbed his cheek.

"Ex-girlfriend," she yelled, as she walked out the door.

Jock stared at Dylan in confusion.

"Care to elaborate?"

"She gave me an ultimatum. I don't much care for ultimatums."

"What did she say?"

"It was the drink or her. I think it was intended as a bluff."

❄

"Do you like living with your mum?" Verity asked Anthony at Sapphire's the next morning.

It was a bit of a leading question, Jock thought, the kind grown ups weren't really supposed to ask, but maybe it was a grandmother's prerogative.

Anthony fidgeted in his seat. "It's OK."

"But you miss your dad?"

"Not really."

Luckily, Simon was not in earshot.

"Well, he misses you," Verity said. "So do I for that matter."

"Dad's fine. He's got Angie now. Hey, maybe you should get a boyfriend, Grandma?" He hesitated just for a fraction of a second. "Or a girlfriend?"

"Cheeky!"

"I like coming for the holidays."

"And you like living with your mum?"

"Like I said, it's OK. I wish I didn't have to go to school, though."

"What's wrong with school?"

"It's tiresome."

"That's what your dad used to say."

"Did he?"

"Yes. Still does sometimes."

"But he's a teacher! Grandma?"

"Yes?"

"Can I have another biscuit?"

"Why are you always hungry?"

"I'm a growing boy."

"Go on, then."

Jock looked up just in time to see Anthony dunk his biscuit into Verity's tea.

"Maybe we should have a word with Morgan," he said to Dylan, as he watched the CCTV clip for the billionth time. "It looks like she's the one who served Claire."

Dylan frowned. "Do you think we can trust her? She's kind of snarky."

"It's in her interest to find Sapphire, isn't it? So she can come back and run this place again."

"I suppose. But don't blame me if she bites you."

"She doesn't bite!"

"All women bite. Take it from me."

Jock glanced around. "Morgan, do you have a minute?"

"What do you want?" She pushed her headband back into place.

"I just wanted to ask you to look at something, but if you're busy, we can do it later."

Morgan snapped her gum. "Now's fine."

She seemed only too happy to sit down and rest her feet, in spite of the fact that there was a pair of hippies waiting to be served at the next table.

Dylan pressed play on his phone and they all watched the woman they thought was Claire, as she talked to Morgan at the counter.

Morgan looked at him with suspicion. "Where did you get this, you perv?"

"We're just trying to find out what happened to Sapphire," Jock said quickly. "Do you remember the woman in this clip? She came into the shop on the day of the May Fair."

"Yeah, I do remember her, actually. She was a bit weird. Kind of pale and smelly."

"What did she smell of?"

She wrinkled up her nose. "She stank like a dead skunk's armpit. She was putting the other customers off their food."

"Do you remember anything else about her? Anything at all?"

"She didn't talk properly. Just sort of mumbled. And she didn't have any money either. But I let her off, given the circumstances. I thought she was probably homeless."

"Wait, there's more."

They all watched as Claire finished her tea and then stuffed the cup and saucer into her handbag.

"The cheek!" Morgan cried. "And to think I was nice to her!"

"Why do you think she did that?" Jock asked, after Morgan went back to work.

"Who knows? Maybe she took it for Sapphire."

"Why would she want a cup and saucer?"

"I don't know. Maybe as a memento?"

"A bit weird if you ask me."

"The whole thing's a bit weird."

"Tell me about it. Hey, you got that tenner you owe me?"

Dylan searched his pockets and came up empty.

"How do you always manage to be skint?"

"Dunno. It's an art."

Shaking his head, Jock went up to the counter to pay.

"I met Dylan's ex last night," he told Angie, as he waited for his receipt.

"Efa? Lovely girl. Too good for him."

"You think? She slapped me round the face!"

He expected her to laugh, but instead, her face grew serious.

"He hasn't told you, has he?"

"Told me what?"

She shook her head. "He runs against the wind, that one. He's got cirrhosis of the liver, Jock. That's why Efa left him. It was the only way she could think of to stop his drinking."

Jock stared at her. "So that's why she slapped me when she saw me giving him a pint. She thought I was encouraging him. But I didn't even know. He never told me."

"Knowing Dylan, he probably didn't think it was relevant."

"Not relevant? I never would have drunk with him if I'd known."

Angie shrugged. "The way I look at it, he's going to drink whether you're there or not. So you might as well keep an eye on him."

Jock shook his head. "No thanks. I don't need that on my conscience."

※

"Do you have to bring the gun?" Claire asks.

"I told you, it's just a precaution, in case anything goes wrong."

I look back down my list. "We might need duct tape. I'll see if I can pick some up at Homebase later in the week."

"When are we going to do it?"

"Soon." Claire doesn't enjoy the planning stage as much as I do.

"I still think we should go at night."

"No, it has to be daytime. We have to be able to see what we're doing. Besides, if we go at night, we won't get her alone."

"I just don't want to get caught. They'll take me away from you."

"Don't worry. No one's going to take you away. Not ever."

I can't decide if Claire's smile is genuine or fake.

23

Gabriella was hard to miss in her lime-green dress and matching wedges. Her jewellery clanged as she walked and the ancient librarian tutted under her breath.

"You found us alright, then?" Jock said.

"Yeah, no problem."

"Thank you for coming. It's so much easier to talk in person."

He led her over to the bank of computers where they were sitting.

"This is my friend, Dylan." He wished Dylan would sit up straight for a minute. "He's the one who found the video clip."

"Where are your shoes?"

"Oh, I don't really do shoes. They constrict my toes. Bare feet are comfortable feet, I find."

She gave him a look. "Bare feet are smelly feet."

"It's okay, he's harmless."

Jock wished he didn't also stink of vodka from the night before. At least, he hoped it was from the night before. Dylan didn't usually drink before lunch, as far as he knew.

"Why don't you take a seat here?" he said to Gabriella, planting himself in between them. He played the clip for her.

"Yes, it's much clearer on this big screen than it was on my phone," she said.

"And?"

"And it's Claire. I'm sure it is."

"How sure?" asked Dylan. "Percentage-wise."

"I don't know – about ninety-nine percent?"

"So there's still one percent of you that isn't sure?"

"Only because it seems so unlikely. I mean, if this is genuine, then it's huge. My father couldn't have killed her if she's still alive, could he?"

"What about all the other May Queens?" Jock said. "What if they're still alive, too?"

"Hold your horses," Dylan cautioned. "We don't want to get over-excited. We haven't got definitive proof that this is Claire yet, let alone any idea what it means."

Gabriella adjusted one of her large hoop earrings. "All I know is we haven't had any death threats since Sapphire disappeared."

"Death threats?" Jock scanned the room.

She nodded. "We used to get them all the time, ever since Dad was arrested. You'd think they'd stop when he died, but they didn't. People seem to think the family of a serial killer is fair game."

"That's awful. Did you go to the police?"

"Of course, but they've never found the person responsible. They just keep telling us that people who make death threats rarely carry them out, like that's supposed to be a comfort. Rarely isn't never, is it?"

"No. No, it's not."

"What kind of threats did you get?" Dylan asked.

"Letters – the old-fashioned kind, typed on a computer, addressed to Mum, mostly. We moved house a couple of years ago and they still knew where to find us. Whoever sends them seems to know us and our routines. They put in these little details to freak us out."

"Like what?"

"Like they'll say, 'I hope you had fun at bingo last night. I wouldn't think of going there again if I were you.'"

"They don't want you to play bingo?"

"That's just an example. It could be the tanning salon or Asda or anywhere really. They want to make us scared to go out."

"Do the police have any idea who sent the letters?" Dylan asked.

"Not really. Dad's name is out there. He's notorious. It could be someone connected to the missing May Queens, a friend or a relative maybe. Or it could just be some sicko who's latched onto us because we've been in the public eye. I've even wondered if it's the May Queen Killer himself." She fell silent for a moment, as if debating something in her head. "There are a couple of things that have always nagged me."

"Go on."

"It's just that Dad was the one who suggested Claire sleep over the night she disappeared. He said it didn't make sense for her to go all the way back to her house, when we lived nearer the club."

"And you think that incriminates him?"

"It makes me uneasy." She fiddled with her ponytail. "No one wants to believe that someone they love is evil, even more so when that person is no longer around to defend themselves. If my dad really was a monster then he never showed that side to me or Mum."

"Was there anything else about Claire's disappearance which sticks in your mind?" Jock asked gently.

"Nothing major, but …"

"Go on."

"Well, the night Claire disappeared, I'd laid my clothes out on a chair by my bed, so I wouldn't have to wake her if I woke

The Perfect Girl

up first. She had a tendency to sleep late and I've always been an early bird."

"Right."

"Well, the thing is, when I went to get dressed the next morning, my socks were missing. I wouldn't care, but they were my Pringle ones. I never did find them. The police didn't either. I know, it probably has no relevance whatsoever, but I just can't understand what on earth happened to them."

Jock exchanged a glance with Dylan. He had the feeling they were thinking the same thing - that Claire's abductor could have stuffed them in her mouth to keep her quiet, or else used them to tie her up. He didn't say it, though. There was no need to upset Gabriella.

"Jock, I told you all this because I want you to know all the facts. But what I really want is for you to prove them all wrong and to find out that my dad was innocent."

"We'll do our best."

Dylan nodded. It was the most serious Jock had seen him.

"Do you think it's going to rain?" Gabriella asked, as they left the library.

"Nah," Dylan said, kicking a can along the road.

"It is a bit cloudy," Jock said. "Ow!" he cried out in pain as a small stone hit him in the forehead.

"Quick, inside!" Gabriella yelled, fending off the tiny rocks with her hands as a barrage of hail assaulted them. Dylan shot ahead, into Fleckford's only McDonald's but Gabriella was as unfit as Jock and they were both puffing and panting by the time they reached the restaurant.

"Bloody hell! That was sudden!" Jock gasped, as they sheltered in the doorway, watching the hail batter the glass.

"Do you want to get something to eat?" Gabriella asked, as they stood there shivering. "Those burgers smell lush!"

Jock smiled. "Why not?"

"Not for me," said Dylan, but Jock knew his game. He

wouldn't order a thing, but then he would pick at their food. Crafty sod.

"I wouldn't have thought a place this small would have a McDonald's," Gabriella commented, as they waited their turn.

"It's the last one before the Welsh border," Dylan told her proudly. "There's a sign on the door."

"Wow! We'd better stock up!"

"You know, I make a point of visiting a McDonald's in every place I go," Dylan went on. "It's sort of like a cultural experiment."

"Are you serious?"

"Deadly."

"Why?"

"Well, it's a point of comparison, isn't it? I like to see what's the same and what's different."

"As hobbies go, that's pretty sad," Gabriella said with a laugh.

"You know what I like about this one?"

"No, but I'm sure you're going to tell us."

"The sign on the toilets."

"Lovely."

"No, look. Instead of the standard 'toilets', it says 'tolets'."

"Did the 'I' drop off?"

"No, it was never there. Look, the 'O' and the 'L' are too close together to fit an 'I' in there. It must have been printed wrong."

"I wonder how many other McDonald's have a misspelled toilet sign?"

"None that I've ever been to, which leads me to suspect that something happened to the original sign and they had to replace it. Look, it's not even in the standard font."

Gabriella cracked a grin. "You really are a huge nerd, aren't you?"

Dylan ran his hand through his hair, which was now flat from the rain. "Just observant is all."

"What shall we get?" Jock asked.

"The chicken's good," Dylan murmured.

Jock ignored him. If Dylan wanted chicken, he would just have to buy it himself.

"The coffee's good here," Gabriella said. "Just don't spill it on your lap because it hurts like hell."

They paid for their food and carried it over to one of the tables. They had just sat down to eat when a couple more people burst through the door. Even with his hood up, Jock recognised Simon straight away.

"Lovely weather!" he called.

"Marvellous," Simon grunted. He and Anthony were both soaking from head to foot.

Anthony scanned the menu with hungry eyes. "Dad, can I have a burger?"

"Now we've talked about this ..."

"Aw, go on Dad! I'm starving."

"You can have a bean burger."

"A bean burger? That's pants!"

"A bean burger and a milkshake. That's my final offer."

Simon held out a crisp ten pound note and Anthony snatched it without hesitation.

"Get me a coffee while you're at it. I'll get us a table."

"Why don't you join us?" Jock asked. "There's plenty of room."

He glanced at Gabriella. "You don't mind, do you?"

"Course not. Who's your friend?"

"Oh, this is Simon."

"Simon, Gabriella," he said, as Simon pulled up chairs for himself and Anthony.

"And what do you do, Gabriella?" Simon asked.

She smiled proudly. "I own an art gallery."

"Really? That sounds interesting."

She glanced at Anthony, who was standing, or rather fidgeting, in the queue. "How old's your boy?"

"Nearly twelve."

"He's quite small, isn't he? I would have thought he'd inherit your build."

"Yes, well, there's still time."

He sounded little irritable. He was probably sick of talking about his height.

"Whose phone is that?" Gabriella asked, as the table vibrated.

Jock fumbled in his jacket pocket. "Excuse me, I'd better get this." He walked over to the door to take the call.

Glancing back at their table, he saw that the conversation was flowing. You'd think they'd all known each other for years, the way they were going on, Gabriella gesticulating wildly and Simon nodding and laughing.

"Who was that?" Dylan asked when he got off the phone.

"My editor. She wants to know when I'm going to send her the rest of the novel."

"Haven't you finished it yet?"

"Nowhere near!" He wolfed down the last of his burger and jumped to his feet. "If you'll all excuse me, I'd better get to it. Thanks again for coming, Gabriella."

"Yeah, I'll see you again, I'm sure."

❄

"FANCY A PINT?" Dylan asked as Jock walked through the bar that evening.

Jock swallowed. "No thanks. And I don't think you should either."

"What are you talking about?"

"Look, I haven't been much of a friend to you, letting you go on like this ..."

"Wow! You're sounding really girly right now. I could

almost fancy you. Who's put you up to this? I bet it was Angie."

"She did mention the small matter of your diseased liver."

"Hey, it's not as bad as it sounds."

"It's exactly as bad as it sounds! You're drinking yourself to death, Dylan, and I'm not about to watch."

"I'm not asking you to watch. I've got my own YouTube channel for that."

"I'm serious, Dylan."

"Wow! If I didn't know better, I'd say you were morphing into Simon. Except you're growing out rather than up."

"Dylan—"

"Shh! If you're going to start talking to me about endangered species, you can save your breath. I've already heard it all from Simon and I'm in favour. Who needs pandas anyway? Concrete over the rainforest, I say. The world could use more parking."

"Have it your way."

He left Dylan at the bar and trudged upstairs to his room. He positioned himself by the window and stared down at the tea shop, watching people go in and out until Angie packed it in for the night. He would rather have sat in the bar with a pint but at least this way he didn't have to answer to his conscience.

❄

THE NEXT MORNING, Jock walked into the library and sat down in an empty carrel. It didn't take him long to get into his groove, his fingers flying across the keys as if they were hot to the touch. He hadn't quite figured out how his murderer had killed his victim. He was pretty sure he knew who had done it and where, but until he worked out the method, he couldn't be sure. His mind worked rapidly. A fresh bolt of inspiration flashed through his mind and he almost had it, when he heard the scrunching of paper. He looked up sharply. Someone sitting across from him was not having a good time. That was about the seventh time he had heard paper being scrunched. Typical! Now he had lost his train of thought. He had just worked out that the murder weapon would have been concealed in the icebox because ... For the love of God! More scrunching! Couldn't people cock up quietly? Yet again, he turned back to his laptop and willed himself to concentrate. Yes, that was it: the icebox was necessary, because without it, the murder weapon would have melted and then ... What was that noise? It sounded like fingernails being scraped across a chalkboard. Ugh! There it was again. How was he supposed to work with that going on? As much as he hated confrontation, he was going to have to have a word with this person. Or better still, report them to the librarian. That way he could stay out of it. He didn't like to make enemies. You never knew what some crazy person might do.

He got to his feet and casually walked past the carrel opposite so that he could catch a glimpse. He saw a pair of muddy boots up on the desk. The man's face was hidden behind a men's magazine. Honestly, some people had no respect for the library. As he watched, the man casually scraped his fingernails down the side of the desk then tore a page from the magazine and scrunched it up loudly, tossing it onto the pile on his desk. Jock whipped the magazine away.

"Oi! I was reading that!"

Just as he had thought. It was Dylan, with an indignant pout etched into his idiotic face. He should probably have punched him by now.

"What the hell do you think you're doing?" he hissed. But instead of answering, Dylan continued to play Pacman on his phone.

"Dylan!" he was loud enough to make a couple of people turn and glare.

Still, Dylan refused to look up.

"This is ridiculous!"

He stalked back to his desk and swept all his stuff back into his bag. It was hard enough, having Sapphire constantly on his mind. There was no way he could concentrate while Dylan was here being a total twonk.

He trudged back down the hill to Sapphire's. The tea shop was quieter than it had been for a while. The number of journalists had dwindled over the weekend, not surprising considering there hadn't been any significant developments since Simon was released almost a week ago – nothing that had been made public, at least. Jock wondered if the police knew what he and Dylan knew. What if they didn't? He wondered again if he should tell them. Was it really worth keeping quiet just for Dylan's sake? Especially now he was being such a pain in the bum.

"What can I get you?" Angie shifted her weight from one foot to the other. He tried not to stare at the pencil sticking out of her bun. Did she know it was there or had she stuck it there momentarily and was now wondering where it was?

"Jock?"

"A cup of tea and a slice of Battenberg, please."

"I'm sorry, we're out of Battenberg."

"Oh!"

This had never happened before. Bronwyn always made a plentiful supply. Angie nudged him and he saw Dylan sitting at a nearby table with three whole Battenbergs in front of him. His cheeks were suspiciously red and his hair damp with sweat. He must have legged it down the hill to get there first.

"I must admit, I wondered what he was up to," she said with a sigh. "I know for a fact he's not a big fan of marzipan."

Jock folded his arms. Dylan wasn't just being an arse. He was being a pimple on the arse of an arse. And how he longed to pop him.

"All this because I told him I wouldn't be his drinking buddy anymore."

"Pillock!" Angie said.

"Prize bloody pillock!" Jock agreed. But he was hurt, all the same. It wasn't fair that he was being punished for being a good friend.

A little later, Angie walked out of the kitchen holding a Spider-Man cake, which she set down in front of Anthony.

"Wait, wait!" Simon said. "Does anyone have a lighter?"

"Dad, that's really not necessary." Anthony sounded embarrassed. "It's not even my birthday!"

"What's with the cake, then?" Jock asked.

"Anthony has to go home tomorrow," Angie said in a low voice. "And Simon won't see him again till the summer holidays, which means he'll miss his birthday."

"Jock? Lighter?" Simon said.

"No, sorry. I don't smoke."

Several people made apologetic faces.

"Where's Dylan when you need him?" Simon muttered.

"He's just left," Angie said.

"Well, what about Morgan? She smokes like a chimney."

"She's late."

"Oh, come on!"

"It's alright, Dad!" Anthony said, touching his arm.

"Shh!"

Angie flicked on the light on her iPhone and began to sing. "Happy birthday to you …"

Anthony's ears burned as everyone in the shop joined in.

"What's the matter? Didn't you like your cake?" Verity asked her grandson, while Simon was in the gents.

"But it's not my birthday! And I'm into robotics and space stuff now. Spider-Man's for kids."

"Can't you go along with it, just to make your dad happy?" Verity said.

"I'd rather have my present early."

"Then you'd have nothing to look forward to on your actual birthday. Though, if I were you, I'd start dropping a few hints about what you'd really like. Otherwise you might end up with more Spider-Men."

"There's only one Spider-Man, Grandma."

"Break it to your dad gently, won't you? I think he still likes Spider-Man."

"I didn't say I didn't like him."

The old lady smiled.

"What's all this really about?" Verity asked, as Simon paid. Anthony was at the jukebox, jamming the last of his holiday money into the slot. They would probably be paying the price in bad music for the next half an hour.

Simon sighed. "Kym wants to take him to Australia for the summer, so we might not get to see him again till October."

"Then you must stand up to her! Say no!"

"I don't want to do him out of a holiday. It will be an experience for him."

"Yes, but it doesn't have to be all summer, does it? We hardly get to see him as it is. It's no wonder he ran away. It's important for a young boy to see his dad."

Simon looked away. "It never did me any harm, not having my dad around."

Verity frowned. "I'm not so sure. Look at you. You spend your life obsessing about some tiny hole in the ozone layer."

"It's the size of North America!"

"All the same, do you want Anthony to grow up like that? Filled with existential angst?"

"Actually, I'd be very proud."

"Yes, I'm sure you would."

❄

AFTER THE DISASTROUS meeting with her dad, Gertrude wanted to go home to England. She gave her notice at the cafe and booked herself a flight for the following week. Her boss, Sondra threw her a party and they drank wine and danced until two in the morning.

"We shall miss you," Sondra told her, wiping a tear from her eye. "You're the best waitress I ever had, despite your atrocious French."

"I'll miss you too," Gertrude said. "This has been the most incredible experience. Maybe I'll come back again next summer."

"Make sure you do."

She'd felt a little forlorn as she took the taxi to the airport. Despite the awful meeting with her dad, she was very fond of the island, and she'd meant it when she'd told Sondra she would like to return.

The taxi driver helped her offload her luggage and she tipped him a bit too generously. The airport was quiet that day and she got through check in quickly, then decided to have one last cup of coffee. Of course, they had coffee in England too, but it didn't taste or smell quite the same as it did here. As she sat, hugging her cup, the voice on the loudspeaker announced the details of the next flight, first in French then in English.

"Flight 9012 to Milan will be boarding in ten minutes. Gertrude, stop slurping your coffee!"

What?

She sat up, but no one else seemed to have heard the strange announcement. She opened a packet of sugar and stirred it in. She took a sip, but it didn't seem any sweeter, so she added a second.

"That's too much sugar!"

She looked up. This time the voice hadn't come from the loudspeaker, but from a man in a green raincoat who happened to be walking by. She watched him closely but he didn't look back.

It started to rain outside and she relaxed once more as she watched the water trickle down the windows. Rain had always had a calming effect on her, as soothing as any massage she'd ever had. Finally, they called her flight. As she walked towards the gate, she heard another voice in her ear.

"Not you, Gertrude. This plane's not for you."

She turned around but there was nobody there. Then she caught sight of the screen next to the gate. Instead of displaying the flight number and destination as it had a moment earlier, it now read:

'Not for you, Gertrude!'

"Can I see your boarding pass, please?"

The flight attendant held out her hand.

Gertrude looked past her, at the people descending into the tunnel. The man in the green raincoat looked back at her and made a slashing motion across his neck.

"Not for you, Gertrude!" came the voice over the loudspeaker.

"Boarding pass?" the flight attendant repeated, with practised patience.

Gertrude leaned heavily against the desk.

"I ... I've changed my mind. I don't feel well. I don't think I should travel."

A first-aider was called, accompanied by a couple of security guards, who seemed suspicious of her story. Her bags were located, searched and returned to her. The first-aider declared her fit to fly, but she declined the offer of a later flight. Instead, she called herself a taxi, travelled back to the café and begged Sondra to let her stay.

She hadn't realised she was ill, not at first. It was only the next time it happened, a few days later, that she began to see it. The man in the green raincoat came into the café and plonked himself down at a vacant table. She glanced at the other waitresses, but no one went up to take his order. Finally, she approached him. He leaned forward and looked right into her eyes.

"Daddy never loved you!"

"You're not real," she told him and went on with her work.

She didn't want to admit to herself she was ill, but she knew she had to confront the problem before it got worse. Once she lost sight of it, it would mess her up until she could no longer distinguish between fiction and reality.

It pained her to make that first appointment, physically stung her throat to make the call. Her fingers throbbed as she held the phone to her ear and her voice echoed as though there were a tunnel running through her head.

Her illness exhausted her, robbed her of all her energy. It was so much easier to stay in bed. She hid under the covers and tried not to think of her mother and all the years she had wasted. Then the phone purred in its cradle. She grabbed it on instinct. Heard the concern in Sondra's voice:

"I thought you were coming in today? Gertrude? Is something wrong?"

Excuses formed on her lips. She didn't have to explain herself to Sondra. She didn't have to do anything. She could stay in bed forever if she liked.

"I…"

"Gertrude, what is it?"

She pressed the phone to her chest and the room filled with thunder. She rocked back and forth, willing the noise away.

"What is it, darling? Tell me what's wrong?"

Gertrude took a deep breath. She felt the tension in the air. She had felt this way before, just before a storm. She had to shout to make herself heard over the thunder. The thunder that only existed in her head.

"I think I'm losing my mind."

She didn't wait for Sondra's reply. It was too overwhelming. She set down the phone and lay back against the pillows, wondering if she'd done the right thing. People hadn't always been kind about her mother. They hadn't always understood.

There were those who avoided her in the street, actively crossed the road if they saw her coming. Acted like she was a vicious dog off its lead.

Her mother had never hurt anyone in her life. The voices had taunted her, and only her. They told her how worthless she was, how disgusting. Gertrude had hated her mother's voices, and she hated her own even more.

"What do you want from me? What do you bloody want from me?"

"Gertrude? It's me, Sondra! Open the door."

Looking around, Gertrude saw the place from her eyes. Saw the hairbrush she had thrown at the wall, the fruit rotting in the bowl. She hadn't been hungry, these last few days. Hadn't been able to bring herself to eat.

"You're going to have to open the door, darling."

She heard the kindness in her voice. It seeped in, filling the whole room with the scent of palma violets. She took a couple of deep breaths to steady herself, then dragged back the covers and staggered across the room to the door.

***

Sondra drove her to the medical centre and gave her name to the stern-faced receptionist. There came a volley of French which Gertrude couldn't begin to follow, before Sondra ushered her into a seat in the waiting room. She tried to talk to her, but Gertrude struggled to hear her over the noise of the clock ticking impatiently on the wall.

"You shouldn't be here. You should at the cafe."

Sondra rubbed her back. "Don't worry about that. I closed it for the morning."

The doctor came out, and Gertrude gaped at him, unable to pick out any of his features.

"It's OK. Dr Mannuzza is going to help you. We have to go in now, Gertrude. It's the only way to get better."

If it weren't for Sondra, she wasn't sure she could have made that initial step. The doctor wasn't scary as such, but his face kept shifting. She would get flashes of his features, glimpse an eye or the tip of his nose, then they would disappear again, as if his entire being was unstable.

The doctor listened gravely as she described her symptoms and nodded.

"We'll need to do some tests but it seems likely you are suffering from schizophrenia."

"Just like Mum."

She fell into Sondra's arms, the blood pumping in her ears.

"You've been under a lot of stress so perhaps it's not surprising this should happen now. It suggests your mind has had the time to process things, and grieve for the sister you lost."

"Do you think my illness was inevitable?"

"I don't believe anything is inevitable, Gertrude. But with your mother's history, I'd say you were predisposed."

She looked down at her lap. She had abandoned her mother to come to this paradise, but she couldn't escape her destiny. It had simply followed her.

"I'm never going to be normal, am I? I'm going to end up alone and crazy, just like my mum."

The doctor shook his head. "If you take good care of yourself, your prognosis could be quite different. Above all, you need to stay positive. Don't let this take over your life."

Sondra handed her a tissue and she blew her nose. The doctor rattled on about her next steps. He talked too long, and her tired brain struggled to take it all in. Sondra whipped out her pad and scribbled it all down, as if she was taking an order at the cafe.

"Don't worry, Gertrude. I'm going to help you. You'll get through this, just you wait and see."

Gertrude's heart swelled with gratitude. In her entire life, no one had ever stuck up for her before. Certainly not her family, or any of her friends from school. She cleared her throat and sat up a little straighter. She had worked too hard to let her life fall apart now. She was going to tackle this head on.

As the weeks flew by, she became used to her altered self. She found that the anti-psychotic drugs eased the symptoms considerably. She was careful to avoid alcohol, or anything else that could screw up her meds, and she felt she had it under control. She still heard things that were strange and unpleasant, and couldn't quite ditch the man with the green raincoat, but the important thing was that she knew what was happening. She knew what was real and what wasn't.

❊

DYLAN WENT OUT of his way to ignore Jock. He would walk out of his room just as Jock was leaving his and very pointedly push past him, letting the hall door slam in his face. Jock responded by throwing himself into his work. Still, without Dylan to distract him, it looked like he was going to meet his deadline. He became so engrossed in finishing his story that it took him a couple of days to notice that he was no longer running into Dylan everywhere he went. Dylan wasn't just pretending to ignore him. He really was ignoring him.

Enough was enough, Jock thought, as he typed the last few sentences into his laptop. It was time he had a proper talk with Dylan. He didn't know how much longer he was going to be staying in Fleckford and it seemed ridiculous to leave it like this.

The thought of leaving without finding Sapphire haunted him too, just as Stavely had said it would. He was carrying on with his life as best he could, but it had been three weeks now and he was beginning to accept that this might not end well.

He dropped his bag off in his room, took a much-needed

shower, then headed back down to the bar. It was about seven o'clock, around the time Dylan would usually be sinking his third or fourth pint. He would be just starting to argue with anyone who would listen about politics or religion or anything else with the slightest whiff of controversy. Jock braced himself for raised voices, but Dylan wasn't there.

"Have you seen Dylan?" he asked Neil.

"No."

"He hasn't been in tonight?"

"He hasn't been in all week. Maybe he's found himself a new local."

"What could be more local than this?"

Neil met his eye. "Didn't he tell you? He moved out."

"When?"

"End of last week. He still owes me a month's rent, the git."

"Did he leave a forwarding address?"

"Ha ha! That's a good one!"

"So you've no idea where he is?"

"I'm sure he'll be in touch – when he wants something."

"Yeah, I suppose."

"If you hear from him, tell him I want my money. Unless you're good for it?"

"Yeah, right!"

He bashed out a text on his phone but with the mood Dylan had been in lately, he would be lucky to hear from him. If only he didn't care.

He wandered outside. He had seen posters advertising a screening of *The Godfather* at the village hall. There was no guarantee that the projector would be working any better than last time, but he liked their cake and there was nothing better to do.

To his amazement, the queue was out the door. He heaved a sigh. Did he really want to join a queue for a film that might not even be showing? As he hovered at the back, not quite sure what he wanted to do, he spotted a woman with a familiar black ponytail.

"Gabriella!"

She didn't turn around.

"Gabriella!" He shouted a bit louder. "Gabriella!"

He ran to catch up with her. "Hey! I thought it was you!"

"Oh, hi, Jock!"

"What brings you back to Fleckford?"

"I'm here on business." She gave him a breezy smile.

"Really?" How much business could she possibly have in Fleckford? And at this time of an evening.

"I'm sorry, I'm running late for a meeting," she said with an apologetic smile. "But I'll give you a ring later in the week, OK?"

"OK."

He watched as she hurried off towards the Cherry Tree Hotel. If he hadn't looked back, he would have thought she had gone in, but he did glance back, just in time to see her dash across the road into McDonald's. Not the most obvious place for a business meeting. So what was she really doing in Fleckford that didn't involve him?

24

Warm, midday sun shines on my back as I remove the first frame from the hive. This disused field with its high hedges is the perfect place to keep my bees and I don't even have to pay rent.

"How are we today, my little beauties?" I ask, as the bees buzz around me. Such industrious creatures. Perhaps that's what I like about them. If there's one thing I can't stand, it's a sloth.

I prop up the frame and peer in. The sunshine lights up the hive, illuminating all the little details. The bees watch me as I inspect for eggs and larvae. The queen bee is alive and well. She looks up at me with respect as the worker bees attend to her needs. I breathe in their wonderfully rich, butterscotch smell. Unlike her, they are all disposable.

❈

IT TOOK a year in Corsica before Gertrude felt ready to return to England. She thought long and hard about what she would like to do and settled on opening a café of her own, a traditional English tea shop, selling fresh cakes and scones. She already knew how to bake, but the glamorous French women had taught her so much about elegance and charm. She now knew how to hold herself and how to walk, how to make every customer feel special by making the effort to come and talk to them.

She was confident of getting the loan she needed. She had written Claire's proposal for the ballet school, after all, and she still had it on her computer, along with a ton of other useful documents. She could use them as a basis to build her own business case. She would need one if she was going to convince a bank manager to back her. No one had ever said no to Claire, and they wouldn't say no to her either. She would find herself a new town, somewhere people didn't know her, or her family. Somewhere she wouldn't be weighed down by her past.

She didn't look like her old self anymore and she had developed a new persona. She stood tall now, every movement confident and deliberate. She dressed in beautiful fifties-style dresses and her body glowed from the warmth of the Corsican sun. She had dyed her hair sunflower blonde and she'd banished the sadness from her eyes with the help of coloured contact lenses. She had Claire's eyes now, a dazzling brilliant blue that made people want to hold her gaze.

There was one last change she needed to make. Throughout her life, she had been blighted with the name Gertrude Scutter. Her father couldn't very well help his last name, but he had insisted on naming her after his mother. Apparently, she had loved her name, but Gertrude hated it. It felt dowdy and boring. That awful name was like a chain around her neck. She was filled with shame every time she had to introduce herself. She didn't even feel like a Gertrude anymore. She needed something more glamorous, more inspiring – the sort of name that made people look twice. She wanted a name that sparkled, a name like … She paused in front of a jeweller's window and glanced down at the rings and necklaces on sale. Sapphire! It was perfect. Her new name would be Sapphire. She glanced up at the name of the shop.

Butterworths the Jewellers. That was it! Sapphire Butterworth. It had a ring to it. She already felt like a somebody.

By the time she opened the tea shop, Gertrude was well-accustomed to her new name. Only once did she let it drop, when making an appointment at the hairdressers. She quickly corrected the mistake, ignoring the confused look on the receptionist's face.

Anytime she felt like she wasn't good enough, she just asked, "What would Claire do?" Claire had always assumed things would work out for the best and up until her disappearance, they had. Now she had gained in confidence, she felt the same was true for her. You couldn't sit around feeling sorry for yourself. You had to make things happen and that was exactly what she intended to do.

※

JOCK'S PHONE bleeped with a message. His heart leapt as he realised it was from Dylan.

'Housewarming, 8 PM tomorrow. Wear a tie. P.S. – I'm registered for gifts at John Lewis.'

Typical Dylan, Jock thought – rude and to the point. But he hadn't even included his new address. Had he just forgotten or was Jock expected to work it out? He re-read the message. No explanation, no apology. He ought to be royally pissed off, but he just felt relieved. Dylan was talking to him again, at least for the time being.

He shouldn't reply. He knew he shouldn't. He should at least leave it till morning, but his eager fingers betrayed him.

'Just don't expect me to drink,' he typed back. 'P.S. – I don't have your new address?'

He immediately regretted it. Why had he bloody well replied? It made him look overeager. He should have played it cool, let Dylan sweat a bit. Now he would think he had won.

It wasn't until quarter to six the next day that Dylan

finally deigned to send him directions. Jock had already showered and put on a clean shirt. He didn't know why he was going to so much trouble but he had no idea how posh this party might be, or who would be there. He might as well make an effort.

Dylan's instructions were odd and erratic, leading him past the square and down to the canal. Surely this couldn't be right? He held his phone high in the air, but he couldn't get a signal. It was growing dark as he followed the footpath over the bridge. It was as still and creepy as it had been the day Sapphire disappeared. He felt a shiver run up his back as a twig snapped behind him. Glancing back, he could just make out two shadowy figures. He quickened his pace, but they were gaining on him, matching each of his strides with longer ones of their own. He was almost at a run when he felt a gloved hand on his shoulder.

"Jock?"

"Angie?" He sagged with relief.

"I'm sorry! Did we make you jump?"

Even in six-inch heels, she only came up to his chin.

"Sorry," came Simon's voice behind her. "We're looking for Dylan's place. I take it you are, too?"

"Yes."

"Oh man! You thought I was the May Queen Killer, didn't you?" Angie said. "I'm sorry. I know it's not funny but it's just so ridiculous!"

She shone her mobile phone down at the ground, revealing her fluffy pink stilettos.

"It's fine," he insisted, but even with company, the canal bank was eerie. The last place he would want to stand about having a chat.

"Look! There's a rat having a swim!" Angie pointed at the water.

Jock followed her gaze. He could just make out a small creature paddling with its front paws, its tail high in the air.

"Ugh!" He had always hated rats. "What are we doing here?"

"Well, according to Dylan's instructions, we need to go under the bridge," Simon said.

Jock eyed the gap between the bridge and the canal. "Not bloody likely!"

"Oh, it'll be fine," said Angie. "Just hang onto me."

"And what about you?"

"I'll hang onto Simon. Come on, let's go."

Jock wanted to protest, but Angie took him by the arm and pulled him under the bridge. She had an enormously long stride for a short woman. It must be the shoes. He almost had to run to keep up.

"It's pitch black!" he said, his voice strange and echoey.

"It's OK. Just hang on tight," Angie said. "Dylan's place should be just the other side."

He closed his eyes and allowed her to guide him along. They emerged on the other side to find a dark red narrowboat, the Kingfisher, decorated with lights and streamers.

"Is this it?"

"I was expecting a cottage," Angie admitted.

"Me too," Simon said. "But this is much more fun!

"Hey, do you think Dylan painted these?" Angie asked, pointing to the childlike illustrations of flowers and castles on the side of the boat.

"Most definitely not," said Jock. "They'd be a lot less PG if he did."

Dylan stood on the deck, clutching a glass of deep-red wine. He had a good-looking woman on either side of him. Jock suspected he was paying them for their company. It was just the kind of extravagance he would indulge in.

"Come on up!" he called out in a princely manner.

Jock wondered how much of that red wine he had had to drink. Still, he followed Simon and Angie on board.

"Nice place," he greeted Dylan coolly.

"Nice tie," Dylan said with a snort.

"How come you're not wearing one?"

"Ties are for tossers."

Jock glanced around. None of the other guests were wearing ties. He tugged his loose and shoved it in his jacket pocket.

"I bought that specially," he told Dylan.

It had only been a quid from a charity shop, but Dylan didn't need to know that.

"Shut up and have a drink."

Jock's heart sank as he clocked the drinks table. There was a ridiculous amount of booze: dozens of bottles of wine, several cases of beer and nothing but bacon rinds and pork scratchings for snacks.

He watched as Dylan poured a glass of white wine for Angie.

"What can I get you?" he asked Jock.

"You got any lemonade?"

"Under the table."

He found a case of soft drinks and grabbed one. He wasn't particularly thirsty, but it gave his hands something to do. He was damned if he was going to drink tonight, after all Dylan had put him through.

He watched as Dylan downed his wine and poured himself another.

"Seriously, Dylan. When are you going to stop drinking?"

"Never."

"But you're making yourself ill. Don't you know you could die?"

A sulky look came over Dylan's face. "I don't need this tonight. This is supposed to be a party."

He started to walk off, but Jock grabbed his arm. "Just tell me how bad it is."

The sulky expression turned to anger. "Have you been Googling my condition?"

"Of course I have and I'm horrified. Don't you know what you're doing to yourself?"

"You only live once, right?" Dylan attempted a smile and failed. "My doctor says I need a liver transplant."

Jock slumped down on the bench. "God!" He had known it was bad, but not this bad. "How long's the waiting list?"

Dylan sat down beside him, still nursing his wine in his hands. "They're not going to give me one, Jock. I drink."

"So you're just going to keep on drinking?"

"I might as well, mightn't I?"

They sat in silence for a few minutes until one of the girls Dylan had been with earlier stomped over and demanded he change the music. Jock drifted down to the bow of the boat. He leaned over the side, enjoying the gentle breeze.

"Do you miss her?" Angie asked, appearing at his side.

For a split second, he didn't know who she was talking about.

"It's OK, I miss her, too," she said, wrapping her scarf tighter around her neck to prevent it from blowing away in the breeze.

His memory of Sapphire was fading, replaced by snippets from the newspapers and headshots printed by the press. None of them represented the bold, confident woman he remembered, the woman who made everything stop just by walking into the room. But it was different now. She had become some kind of an enigma, a puzzle that nagged at him to be solved.

Angie gazed intently into her wine glass, as if it were a crystal ball.

"She loved a good party. Loves, I mean," she said quickly. "Why do I keep doing that?"

Dylan wandered over with a bottle of wine in his hand. "More white, Angie?"

"Go on then."

She turned back to Jock. "Come on, let's mingle."

They walked over to where Simon was standing with Bronwyn.

"Simon was just explaining the impact of climate change to me," Bronwyn said, her eyes a little too wide.

"Sounds riveting." Dylan topped up her glass. At the rate he was going, everyone would be trolleyed within an hour.

Bronwyn brought the glass to her lips. "What shall we drink to?"

"How about Sapphire?" said Simon.

"Sapphire doesn't even drink," Angie pointed out.

"Much like myself." Dylan cracked up at his own joke.

Bronwyn laughed, but Angie and Simon exchanged worried looks. Jock wondered if they knew how bad it had got.

"That's better," Dylan said. "Now, who wants to dance? I've got a ripping Madonna CD."

"What's a CD?" Bronwyn asked.

Dylan palmed himself in the face. "Oh God, I'm getting old!"

That didn't stop him from showing off his dated dance moves, though.

"Come on, Jock! Get on the dance floor."

"Not me. I've got two left feet." Not to mention the fact that he was stone-cold sober.

"Same here," Simon said. "Besides, drinking and boats don't mix. If you look at the statistics—"

"Man, I wish you'd both lighten up," Dylan complained, topping up everyone's glasses again.

"Hey, I've barely started the last one!" Angie protested.

"Really?" Dylan looked genuinely surprised.

"Maybe you'd better slow down a bit," she said softly.

Simon glanced at the huge arsenal of drinks. "Yeah, you don't want to run out."

"I take it the loo's downstairs?" Jock asked.

"I usually just aim over the side," Dylan said.

"But there must be an actual loo?"

"Downstairs. If you're going down there, can you grab some crisps?"

"OK." At least he hadn't asked him to bring up more booze.

He climbed down the narrow stairway and dropped into the cabin. He really did need the loo, but he was also curious to see Dylan's new living quarters. He found a small galley kitchen and a cosy little lounge area, which he supposed must double as a bedroom. He looked about for the loo, but all he could see was a cupboard. He tried the handle. The tiny cubicle doubled as both a loo and a shower. He pushed his way in. It wouldn't have been quite such a tight squeeze if it weren't for the fact that the door opened inwards, forcing him to press himself against the wall so that he could close it behind him.

How does Dylan live like this? He used the toilet and then rinsed his hands in the doll-sized basin. There was no towel, so he had to dry his hands on his trousers. He was just about to pull the door handle when he heard voices in the cabin – a man and a woman. He could just make out a little of their conversation – a conversation he clearly wasn't meant to hear.

"We should know within a couple of days."

"I don't think I can wait that long."

"We have to."

Slowly, he opened the door. Simon was unmistakable, even from the back. But what was Gabriella doing here? She and Simon barely knew each other, so what could they be talking about with such intensity? Whatever it was, his instinct told him to leave them to it. He looked at the stairs and tried to calculate whether it was possible to make it up to the top without them noticing. They had their backs to him. With any luck, he could just slip out.

He crept along, quietly as he could, careful not to breathe too loudly. He was almost at the stairs when the boat jolted slightly and his hip caught the bookcase. A jar of pennies slid off the counter. He put out his arm to catch it, but only succeeded in sending it clattering to the floor.

Two heads whipped round. Simon's eyes met his. His look was deep and penetrating, as if he were trying to suss out how much Jock had overheard, how much of a problem he was going to be. Leaving the pennies on the floor, Jock grabbed the nearest rung of the steps.

"Wait!" Simon's voice boomed after him.

Jock tried to pull himself up the ladder, but it was too late. Simon had him by the ankle.

25

Jock glanced back over his shoulder. Simon looked worried rather than angry.

"Just wait. Let me explain."

"Then let go of my foot," Jock demanded, his heart beating hard in his chest. If there were nothing to worry about then why was Simon manhandling him? Simon loosened his grip and Jock moved faster than he had ever moved in his life. Simon was a lot fitter than him, but climbing the narrow staircase was not easy for such a large man. As he struggled with his footing, Jock scurried up the ladder.

"Hey, you forgot the crisps!" Dylan chastised him, as he hoisted himself onto the deck.

"Get them yourself, you lazy git!"

He swung his leg over the side and hopped down onto the riverbank.

"Hey! Where are you going?"

"Got an early start tomorrow."

"But you don't even work!"

Jock did not bother to reply. He glanced back one last time and saw Simon's head pop up above deck. He glanced left and right. There was no way he was going back under that creepy tunnel, so he followed the canal path in the opposite direction, running at first then walking when his side started to ache. He walked further and further out of his way until he reached a pub called the Green Man. The lights were on and there were people smoking and drinking outside, just inches from the canal. He paused to catch his breath. He didn't think Simon was following but he wasn't taking any chances. He went in and asked the barmaid to call him a taxi.

"Do it yourself, love. There's a payphone over there. But what's your rush? Why don't you buy me a drink first?"

❄

IN THE BROAD light of day, Jock felt like a prize chump. Simon wouldn't harm him, especially after what he had done for Anthony. If he weren't such a coward, he would have just let them explain. Now it was going to be embarrassing and awkward. He had a good mind to leave Fleckford early. He checked his phone and found he had six missed calls from Dylan and a drunken message telling him to get his arse back to the party, then a second one to tell him he was an inconsiderate bastard and a final one to say that he was missing the stripper. Dylan sounded so drunk by then that he probably wouldn't even remember calling.

As much as he wanted to just pack up his stuff and go, something was stopping him. He stood in front of Sapphire's tea shop, debating whether to go in. He couldn't see Simon in there, but you never knew when he was going to walk in.

"Morning, Jock. Did you enjoy the party?"

He almost jumped out of his skin as Gabriella walked up to him. She was still wearing the clothes she had had on the night before.

"It was OK." He backed away a little.

"You left really suddenly."

"Yeah, I was getting a headache."

"You look fine now."

"I'm much better, thanks."

"Well, are you coming inside?"

He glanced up and down the street but there was no sign of Simon.

"Come on, I won't bite."

"After you."

They walked in and sat down. Angie fluttered over. "Who's your friend?" She gave him a curious look.

"This is Gabriella." He took care to omit her last name.

"Nice to meet you," Angie said. "You look kind of familiar."

"Yeah, I think I saw you at the party last night."

"Ah! So you know Dylan?"

"Afraid so."

"Can I get you some tea?"

"I'll have a cappuccino, please."

"I was surprised to see you last night," Jock said to Gabriella, as Angie walked off towards the kitchen.

"Yes, well, I bumped into Dylan and he invited me. It was a really last-minute thing."

He watched her closely, convinced there was something she wasn't telling him. Gabriella had a gallery to run, so why was she hanging around?

"Here you go!" Angie set Gabriella's coffee down in front of her.

"Hey! This isn't a cappuccino! It's an Americano with squirty cream on top."

A hush fell over the surrounding tables. It wasn't often a customer complained. It just wasn't done.

"What's the difference?" Angie sounded defensive.

"That's what you get for ordering coffee in a tea shop," Jock said, trying to make light of it.

"No one's ever complained before." Angie dabbed her eye with the corner of her apron and flounced off to the kitchen.

"Oh Lord! Now I've gone and upset her," Gabriella said.

"I wouldn't worry. She'll get over it."

She took an experimental sip and pulled a face. "It really is a terrible cappuccino."

"You and Simon looked like you were hitting it off last night," he said, changing the subject. "What were you talking about?"

"I really can't remember." She stifled a yawn. "Anything's fascinating after a few tequilas."

"Hmm!"

But she hadn't looked particularly drunk. Her refusal to answer his question only fuelled his curiosity. What had she and Simon been up to on Dylan's boat? Or was he better off not knowing?

A little while later, Bronwyn appeared with a second cappuccino, which looked much like the first.

"I'm sorry, I can't drink this." Gabriella rose to her feet. "I'll see you later, Jock."

He opened up his laptop. He had barely begun typing when someone flung a smelly slipper down on the table in front of him.

"Morning, Dylan," he said without looking up.

"Cinders."

"What?"

"You left the party in a bit of a hurry last night."

"Something came up."

Dylan plonked himself down beside him. "Man! That stinks!"

"It's your slipper, isn't it?"

"Never mind that. What happened?"

"Did you notice anything going on between Gabriella and Simon?"

Dylan laughed. "I don't think so."

"You didn't see them. They were being really secretive

down in the cabin and they jumped apart as soon as they saw me."

"Maybe they've found something. About the May Queen Killer."

"But why would they keep it from us?"

"I don't know. It's an interesting development."

Dylan closed his eyes and lay his head down on the table.

"Hey, are you alright?"

"To be honest with you, I'm experiencing a real katzenjammer."

"I wish you wouldn't drink."

"I wish you wouldn't nag."

"Shall I ask Angie for one of her disgusting concoctions?"

"You do and you're a dead man."

Dylan put his feet up on the chair opposite, knocking something to the ground. He glanced down to see what it was. "Oh, nice handbag, Jock."

Jock leaned over and saw a leather bag. It was butter soft, with a fancy gold clasp.

"Must be Gabriella's."

"I'll put it behind the counter if you like," Angie said, appearing with one of her hangover cures.

Dylan winced. "What are you, psychic, woman?"

"Not really. I saw you walk in, looking like you had blisters for eyeballs. Besides, I know how much you put away last night."

"I really don't—"

"No arguing. Just drink it."

"Tell her to leave me alone, Jock."

Jock shook his head. "You take your medicine. I'll ring Gabriella and tell her about her bag."

He opened his laptop and checked his emails. His mum had sent him a reminder about his sister's birthday. There was really no need. Keeley had been dropping hints the size of elephants. He wasn't likely to forget.

The Perfect Girl

"Buying yourself something nice?" Dylan asked as he browsed the web for women's jewellery.

"I need a present for my sister."

"What does she like?"

"Money."

"Then why don't you just give her some money?"

"Because then she'll know how much it cost."

"I tell you what: we should go to Pepper Hill. They have some nice little boutiques there, full of the kind of shiny crap women like."

"It has to look like quality."

"It's nice stuff. Handmade. Unique."

"How are we going to get there? Wasn't your car repossessed?"

"Not a problem. It's on the canal."

Jock smiled. "Sounds like a plan."

"When do you want to go?"

"Can we do it tomorrow? I've got a meeting with my editor in half an hour."

Actually, he was a bit surprised Hilary was coming up to see him again. He had sent her the finished draft of his book the night before. It still needed work, but he was pleased with it and he felt he was ready for her input. But instead of taking a couple of days to get back to him like she normally did, she had been on the phone first thing in the morning.

"Jock! Are you still in Fleckford?"

"Er, yes. Yes, I am, actually."

"Well don't go anywhere. I'll be there at eleven."

"OK."

"And don't show anyone the manuscript. No Instagram sneak peaks, no Twitter previews."

"I've no idea what any of that is."

"Good. That's good."

***

"Thanks for coming," Jock said when Hilary arrived. She wasn't smiling. Actually, she looked a bit worried.

"Well? What did you think? Let me pour you some tea."

"I don't want any tea, thanks. I found it rather disturbing," She smoothed her skirt down over her knees. "I mean, where are you getting your ideas? I wouldn't have thought you had it in you."

"You'd be surprised."

"Why did you kill off the detective's mother?"

"She deserved it."

"Don't you think Audrey would be more upset if her mother was murdered? I find it odd that she just carries on with the investigation."

"She's not upset. She's relieved. Her mother was an awful, spiteful person and now she's gone, Audrey's free to get on with her life. Don't you see? Her mother's death makes her a better detective. She's finally allowed to focus."

Hilary drew a breath. "But she goes on to shield the killer. Don't you think that's overstepping the line? I mean, we've been marketing you as the next Agatha Christie. Do you really think Miss Marple would behave this way?"

"Audrey is not Miss Marple," he said emphatically. "She's her own person. It's time she stepped out from Miss Marple's shadow."

❄

I LEAN over the fence and fiddle with the lock. It won't budge.

"Must be padlocked," I say with a frown. "You'll have to climb over, Claire."

Obediently, Claire gets the step ladder from the boot and climbs over. It must be a bit of a drop the other side, but she manages it OK.

"Come on, open the gate before someone sees."

"I'm trying!"

I start to look for an alternative point of entry, when she finally opens the gate.

"Don't forget to put the ladder back in the boot," *I tell her, as I walk inside.*

I set the box down behind the shed. Nobody can see us there. There are tall hedges on either side of the garden and the curtains are still drawn.

"No movement from inside," *I say when Claire returns.*

"Maybe she's still asleep?"

"Old people rarely lie in."

"Then why are the curtains closed?"

"She's probably still in her dressing gown."

We carry the box down the garden, stopping outside the back door.

"How are we going to get in?" *she asks.*

I produce the key from my pocket.

"Where did you get that?"

"Let's just say the opportunity fell in my lap."

As quietly as I can, I unlock the door and step into the kitchen. The wall is tiled in a disgusting shade of mustard yellow, with olive-green cabinets and hot-pink door knobs. There are definite signs of life: the smell of recently burnt toast, a tell-tale coffee ring on one of the surfaces and a pile of dirty plates next to the sink. The TV blares from the living room. Claire sets the box down on the kitchen floor and we peer in. In complete contrast to the kitchen, this room looks dated, with a brick chimney place and portraits of ancestors on the walls. She's in there, watching the news.

The remote is lying on the arm of the sofa. I grab it and switch off the TV.

"What the ....?"

Her face registers first surprise and then horror. We must look quite frightening, dressed in our white, protective gear, with gloves, masks and veils over our heads.

"Who are you?" *Daphne whispers.* "What do you want with me?"

26

She can't see my face, not in these clothes. She can't see Claire's either, which is just as well. She knows Claire, or at least she did once, before Peter was accused of killing her.

"I can't believe that after all these years you still have no idea who I am." I look at her in disgust.

"You're the one who sent the letters aren't you?" Her voice breaks slightly, betraying her fear.

"I don't know why you're so surprised. I told you I was coming. I always told you I was coming."

She backs away, towards the mantelpiece.

"I've been watching you," I tell her.

"Since Peter died?" Her eye flickers towards a little table where her iPhone is charging. She's thinking of making a grab for it, I can tell.

I laugh bitterly. "No, not just since Peter died. I've been watching you for much longer than that."

"I sensed it."

Her eyes dart to the table again. She must think I'm stupid. I grab the phone and whack it against the brick wall of the chimney then fling it into the grate, where it nestles among the coals.

"Dial 999," she says, her voice clear but shaky. My head jerks in the direction of the broken phone. To my alarm, the screen lights up.

The Perfect Girl

"Calling, 9 ... 9 ... 9," it says in robotic fashion.

"How did you do that?"

"It must be voice-activated," says Claire. "Look, it's dialling."

"Turn it off! Turn it off!" I grab it out of the grate and stomp down hard with my boot, kicking it until the display cracks.

"The police are on their way," Daphne says triumphantly. "I think you'd better go."

Claire looks at me in panic.

"She's bluffing." I shove Daphne to the floor. I'm not sure if she is or not, but we're not leaving until the job's done.

A tiny Yorkshire Terrier flies into the room, yapping its head off. I'm surprised it didn't bother us before now, but it looks a bit past it. The dog is no threat, but it keeps jumping up at me and its yapping is really getting on my nerves.

"Shut up! I can't think!"

I boot it across the room.

"Coco!" Daphne cries, as it lands in a heap on the floor. It gives a pathetic little whimper then falls silent. I glance over. I didn't mean to hurt the dog. I just needed it out of the way.

"You should have called him off," I tell Daphne, who is bawling her stupid eyes out.

I turn to Claire, who's watching with a mournful expression. "What are you waiting for? Spray her!"

"No!" Daphne backs away as Claire aims the bottle at her. She covers her eyes, but the spray just keeps coming.

"What is that?" She coughs, falling back onto the sofa.

"It's just deodorant," Claire says. She sounds apologetic.

"Keep spraying! Don't stop until the bottle's empty!"

Daphne has her hands over her face so she doesn't clock what I'm doing as I set the box down in the middle of her living room. I slash the tape it's wrapped in and let the sides of the box collapse.

"Be free, my little beauties!" I whisper.

A cloud of bees escape, confused and disorientated. The ceiling changes from white to black as more and more of them appear. Hundreds, maybe thousands of them, all loose in Daphne's living room. It doesn't

229

take them long to find her. *The deodorant is pungent. She screams and tries to swat them away, making them angry. Soon she is just a writhing black blob. The dog pulls itself up on its wonky legs and wobbles towards its mistress. It makes a pathetic attempt to paw at the bees, before it too is swallowed up in the black cloud.*

Claire and I back away towards the door. There are plenty of bees buzzing around us, but our clothes protect us from the worst. Not that I'm worried about a few bee stings. I take one last look back at Daphne but I can't see her for bees.

"Come on! We've got to get out of here!" Claire says. "I think I can hear someone in the driveway."

"Wait!" I pull my phone from my pocket. "I need to take a picture."

※

Jock refused Dylan's hand as he climbed onto the boat. He wouldn't put it past him to give him a friendly shove into the water. Dylan started the boat up and soon they were cruising along.

"I'll let you steer for a bit if you like?"

"OK." It seemed pretty easy. Still, he felt a little nervous as Dylan disappeared down into the cabin. What if he lost control and couldn't stop? He pulled nervously at the tiller as another boat came into view. For a moment, he wasn't sure whether he was supposed to pull left or right, but before he could make a decision, the other boat moved over. Jock relaxed and began to get a feel for the boat. By the time Dylan resurfaced, he was steering gently up river and he still hadn't hit anything. In fact, he was starting to enjoy himself.

"Come on, Jock. I'll show you how it's done," Dylan elbowed his way in.

"I'm fine," Jock said through gritted teeth. He didn't really want to give up the tiller, but he supposed he had to, seeing as it was Dylan's boat. He let go and stood to one side, watching as Dylan steered with confidence. Come to think of it, Dylan did everything with confidence.

"Are you sure you're not going too fast?" he asked, as he felt the boat judder.

"Whoever heard of speeding on a narrowboat?" Dylan let out a laugh. "I could walk faster than this."

"There must be a speed limit."

"Do you see any police?"

The boat was starting to swing about from side to side, causing a bit of a tide to wash up on the bank.

"Dylan, you need to slow down! Slow down or I'm getting off."

He looked over at the bank, wishing it was low enough for him to jump onto. To his relief, Dylan actually slowed down.

"Why don't you drive again for a bit? I'm getting bored, anyway. I'll get us a couple of drinks."

Jock smiled and resumed steering. To his immense surprise, Dylan returned a few minutes later with a couple of cans of coke.

"I don't think I've seen you drink a soft drink before, apart from tea, of course."

Dylan shrugged. "I don't have to drink all the time, you know. In fact, I almost never drink on Sundays."

They found a mooring on the bank at Pepper Hill and tied the boat securely.

"Do you know the place well?" Jock asked as they climbed up the steps and walked along the narrow lane.

"Yeah, Efa used to drag me round here quite a bit. It's all posh boutiques and art galleries. It hasn't even got a proper pub, just a sodding wine bar where they charge you three times the normal price just because the carpets don't smell of armpit."

"I can see the appeal."

"Here's the jeweller's," he led him into a shop with little glass cabinets containing rings and necklaces.

"Hey, these look pricey."

"You've got money, haven't you?"

"I thought the whole object of this trip was to get something discounted?"

"Oh! Was it?"

The saleslady looked familiar, but Jock couldn't place her until she took off her glasses and pointed to the door. So that was why they were really here, so Dylan could spy on his ex-girlfriend and generally be an arse.

"Don't be like that," Dylan wheedled. "Jock here is after a present for his sister."

Efa scowled then, catching a look from her manager, transformed her face into a smile.

"What sort of thing are you looking for?"

"A necklace or something."

"What does she like? Gold or silver?"

"I don't really know."

"What's her dress style?"

"Smart chav."

She smiled slightly. "In that case we're probably talking gold. Let me show you what we have in the Tombstone range."

"Sounds a bit goth."

Efa removed a gleaming gold necklace from its box.

"Believe me, a goth wouldn't be seen dead in this."

Jock tilted his head. He had no idea if Keeley would like it but he felt compelled to make a purchase.

"I'll take it."

Her smile widened and she slipped it back into the box. He cringed at the number that flashed up on the till but handed over his credit card regardless.

"I can't believe you put me in that position," he complained to Dylan as they left.

"What are you talking about? You got what you came for, didn't you?"

"Yes, thanks. At quadruple the price. I'll probably have to mortgage my flat to pay for it."

"Or just scribble another book. You'll be fine."

"You still shouldn't have taken me to Efa's shop. There are plenty of other places we could have gone."

"What's the big deal? We were probably doing her a favour. It's not like she had any other customers and she's on commission, you know."

"It's stalking, or harassment at the very least."

"What harassment? I barely said a word."

"That's because you were staring so hard."

"Well, what am I supposed to do? I never see her anymore. She was my world, Jock. And then she walked out on me."

Dylan clearly enjoyed playing the victim in this scenario. The way he talked, you would think Efa had betrayed him. His drinking didn't seem to figure into it at all.

"You have to accept that she doesn't want to see you anymore."

Dylan kicked a pebble into the road. "You're a heartless man, Jock. You really are."

"I thought you were moving on. What about those women from the party?"

"Oh, them! They were just a bit of fun. I'm a one-woman man really."

"But she's left you!"

"Yeah! It's going to be a long, lonely existence."

"You should really leave the poor woman alone. Don't you know there are plenty of fish in the sea?"

Dylan looked astounded. "Fish? What do I want with a fish? You can't sleep with a fish. And who'd even want to? I've never understood the whole mermaid thing. Swim back into the sea, Ariel, before someone catches you and has you on toast."

Jock looked at him out of the side of his eye. "Have you quite finished?"

Dylan shrugged. "Man, you've some cock-eyed notions."

Dylan's shoes squeaked loudly as they walked along the pavement. The high street was eerily silent, as if everyone had gone inside and locked their doors. There was no one out mowing their lawn or even walking the dog.

"Where is everyone?" Jock murmured.

"Maybe they're all in church."

It seemed unlikely. Organised religion was a minority occupation in these parts. It didn't seem plausible that the entire population of Pepper Hill had suddenly seen the light.

"Hey, Gabriella's gallery is just along here," Jock said. "Do you want to see it? She's got some really trippy paintings."

"Not particularly. Art galleries bore the pants off me."

"It's modern art."

"Ugh! The worst kind! Self-indulgent tat! They get a monkey and stuff it with recycled tyres and then sell it to some sucker with more money than sense."

Jock shrugged. "I thought you'd like it. You draw some pretty surreal stuff yourself."

"I keep my doodles in my pad where they can't hurt anyone."

"You really are odd, you know that? Let's just see if Gabriella's there. Might as well say hello since we're here. Besides, I still want to know what's going on with her and Simon."

"You think he's having a left-handed honeymoon?"

"I don't know. There's definitely something going on there."

"Very well, call her if you must. But I think it's highly unlikely that Simon would cheat on Angie with that salad dodger."

Gabriella had her feet up on the till. She was so intent on

the trashy novel she was reading that she didn't hear them come in.

"Good book?" Jock asked.

She snapped it shut. "Not particularly."

She glanced at Dylan who was lingering in the doorway. "What can I do for you boys?"

"We were just passing." Jock tried not to stare at the cow's head, peering out at him from a large canvas on the wall.

"Is that one new?"

She nodded. "Came in last week."

"Disturbing, isn't it? That looks like real blood dripping off its tongue."

"That's because it is. The artist also used real dung."

Jock moved away. "Thought I caught a whiff."

"Hey, I wanted to thank you for finding my bag. I got halfway down the road before I realised I'd left it. Felt like a right plum."

"No problem."

She glanced at the clock. "I don't mean to be rude, but I was just about to lock up. Mum's expecting me for lunch."

"Don't let us keep you," Dylan said from the doorway.

"Hey, why don't you join us? She always makes too much."

Jock locked eyes with Dylan. "We wouldn't want to put you to any trouble…"

"Honestly, it's no trouble at all. To be honest, Mum gets lonely. She doesn't get many visitors these days."

"You're sure there will be enough food?"

"Absolutely. I'll even make you a cappuccino so you can see how it's supposed to taste."

"Well OK then. Why not?"

Gabriella smiled and grabbed her keys. She glanced over at Dylan, still skulking in the doorway.

"I take it he's house-trained?"

Jock's lips twitched. "I can't promise anything. Maybe you should put down some newspaper?"

Gabriella's laugh echoed around the shop. "Just give me a minute while I shut the shop."

"Do we have to?" Dylan murmured, as they stepped outside.

"Don't be such a misery guts. It'll be fun."

They waited as Gabriella pulled down the shutters.

"Right boys, we need to turn left at the Lipo Clinic and then right at the Happy Puppy dog jewellers."

They followed her around the corner and down a long, winding road.

"Are we nearly there yet?" Dylan moaned. "I've got a stone in my shoe."

"Why don't you take it out then?"

"I can't. It's character forming."

"You're definitely an acquired taste, you know that?"

Gabriella was a good way ahead of them by now. She waved her arms to indicate that she was turning into a quiet cul-de-sac. Then she walked up the path to number six and rang the bell. She didn't wait for an answer. She produced a big, jangling bunch of keys and unlocked the door. Then let out the loudest scream Jock had ever heard.

27

It was adrenaline rather than courage that propelled Jock forward, over the gravel path and into the house. He shrieked as a couple of bees whizzed past his ear and he ducked down for cover. It wasn't him they were interested in, but their freedom.

"Quickly! This way!" Gabriella charged down the hall into the living room at the back of the house. It took Jock a moment to realise what he was looking at. At first, it was just a blurred, black mass and then he saw the body, covered from head to toe in bees. The bees didn't look much better off than the body. Some of them were struggling and flapping their wings, but few looked particularly lively. Once they had stung their target, that was it for them, their lives were over.

"Come on, Mum! You've got to wake up!" Gabriella grabbed a magazine and used it to shoo the bees off her mother's face.

Jock's legs shook beneath him. He was not equipped to deal with this. He was a thinker, not a doer. He couldn't cope with emergencies. He looked at Daphne and tried not to retch. "Have you called 999?"

"Of course I bleeding well have! They're on their way."

He was vaguely aware of Dylan opening doors and windows, attempting to drive the bees out of the room.

"Are they still on the line?"

"It's on loudspeaker, for all the good it's doing."

He leaned towards the phone. "Is there anything we can be doing?" he asked the operator. He couldn't hear much over all the commotion, so he pressed the receiver to his ear.

"Have you checked that her airways are clear?" he asked Gabriella.

"They are now," she said, as her mother let out a long cough. "That's it, Mum. Spit 'em out."

"That's good. Now we need to get her into the recovery position."

He forced himself to move towards Daphne. Most of the bees appeared to be dead or dying, but a few still flew around, hampering their efforts to help. He tried not to cry out as one of them stung him on the back of the hand. He pulled back. It smarted, but how much pain must Daphne be in, covered from head to toe?

"We need to get her on her side," he said to Gabriella.

"OK, let's roll her."

He got down on one side and Gabriella on the other. It was hard to see where to hold. The entire length of her flesh was covered in bees.

"OK, on three," Gabriella said. "One, two …"

But before they could roll her over, Dylan came charging back into the room and sprayed them all with a garden hose. The water caused a cloud of bees to rise up in the air. Several fell to the floor, dead, whilst others flew for the nearest window. The majority of them seemed to head for the front door, where Dylan had turned a light on.

Jock looked down. It had worked. There were far fewer bees on Daphne now, although they were all now covered in cold water.

Daphne opened one eye.

"She's waking up!" Gabriella exclaimed. She glanced at Dylan, who was still clutching the dripping hose. "Will you get that out of here?"

"You're welcome!"

"And get some blankets, will you?"

"Where from?"

"Just go upstairs and grab them off the beds."

"Do you remember what happened?" Jock tried not to mind how his damp clothes clung to his body.

Daphne mumbled something unintelligible.

"She can't talk. She's been stung in the mouth."

Dylan came back downstairs with a duvet and laid it over Daphne. "Don't worry, you're going to be OK," he said softly.

Her eyes crinkled slightly, as if she were trying to smile.

"She's trying to speak." Gabriella tried to take her mother's hand. "Go on, Mum. I'm listening."

The injured woman let out a murmur.

"What's she saying?" Jock asked. "Sounds like … cocoa."

"She's asking for her dog."

Jock looked around the room.

"Haven't seen a dog."

"Coco!" Daphne closed her eyes, as if it were all too much of an effort.

Gabriella squeezed her own eyes shut. "Please, God, let her live."

"The ambulance is here!" Dylan called from the doorway.

"Thank God!"

Jock moved to the side as the paramedics dashed in. They were swift and professional, instantly taking control of the situation, but even they couldn't hide their horror at the vision before them.

"Never seen anything like it," one of them said, shaking his head. It was only as they carried Daphne out that they noticed the tiny terrier that had been lying at her feet.

"Oh, Coco!" Gabriella wailed.

Dylan put his ear to the dog's face. For a moment, Jock thought he was going to attempt CPR.

"I'm afraid he's dead."

They followed the ambulance crew outside and watched as Daphne was loaded into a neon-yellow ambulance. The paramedics squeezed inside, but there was no room for Gabriella.

"I'll drive you to the hospital if you like," Dylan offered, stripping off his shirt. "You're in no state to drive yourself."

"Thank you. I'll just grab some clean clothes. I'll see if I can find some for you two, too. We can't go like this."

She returned with a couple of oversized T-shirts and jogging bottoms. Jock balked slightly as he realised the probable source of the clothes.

"Did these...?"

Gabriella met his stare. "Belonged to my dad, yes. But don't worry, I don't think he'll be needing them in a hurry."

Jock glanced at Dylan, but he had already stripped down to his boxers. Grimacing slightly, he followed suit. The clothes smelled a little musky, as you might expect after five years. But he could still detect a slight whiff: the distinct combination of aftershave and body odour that made a man's smell unique. He shuddered as he imagined Peter Helston's ghost appearing in front of him to claim back his clothes.

"Come on, let's go." She grabbed the keys to her Ibiza and placed them in Dylan's hand.

"Do you think this is a good idea?" Jock asked in a hushed tone as they followed her out the door.

"How else are we going to find anything out?" Dylan said under his breath.

Jock sat in the back of the car and stared out the window. Any minute, Gabriella was going to start crying again and he had no idea what he was going to say. Women's tears made him very uncomfortable. He wondered how long it would be until Dylan's sense of duty wore off. Because the Dylan he had seen today was not one he had ever encountered before. He had been kind and quick-thinking – compassionate, even.

❉

"I thought that went rather well," I tell Claire, as we struggle out of our protective gear. She whips hers off in seconds then helps me to peel off mine and we shove it all onto the backseat. I get a prickly feeling in my back and relish the sensation. I only have a few stings, but the back one's a wowzer. It jabbed me at such an angle it almost took my breath away. I have never felt so alive.

Claire's looking back at the house.

"Did you see her face?"

"She had this coming. She's always had it coming."

"I know, I know. I just didn't think it would be so ... brutal."

"Claire, are you–?"

Suddenly, she is puking into her lap.

"Bloody hell!" I toss her a-cloth. "Clean yourself up, woman! You're a disgrace."

"I'm sorry," she sobs. Globules of puke dangle from her hair. The smell fills the car.

"You disgust me." I switch the air conditioning to full blast. I would say more, but I'm impatient for her to start the engine. It's not a good idea to sit around outside the scene of a crime, even if the road is dead quiet. I watch the postman bypass Daphne's house. Just as well, he'd be in for a bit of a shock.

"What have we done?" She rests her head against the steering wheel.

"Let's talk about this later." I notice a curtain twitch. "We've got to get out of here."

"I can't. I just can't."

"Alright, move over. I'll drive."

But she just keeps on sobbing into the steering wheel. Pathetic! I fantasise about throwing her out of the car and reversing over her. Save it for later, I remind myself. Use your personal power. Stay in control.

"I said, drive!"

"Is she going to die?"

"Maybe. Maybe not. It doesn't matter either way."

She bawls even more. Big, ugly sobs. The salty tears gush from her eyes.

"What now? What is your bloody problem?"

"You wouldn't understand." She clutches the steering wheel.

"Oh, will you put a sock in it!"

"I don't care what happens to me. Nothing could be worse than this."

I grit my teeth. "If you don't step on it, your sister's dead."

"You wouldn't."

"Wouldn't I?"

To my immense relief, she finally revs the engine. It must be the slowest getaway in history. I glance around again as we pull away. The curtain has stopped twitching and I can't see anyone else around. But it only takes one: one person to remember our car, one person to identify its two occupants and provide the police with a description. I had better lay low for a while.

"I don't know how you live with this guilt!"

Claire steers the car down the narrow country lanes. I wince as she gets too close to the hedge. That'll leave a scratch for sure.

"What do you mean?" I check the rear mirror to make sure no one's following us. They aren't, unless the police have commandeered a tractor.

"What can she possibly have done to deserve what we did to her?"

"Are you questioning my judgment?"

"I'm trying to understand."

I just want to get home so that I can play the scene over and over in my head. I'll be fantasising about this day for the rest of my life. The day I finally got even with Daphne.

"There's a lot you don't know about Daphne."

"Tell me."

"She stole someone very precious from me."

"Is she … a killer?"

I laugh out loud. "Daphne Helston? She hasn't got the balls. Not even one."

"Then …"

"She ruined my life. My entire life. She made me the way I am."

The air conditioning isn't doing it for me. I open the window. There's nothing quite like the feel of wind in your hair or the smell of blood on your hands. We turn round the corner and finally lose the tractor. I watch as it chugs off into the field. I could never drive something that slow. It would drive me crazy. Claire leans forward to adjust the Sat Nav.

"Claire, you're driving too close to the canal!"

28

I'm about to grab the wheel when Claire pulls back into the centre of the road.

"It's a bit narrow here," she mutters.

She's lying. She was driving close to the edge on purpose. She's thinking about offing us both. Again, she veers a little too close to the canal. A little too close and a little too fast. She's trying to get up the courage. I grip the door handle.

"If you kill us, Getrude dies, too," I say through clenched teeth. "No one knows where she is, remember? Do you want your sister to die?"

Claire takes a sharp breath. I can almost hear the cogs whirring. She's on a sharp learning curve. I've pushed her too far before she's ready. I'm going to have to find a way to rein her back in.

"Things are going to change."

"Just let my sister go. We should never have taken her."

"I can't keep doing this forever."

She sneaks a peek at me. I've got her attention.

"I just need to get a few more things out of my system. Settle my affairs. That was what today was about."

She looks hopeful.

"I'll help you," she says. "You can do this, I know you can."

We ditch the car and take the boat back to the warehouse. I think

Claire's expecting a cup of tea when we get back and a little cry on my shoulder but I'm way too angry. We take the lift up to her room and I go in with her, wrinkling my nose at the stale smell. I wait till she sits down then I leave abruptly, bolting the door behind me.

"Hey, let me out!"

She hammers on the door. She's got too used to her freedom. It is time to remind her how all this started, how I came to wield such power over her.

"You can't leave me in here!"

Oh, but I can.

I wasn't lying. Things cannot go on like this forever. I have misjudged her. She has become an unknown quantity like her sister or more likely, because of her.

❄

"I JUST COULDN'T BELIEVE IT," Gabriella said. "I opened the front door and a swarm of bees flew out. I don't know how I managed to dodge out of the way, but they shot right past me like they wanted to escape. That's when I found Mum. She looked awful, just covered in bees. She had her eyes closed and for a moment I thought … I thought she was …" She squeezed her eyes tight shut, unable to finish her sentence.

Jock made sympathetic noises and glugged his terrible vending machine tea. He wasn't entirely sure what he and Dylan were doing here. Gabriella should really have friends or family with her, not them, but she seemed too upset to care about that. She didn't want them to leave, that much she had made clear.

"Just when we thought it was all over," she gulped. "I thought we'd finally be able to move on with our lives. It doesn't make any sense. I mean why did they attack her now, just when another girl's gone missing? Dad can't have had anything to do with it. Not this time."

"You think someone used the bees to attack your mum?"

Jock arched his brows at Dylan. "You can't make bees attack people, can you?"

Dylan frowned. "You'd have to know what you were doing but I think Gabriella might be right."

Jock thought for a moment. "Whoever it was probably got some nasty stings themselves. The police could check with the local hospitals and see if anyone else has been admitted with multiple bee stings."

"I doubt they'd go to a hospital," Dylan objected. "They'd know the police were looking for them."

"But do you really think this was deliberate? That someone used the bees as a weapon?"

"It certainly looks that way."

"So the May Queen Killer is a beekeeper?"

"We don't know if this was the May Queen Killer. But I'm betting there's a connection."

Jock drained the last of his tea and tossed the paper cup in the bin. Why would anyone want to hurt Daphne? Did they think she was the one who had taken Sapphire? No, the idea was ludicrous, laughable even. There was no way.

"Ah! About time!" Dylan said.

"What?"

He looked up as Stavely charged in, tie askew and nostrils flaring. He felt a groan in the pit of his stomach. He should have known it was a bad idea to come to the hospital. How suspicious must he look?

"Have the Welsh Police arrived yet?" Stavely demanded.

"No."

"Good." He turned to Sweep who was just behind him. "Daphne Helston's house is a bit too close to the border for my liking. We don't want some sort of Bridge situation."

Jock had no idea what he was talking about, but he decided it was best not to ask.

Stavely turned his attention to Gabriella. "I understand

that this is a difficult time, but do you mind if we ask you a few questions?"

"I'm not sure I'm comfortable talking to you." She wiped her eyes, leaving a streak of mascara across her hand.

"Come on, for your mum."

"I'm not sure she'd want me to talk to you."

Jock looked from Gabriella to Stavely. "You know each other?"

"Of course they do," Dylan said. "From when Claire went missing."

"Oh."

"And I'd like to know what the two of you are doing here," Stavely said, looking from Jock to Dylan.

"We were visiting Gabriella," Dylan told him.

Stavely leaned in closer. "I'm getting a right whiff from you."

Dylan folded his arms. "We haven't done anything wrong."

Jock nodded.

"Who was the first at the scene?"

"Me," said Gabriella. "But they weren't far behind."

"Did you see anyone out in the street?"

"No, it was very quiet."

"What about you two?" He looked at Dylan and Jock.

"Like she said, it was dead."

"A new garden centre just opened round the corner," Gabriella elaborated. "I think a lot of our neighbours went there for the opening."

"There was a neighbour working on his car just across the street," Sweep said. "He was out there most of the morning, so it sounds like the perp might have gone round the back."

Stavely looked at him sternly. "If there is a perpetrator," he amended quickly.

"You needn't be pedantic on our account," Dylan said.

247

"There's no way those bees got there by accident, not unless they carried their own beehive."

Stavely turned to Sweep. "Right, go down to the cafeteria and get me a roast dinner and tell them not to scrimp on the gravy. I'll also need a beekeeper and plenty of chalk."

"I'm not sure I'll be able to get hold of a beekeeper at this time on a Sunday."

"Well, I need one. In fact, get me all of them. I want a list of all the beekeepers in the area."

"Are they all registered somewhere?"

"No idea! Go and find out."

Sweep nodded without enthusiasm. Stavely reached out and touched his shoulder.

"We need to dig deep to find what we're looking for. And if that means talking to a hundred bloody beekeepers then so be it. Somebody knows who did this."

Sweep stalked off in the direction of the lifts, his long arms swinging at his sides.

Stavely drew a breath. "The back door was open but there were no signs of forced entry. Have you or your mum lost your keys lately?"

"No, and Mum hasn't either. She would have said."

"Could be a pickpocket. Have you left your bag lying about at all?"

Gabriella went red. "I left it at the tea shop!"

"But Angie put it behind the counter," Jock said. "I don't think anyone could have tampered with it."

"It only takes a minute."

"My keys aren't missing."

"They might have taken a copy. You'd be surprised what criminals can do."

"But why? Why would anyone want to attack Mum?"

Jock cleared his throat. "I think it might be because of the TV interview."

Stavely looked at him. "What TV interview?"

"Daphne's. It was about a week or so ago. She made a personal address to the May Queen Killer. Maybe it hit a nerve."

A few minutes later, Sweep came back, carrying a polyester container with steam coming out of it.

"Here you go, sir. Roast beef with plenty of gravy. I even managed to snag you the last Yorkshire pudding."

"Arse-licker," Dylan muttered under his breath.

Stavely took the container. "Did you know Daphne Helston did a TV interview? Why wasn't I informed?"

"I ... didn't know."

Stavely make no attempt to hide his frustration. "Excuse me, I've got a press officer to sack."

He took his dinner and walked off towards the exit. He was almost out the door when he turned back to look at Sweep. "Why are you still standing there? Go and get me that bloody list of beekeepers!"

Sweep whipped out his phone.

"Outside, please," a nurse said, pointing to one of the many 'no mobile' posters dotted around the waiting room.

Sweep sighed and trailed after Stavely.

"They're hiring at Argos," Dylan called after him.

"Piss off!" said Sweep, almost colliding with the automatic door.

Just then, a doctor came over and spoke to Gabriella.

"Your mum's asking for you."

"I can see her?"

"Just for a few minutes. She needs her rest."

While Gabriella was visiting Daphne, Stavely walked back in. "What were you two really doing in Pepper Hill?" he asked, wiping his mouth with his hanky.

"It's very nice this time of year," Dylan said. He tilted back in his chair, his arms resting behind his head.

"Just as long as you weren't meddling in my investigation. I can't abide amateurs."

Dylan's jaw tightened.

"And just because you write doesn't mean you know anything about real crimes," he told Jock. "If any more information comes your way, you give me a ring. Kapeesh?"

Jock was careful not to make any promises. Why should he listen to Stavely? The police hadn't even known about Daphne's interview. It was like they weren't even paying attention.

❈

THE FIRST THING Jock did when he got back to his room was strip off Peter Helston's clothes. He knew he was being irrational, but those clothes gave him the willies.

"We should sell them on eBay," Dylan joked. "People pay good money for morbid memorabilia."

Jock shook his head. "Gabriella might want them back. They did belong to her dead father, after all."

He put on his dressing gown and picked up his wash bag. As he passed the window, he saw Angie locking up the tea shop. The lamplight shone on her hair, changing her honey blonde to a fierce shade of orange. She slipped the keys into her handbag then waved to Simon on the other side of the street. Simon bent down so Angie could wind her arms around his neck, like a zookeeper petting a giraffe. He murmured something in her ear and her giggle echoed down the street. There didn't seem to be any tension between them. Either she was OK with what was going on between him and Gabriella or she was completely oblivious.

❈

SAPPHIRE WAS FRANTIC. It had been days since Claire's last visit. She began to worry that she might be hurt, or even dead. What if they were all alone down here and nobody knew? She lay awake, cold and bored in the darkness. A rat scuttled over her and she booted it off. She was more prepared for them now and quicker with her shoe. She heard Ingrid sniff.

"You OK?" she asked softly, careful not to wake the others.

"I'm sorry. I miss my home and my family. Do you think they're even looking for me?"

"Of course they are!" Sapphire reached out and took her hand. Ingrid's family were not looking for her. They thought she was dead, but telling her so would not help her.

"I'd barely spoken to them since I left Sweden. I was too caught up in my new life, my studies, my boyfriend. We don't have May Queens in Sweden, but I thought the idea was charming. I couldn't believe it when I won. I made the dress myself, you know. It took weeks to do all the embroidery."

"It's beautiful."

"It was beautiful. Now it's a filthy rag. If we ever get out of here, I'm going to light a fire and burn it. How I long to put on a comfortable pair of jeans and a pullover and just snuggle up in front of the TV."

"I miss TV," Sapphire said. "I never realised before how many hours there are in a day."

Ingrid wiped her eyes. "You know, I was watching a really good serial before I was taken. I was only halfway through it. I wish I'd set it to record."

"It's the silliest things you think of. I had a load of washing in the machine. I hope someone's been up to my flat to hang it out. Otherwise it will be all mouldy."

"Come to that, I bet my car's been towed!"

"Hey!"

"What?"

"That's the lift! Listen!"

"Shall we wake the others?"

"No, leave them. It's probably Claire."

They listened, but there was no knock. "That's not Claire!" Ingrid said.

They shielded their eyes as the door burst open.

Clunk! Clunk! Clunk came the boots on the stairs. Then that smell – sweet, earthy, cocoa flavours. A bright lamp shone around.

Through her fingers, Sapphire saw a ghostly figure, dressed from head to toe in white.

Ingrid took her hand and squeezed it. She tried not to shake.

Clunk! Clunk! Clunk!

The May Queen Killer descended into the depths of the cellar and looked around.

"What do you want?" Sapphire asked, her voice trembling slightly.

"Kneel before me."

Sapphire hesitated. She could hear a dog whining in the corridor.

"Just do it," hissed Ingrid.

Sapphire dropped to her knees. She felt a swift kick in the face and she tumbled backwards, smacking her head on the stone floor.

"Are you hurt?" Ingrid asked, springing forward.

"I'm OK." Her head smarted, but she wasn't going to show it. She pulled herself to her feet.

"I want to go home," she said, as forcefully as she could manage.

"You can go – on one condition."

Her heart leapt. "What's that?"

"You leave me your ear."

She shrank back. "You're out of your bloody mind!"

"Maybe. But the offer stands."

"What, you'd really let me go? I don't believe you."

She glanced at Ingrid, who was shaking her head emphatically.

"You don't have to decide now. Have a think about it and let me know."

"Why would you want my ear?"

"Because then I'd still own a part of you."

There was a loud whine from the door and the May Queen Killer turned sharply. "Shut it!"

The dog snarled. It sounded mean and hungry. If only she could turn it against its owner. How much happier they would all be.

"How do I know you'd really let me go?" She blinked at the light.

"We'd do it outside, on my boat. Then I'd drop you off upriver. I know you won't give away our location because I'd still have Claire. And you wouldn't want anything to happen to her, would you?"

"No."

"So? What's your answer?"

"No."

"You don't have to decide now. Why don't you sleep on it?"

29

"What do you think?" Sapphire said, as she and Ingrid lay awake in the darkness. "Maybe it would be better to lose an ear. We're just rotting away in this cellar. I don't know how much longer we can survive with so little food and drink."

"The offer's not real," Ingrid said. "Of course it's not. They just want to torture you."

"But what if it *is* real?" She touched her left ear and then the right, trying to imagine how it would feel to lose one.

"Do you think the offer applies to the rest of us?" Harmony asked. "I was too scared to ask."

"Just stay out of it," Fizz warned. "Offers like that we could do without."

❄

JOCK HELD the pastel pink receiver to his ear and twirled the cable round his hand. It felt odd to talk on a real phone. He hadn't used a landline in years.

Gabriella's voice sounded gruff as she answered the phone, as if she had only just got up.

"Hi, it's Jock. I was just ringing to see how your mum's doing?"

"Oh, hi, Jock. She's a lot better today, no thanks to those lunatics."

"Does she know who attacked her?"

"She said there were two of them, both covered from head to toe in protective gear. Like beekeepers."

"Does she have any idea who it was?"

She hesitated for just a fraction of a second. "Thanks for your support, Jock. I really appreciate it. But it turns out that my dad was the May Queen Killer after all. He brought all this upon us."

"What do you mean? What have you found out?"

"I'm sorry, Mum's calling. I've got to go. I'll call you back later in the week, I promise."

"But..."

She was gone.

"You look serious," Dylan said, as he sat back down at their table. "What's the matter? Has your mum just told you where babies come from?"

"That wasn't my mum on the phone. It was Gabriella. She said she thinks her dad was the May Queen Killer after all. She sounded pretty certain."

"Well, ring her back and ask her to explain, pronto!"

"I tried, but she went all vague and said she was busy. Something's going on with her." He glanced around quickly. "What if the police were right the first time? What if Simon is involved?"

Now it was Dylan's turn to look puzzled. "What have you got against Simon?"

"They were definitely up to something at your party. And Gabriella was so open about everything to begin with. Now she's downright cagey."

"Yeah, but Simon?"

"Just hear me out, OK? What if the two of them are

working together, covering each other's tracks? Or worse still, if he's threatening her to keep her mouth shut?"

"But what would be his motive? We still don't know who attacked Daphne. I don't believe for a minute it was Simon. And I reckon Daphne would have been able to identify him if it was. He kind of stands out."

"What if she's too scared to say?"

He poured himself a fresh cup of tea from the pot. There wasn't much a hot cup of tea couldn't help with. "Even if Simon's not directly involved, I think he knows something – something he's not telling us."

"Maybe."

"So what do we do?"

"We get him pissed," Dylan said.

Jock rolled his eyes. "That's your answer to everything, isn't it?"

"Do you know a better way to get information out of people?"

"The police interviewed him for two days and they didn't get what they needed."

"Well, they didn't try alcohol, did they?"

"I'm not even sure he drinks that much."

"He will if we say it's home-brewed."

"Organic," Jock said. "We'd have to say it was organic. Are you sure there isn't a better way?"

"Not that I can think of."

"How are we going to get him to come out with us, without it looking weird?"

"We'll say it's your birthday."

The lie made him squirm. "Why can't it be your birthday?"

"Because he knows when my birthday was. Bronwyn made me a whiskey cake."

"Nice."

"Yes, it was actually."

"So who's going to ask him?"

"I think it would be better coming from you."

"But you've known him longer than me and I haven't really spoken to him since the party."

"Still, he'd be less suspicious of you."

Jock swallowed and walked up to the counter. "Alright, Simon?"

"Fine, thank you," Simon didn't even look up from his *Guardian*.

He had never found it particularly easy to make small talk with Simon, but now it was worse than impossible. He wasn't sure if he was even listening.

"So, Er … Do you want to go over the Dragon later? For a drink, I mean? It's, um … it's my birthday."

"Me?" Simon scratched his head.

"Er, yeah."

Heat filled his cheeks. He had made it sound like he was asking him out on a date. Oh God, what if that was what Simon thought?

Angie stepped forward, a big smile on her face.

"We'd love to come, wouldn't we, Simon?"

Simon looked at him a little oddly, but he nodded politely and returned to his paper. Jock went back to his table, cheeks flaming. He should have known this wasn't going to work. Simon was too clever to fall for such an idiotic ploy.

Angie disappeared into the kitchen and re-emerged a few minutes later with an entire Battenberg, decorated with pink and yellow candles.

"I wasn't sure how old you were," she whispered, as she set it down on the table. She looked at him, clearly expecting him to provide this information, but he just shook his head. He wished he had never opened his stupid mouth.

He cringed as the entire tea shop sang 'Happy birthday' to him in a loud chorus. Any moment, he expected someone to point out the fib. He glanced at Dylan. It was just the kind of thing he would do. But just this once, Dylan kept quiet.

"Go on, Jock. Aren't you going to blow out your candles?"

Simon's mum smiled at him encouragingly and all the other old ladies waited in anticipation.

"Don't forget to make a wish," Dylan added. Jock caught the look on his face. He was clearly enjoying his discomfort.

※

SAPPHIRE WOKE UP IN A SWEAT, which was quite a feat, since there was a howling gale coming in. The door strained against the wind, making a sound like a tom cat's yowl. She willed the wind to smash the door and pull it right off its hinges, but it remained, steadfast, blocking her and the other May Queens from the outside world.

She was suddenly aware of a movement outside. Was Claire out there? Maybe she was. She had never liked thunderstorms when they were young. She used to scream and hide under her bed with her dolls. Mum would say that Gertrude had summoned the thunderstorm with her wickedness. She had always been a few sandwiches short of a picnic. Claire had been young enough to believe it, though. Maybe she still did.

She pressed her face against the door. "Claire, I know you're out there," she whispered, but there was no reply.

She pressed her ear against the door.

Someone or something was definitely out there. She could hear it breathing. She hoped it was Claire and not a dog.

"What are you doing out there? Why don't you come in so we can talk?"

She waited a while, but there was no answer. Perhaps she had imagined it. She settled herself on the top step and closed her eyes. Minutes ticked by. She had no idea how many. She was just drifting off when she heard a sneeze. She sat up straight.

"Claire? Is it safe to talk?"

There was no reply, but she gabbled on anyway. "If you're out there, Claire. I want you to know that I still love you and I really wish you were here with me. I just want to talk to you. I thought you were dead! Don't you even care what I went through?"

"What *you* went through?" The voice was so unexpected, it made Sapphire jump. "I'm the one who was taken. You just carried on with your life. If fact, as far as I can see, your life got better. I've seen your tea shop. It looks pretty swish. You've been doing pretty nicely for yourself without me."

Sapphire sucked in her anger. What Claire had said was unfair and unjustified, but it was so great to hear her voice again. She had to be very careful. She didn't want to do anything to scare her off.

"Claire, what are we doing here? What do they want with us?"

"I saw your face in the paper. I couldn't believe you were going to be a May Queen, after what happened to me."

"But you … you told them it was me?"

"I was so surprised, I blurted it out."

"I don't get it, Claire. Why don't you want to escape?"

"I do. I just don't know how. I'm sorry I haven't been down for a while. I've been locked in my room since … well, this is the first day I've been allowed out. But I've been told not to come down here. I'm not supposed to see you or talk to you."

Sapphire had to think fast. She knew that whatever she said next was crucial. If she played this wrong, she might not get another chance.

"Just tell me what you know. What's out there? What's keeping us in?"

There was another long pause.

"The doors and windows are locked at all times. I've been allowed out on a few occasions, to ... help with stuff. But never alone."

"How many floors are there?"

"Three, besides this cellar, but the building is full of old machinery and some of it looks dangerous. Worse still, there are Rottweilers. They're trained to keep us in and other people out."

"They don't go for you?"

"They know me. I look after them, but even so, I don't trust them one bit."

"There must be something, anything you can think of that might help us to escape?"

"There's no one here at night, Gertrude. It's just us and the dogs."

30

Claire had given her what she wanted and yet Sapphire's face burned with rage.

"Do you mean to say that we are alone here every night and you never once let us out? We could have escaped, Claire. We could be free."

Claire hesitated. "It's not that simple. Even if we made it out of the building, we'd have to get across the canal."

"I'll swim if I have to."

"Then I hope you're a better swimmer than you used to be. It looks dangerous."

"This is dangerous. We haven't had any food or water in days. You have to get us out, Claire. Give us a fighting chance. If we stay here, we have no chance."

She looked back into the dimness of the cellar, where the other May Queens lay huddled together. Soon they would be too weak to escape.

❄

"Now we need to do this carefully," Dylan warned, as they stood outside the Dragon that evening. "We want him nicely oiled, not blazing drunk."

"The same goes for us." Jock was already beginning to doubt the plan. "I'm not even supposed to be drinking with you, remember?"

"But you'll make an exception, this once?"

"You could just drink coke."

"No way! It'll look suspicious."

"How are we supposed to get him drunk anyway? A six pack wouldn't even touch the sides."

"It'll be easier than you think," Dylan said. "Just because he's big doesn't mean he can handle his booze."

"Are you sure we're doing the right thing?"

"You can never be a hundred percent sure of anything. Are you coming inside or what?"

Neil shot them a dark look and put out his hand.

"I take it you have my money?"

Dylan pulled his wallet out of his back pocket and emptied it on the bar. "It's all there."

"Yeah, in five pound notes. What did you do, rob some kiddie's piggy bank?"

"Money's money isn't it?"

Neil scooped the notes into a brown envelope and slipped it under the till.

Dylan turned to Jock. "You getting the first round in? I'm skint again, I'm afraid."

Angie gave Jock a strange look as he returned from the bar with a round of drinks and set a pint in front of Dylan. Hadn't he told her just the other day that he wouldn't be drinking with Dylan anymore? She must think he was terribly weak. He glanced at Simon, wondering how they were going to bring the conversation round to what they wanted to talk about. He was hoping Angie would mention Sapphire, but she seemed to be avoiding the subject. Perhaps she wanted a night off from her grief. He cast his eyes at Dylan, but he was drinking as if it were a competitive sport, not even bothering to tell any amusing anecdotes. Simon talked plenty, but not about anything the rest of them were really interested in. Jock had nothing against pandas, but Simon's monologue about their battle for survival was so incredibly dull that he found himself wishing they would just become extinct already.

Dylan set the pace, returning to the bar for pint after pint. Simon, meanwhile, hugged the same bottle of cider all night. He seemed more interested in talking than drinking. As he droned on, Jock felt his eyes closing. He rested his head down on the table and was almost asleep when his phone jolted to life, jumping up and down in his pocket like an excited dog.

"Is that the tune from the exorcist?" Simon asked.

"Yeah! That'll be my mum." He switched it off.

"Aren't you going to answer it?"

"Nah! She's always checking up on me. You'd think I was twelve."

"Why don't you just tell her to piss off?" Dylan asked.

"Dylan!" Angie shook her head.

"No, he's right," Jock said. "There's no telling my mum. I tried ignoring her for a couple of weeks but she called the police and reported me missing. So I ended up calling her and now I'm back at square one, with the incessant phone calls and parcels. She even monitors my bank account. I've had to change the password."

Angie whistled. "Your mum sounds like a nutjob!"

"She is! She really is. I just don't know how to handle her. And it's not just me. Since I've been away, she's been bugging my nephew, too. I wish I could get her off his back, but I'm a coward. I've always been a coward."

"To cowards!" Dylan raised his glass.

"But you're not, Jock." Simon said. "What you did for Anthony that day at the station …" He laid a heavy hand on Jock's shoulder. "That was brave. You could have walked past, but you didn't. You stepped in and did something. You put yourself on the line to make sure Anthony was OK. To be honest, I wasn't terribly sure about you before then. You'd seemed a bit weak and needy. But you're not, Jock. You're not."

"You thought I was weak and needy?"

"Sorry, I didn't phrase that terribly well. What I meant was, when it came to it, you really showed what you were worth. You are capable of being brave, Jock. You just have to step up to the plate."

There was a loud thump as Dylan fell backwards and landed on the floor.

"Dylan? Are you OK?"

Simon pulled him to his feet and set him back down in his chair. Dylan did not seem bothered by his fall. He grinned broadly, like he was auditioning for *The Muppet Show*.

"He's going to feel that in the morning," Angie commented.

"He'll be fine," Simon said. "His skull's so thick it would take a jackhammer to harm him."

"Still, I think it's time we called it a night." She slipped on her denim jacket. "Some of us have an early start."

"I'm pretty tired, too," Jock admitted.

"What about Dylan?"

"I'll take him back to his boat," Simon offered.

"Er, no, that's OK. He can doss down on my floor tonight."

"Are you sure?"

Jock nodded. Just in case. Though, if Simon did turn out to be a serial killer, he would have to be the most boring one in history.

❋

I HOLD the spoon in the air and watch the honey drip down onto the crumpets. The little holes remind me of the inside of a beehive. Jock sits by the window, bashing away on his laptop as if it were an old typewriter. Definitely a worker bee, that one. Bronwyn clumps out of the kitchen and smiles at me.

"The tulips are lovely," I say. "They make the place smell really fresh."

"They were Sapphire's favourite, you know."

"Yes, I know." *I try to look sad.* "There hasn't been anything in the news today?"

"No, there's no mention of her. They're all moving on to other things."

"It's gone quiet in here as well," *I note.*

The tea shop is half empty, quite a change from the last few weeks of mayhem.

"I like it better this way."

"Me, too. But it's such a shame we'll have to close down."

I nod. "I keep praying for a miracle."

Glancing outside, I notice young Evan and his mates with their noses pressed against the window of the Dragon. I walk outside and he sidles up to me.

"Can you get us some cider? Usual deal."

"The price has gone up," *I tell him.* "Unless you want to do another little job for me?"

His gold tooth glimmers. "I'm listening."

"I've got a couple of dogs for you to look after. Their owner's planning an extended holiday."

"I don't know. My mum's not going to like it."

"I'm sure you can convince her. They're Rottweilers. Excellent fighters. Could be good little earners for you."

❄

As FAR AS Jock could tell, Dylan had replaced drinking at the Dragon with drinking alone on his boat. Aside from saving himself money, there didn't appear to be any particular advantage to this. In fact, it was probably worse. Even Neil had the decency to stop serving him once he fell off his bar stool. But alone on the boat, there was no one to stop him reaching for one more can, and no one to stop him toppling over the side either.

Dylan shuddered as he took a swig of the alcohol-free beer Jock had brought with him.

"Tastes like tadpoles," he complained but he drank it, all the same. He was only humouring him, Jock knew, but if it was diluting the alcohol even a little bit then it had to be doing some good.

"So when do I get to read this book of yours?"

"I've got a copy in my bag, but it's still a bit rough."

"Hand it over. It'll come in handy in case I run out of loo roll."

"Thanks!"

Reluctantly, he handed Dylan a copy of his precious manuscript. In the past, he had always had plenty of beta readers, but this book was different. Fragile. He wasn't sure he was ready to have Dylan rip it to pieces. Not after the way Hilary had reacted.

Dylan scanned the first couple of pages, his facial muscles twitching in that unnerving way of his.

"Wow! You're really messed up!"

"Which bit?" Jock asked apprehensively.

Dylan folded back the first page and read aloud: "This book is dedicated to my mum, Mavis. I didn't go to school, like most other kids. Instead, my parents home-schooled me. My mother was worried about me hurting myself or catching germs, so I never joined the scouts, never learnt to swim or ride a bike. I never had friends round to play and I never had a girlfriend. I'm thirty years old now and last year, I bought myself a flat in Notting Hill. My mother did not want me to move out, so she told me she was dying. I knew in my heart it wasn't true. She would say anything to keep me under her control. She once told me that no one else would ever love me. Thanks to her, I am alone and a coward. But I am also a writer, and as a writer, I can do anything. I can travel anywhere I want. I can create life. I can even kill."

A slow smile spread across Dylan's face.

"This is dark, Jock. I wouldn't have thought you had it in you."

"Just wait till you read the book."

"I can already tell I'm going to like it," Dylan placed it in the cupboard for safekeeping. "You weren't exaggerating about your mum, then. She really is a nutter!"

"Unfortunately, yes."

"Have you thought of getting a restraining order?"

"Do you think it would do any good?"

"Probably not, but this dedication might just do it."

"I hope so."

Dylan looked at him with something approaching concern. "Just as long as you know what you're doing. Because once you've done something like this, there's no going back."

"I know that."

"Good."

They fell silent for a few minutes and watched a pair of swans glide by, their heads high in the air. A string of fluffy, grey signets followed, one behind the other, all in procession.

"Stuck-up buggers, aren't they?" Dylan said. "You'd think they own the place!"

"Maybe they do." Jock took a long swig of his drink and tore open a packet of pork scratchings Dylan had left over from the party.

"Actually, there was something I wanted to ask you," Dylan said.

"Go on."

"Do you mind if I draw a bit of your blood?"

"Are you serious?"

"I just want to find out if we're the same blood type."

"Why?" But he had a feeling he already knew the answer. "You're after my liver, aren't you?"

"I wouldn't need all of it. Just about sixty percent."

He couldn't tell if he was serious. "I thought you said they wouldn't give you a liver transplant because of your drinking."

"There are ways." Dylan drummed his fingertips on his beer can. "We could go private. Maybe get it done abroad. It would be cheaper that way."

"Would it be safe?" He didn't know why he was even entertaining the idea. The whole thing was ludicrous.

"Safe as houses. Did you know the liver is the only organ that can regenerate itself? Even as little as twenty-five percent of it can regrow to its original size."

"Yet you want sixty percent?"

"What can I say? It's the gift of life, Jock."

Dylan's smile was as wide as a crocodile's. Definitely time to change the subject.

"Can I have a go at driving the boat again?"

"Yeah, why not? Just as long as you don't capsize us."

Jock felt a sense of pride as he steered the Kingfisher downriver. It was much easier than steering a car. Not that steering had ever really been his problem. His mind had an annoying tendency to wander and that combined with the need to avoid other vehicles and objects on the road …

"Jock, watch out for that boat!"

He pulled the tiller back sharply, just in time to avoid a collision.

Dylan pushed him aside.

"Have you had a drink today?"

"Only a couple. I'm still a better driver than you."

They chugged on for a while, enjoying the tranquillity of the water. Most of the boats were tucked in for the night, so there wasn't a lot of traffic. Just the swans, the reeds and the beginnings of a beautiful sunset.

"Romantic, isn't it?" Dylan wrapped his arms around Jock.

"Sod off!"

"Better head back soon."

"How do we turn around?"

"Just keep going. There should be a winding hole somewhere."

By the time they reached the winding hole, inky violet patches had smudged the sky and Dylan had to take over the steering again.

"Bugger!" he said, as they came back to where they had started.

"What?"

"Some dipstick's taken my mooring! We'll have to go a bit further and find another one."

"Oh dear!"

"It's alright. It's not like I own the space. It just makes life easier if I moor in the same spot each night."

They moved on upriver. The trees leaned inwards as the river narrowed and Jock wondered if Dylan knew what he was doing.

"Crikey! We're going to have to moor in Pepper Hill at this rate," Dylan said. "I'd have let you off at Fleckford if I'd known. You're going to have quite a hike home and I know exercise doesn't agree with you."

Jock swallowed. There was no way he was going to walk all that way in the dark. He would spend the night on the boat if he had to.

"Hey! Isn't that Simon's bike?" Dylan asked.

"Where?"

"There, chained to that tree."

"Are you sure?"

"He's the only poser I know with a neon-green saddle."

"He probably has to get it specially made, doesn't he, because he's so tall."

"But what's he doing here at all?"

※

Sapphire pulled a button off her dress and put it in her mouth. She could feel her stomach eating itself from the inside and her mouth was so dry, her lips kept sticking together. She sucked hard on the button and pretended that it was a boiled sweet. A lemon-flavoured sweet, she decided, from a large packet. She could hear the lift creaking as it made its way down the shaft. Would it be Claire, she wondered, or was it the May Queen Killer coming to ask her about her ear?

She braced herself, but even before the door opened, she knew it was Claire from the lightness of her footsteps. Sure enough, there was a knock. The door swung open and Claire held out a sandwich and a cup of tea.

"Thank God!"

Sapphire grabbed the tea right out of her hand and took several desperate gulps, but as for the sandwich, it wasn't enough to feed a squirrel let alone four hungry women.

"Sorry," said Claire, seeing her face. "It's got ham in it, but there isn't any butter. I never was much of a cook, was I?"

Sapphire forced a smile. "What about you? What are you having for dinner?"

"Oh, there should be a bit of food left in the kitchen for me."

Sapphire wondered. Her sister looked pale and gaunt. Her own diet could not be any better than theirs. She turned to go.

"Wait! We have so much catching up to do. Surely you can stay for a few minutes?"

"Better not. I don't want to get in trouble. Maybe another time."

"Stop! There's something I wanted to ask you!"

Claire hesitated. "What?"

"They said they would let me go … if I let them take my ear. Do you think they're telling the truth?"

"No. No, they won't let you go."

"How can you be sure?"

Silently, she pulled off her socks and shoes.

Sapphire gasped.

Claire was missing a toe off each foot. Her beautiful dancer's feet were mutilated.

Sapphire reached out and touched her arm. "I'm so sorry," she whispered.

"It's no big deal." Claire shrugged it off. "It was five years ago."

She watched as Claire walked back up the steps, only now noticing the difference in her gait.

"I'm going to lose my ear, aren't I?" she called after her.

Her sister didn't answer. Sapphire slumped down on the bottom step, still clutching the sandwich, and she probably would have taken a bite if it weren't for the fact that Claire didn't quite shut the door after herself.

She was giving them a fighting chance.

31

There was no time to lose.

"The door's open!" Sapphire hissed to the others. "We've got to get out of here!"

"No!" said Harmony. "It's a trick!"

"Please," Sapphire begged. She stood in the doorway, afraid the door might lock itself if it was allowed to close. Nothing would induce her to go back into that cellar. "We have to go now! This might be our only chance!"

"I can't!" Harmony said. "It's too dangerous!"

"You can." Fizz took her by the hand.

"No. You can't make me!"

"Leave her," Ingrid said. "She's right. It is dangerous. This is a decision we all have to make for ourselves."

"Well I'm damned if I'm going to spend the rest of my life in this rat hole."

Fizz scrambled for the door.

Ingrid hugged Harmony tightly. "We'll send for help as soon as we're out."

"Keep it down!" Sapphire warned. "You never know who's about."

Certain as she was that Claire had let them out intentionally, there was still room for doubt. Claire was an unknown quantity these days and it was hard to know what she might do. What if she had been asked to let them out? It might be a trick, and even if it wasn't, there was no knowing who or what was out there. No knowing if they had any real chance of escape.

"Why didn't she wait for us?" asked Fizz.

"I don't know."

It made Sapphire uneasy. If Claire truly wanted to help them, why didn't she stick around to guide them out? What good was it to leave them to wander around the building when they didn't know the layout?

The lift stopped creaking, signalling that Claire had gone back up to her own floor.

"OK," Ingrid said. "Let's go!"

The feeling of leaving the hated cellar was incredible, if only there were time to appreciate it. They congregated in the dimly lit corridor, which was, nonetheless, several times brighter than their miserable prison. For a moment they stood there, shivering like a row of paper dolls in their pathetically thin dresses. Their bodies looked bony and angular, as if their creator had been too rough with the scissors. They lacked warmth and colour and life. They had no weapons and little strength. They leaned against each other, barely able to walk.

"We can do this!" Ingrid said. She had been locked up longer than anyone. She was the hungriest for freedom.

The walls were a damp, monochrome grey. Dismal as it was, it was amazing to have something else to look at, besides the same four walls. There was a small, dirty window just below the roof. Sapphire could just make out the sky she never thought she would see again. It was a beautiful purpley-grey, almost silver and it was raining a little, slanted drips of water that streaked sideways down the pane.

"Here's the lift," Ingrid called.

Sapphire watched as she pressed the button.

"What's taking so long?" Fizz muttered. She bounced nervously in place.

Sapphire pressed the button again. There was a loud creaking noise as the lift finally descended. It was very noisy. The thick cellar walls must have muffled the noise significantly.

"What if the May Queen Killer hears?" Fizz asked.

"It's too late to worry about that now," said Ingrid.

The doors jolted open and they all jumped back, but the lift was empty. A slight hum came from the overhead light. They shielded their eyes as they crowded in, unable to cope with the glare. The lift stank even worse than the cellar.

"Ugh!" Fizz squealed. "I stepped in a puddle!"

"Which floor do we want?" Sapphire asked. The buttons looked like they had been burnt off, but they still had little backlights on them.

"Ground floor," said Fizz. "I think it's this one." She pressed the middle button but nothing happened.

"Let me try," said Sapphire. She pressed down hard. This time, the doors slammed shut, making them jump. The narrowness of the lift was even more constricting than the cellar. She could almost hear the beating of their collective hearts as it jerked into action then stopped again abruptly.

"Come on!"

She pressed the button again and it jerked back to life.

"*Hola!*"

"What was that?"

"It's just the lift," said Fizz.

The walls vibrated.

"Hold on!" Sapphire hissed.

The lift shot up to the top of the building, hovered there for a moment, then began to descend again, throwing them around the lift. Ingrid reached up and pressed the middle button, but it didn't seem to matter which button she pressed. The lift had a mind of its own.

"*Buenos dias!*" it greeted them as the doors opened.

"Is this the ground floor?" Sapphire asked, looking into the darkness.

"I don't know, but I'm getting out!" Fizz jumped clear.

"We should all get out," Ingrid said. "There's safety in numbers."

Sapphire took a step forward but the lift had other ideas.

"*Adios!*" The doors slammed in her face. She only just managed to jump back in time.

"You should have held the doors open!" Ingrid said. They were moving at a rapid pace, leaving Fizz far behind.

"No way!" said Sapphire. "I don't trust this lift. I think it would have crushed me."

"I know you're in there," said a voice on the intercom.

"That wasn't the lift," Ingrid said.

And then the lights went out.

❉

"It *is* Simon! Look, there he is!"

Jock and Dylan watched the giant figure as he tugged on the ropes of a small narrowboat.

"Is he mooring?" Jock asked.

"No, I think he's casting off, but where would he be going at this time of day?"

"I didn't even know he had a boat!"

"Nor did I. He's never mentioned it."

"Maybe he rented it."

"Maybe."

Jock swallowed. "You don't think he could have Sapphire on board?"

"Oh, please!"

"Then where's he going?"

"I don't know."

They watched as Simon started up his boat and set off upstream.

"Come on, let's follow him," Dylan said.

"What if he sees us?"

"With any luck, he won't. Besides, I doubt he'd recognise my boat in this light. We'll just hang back a bit, give him a chance to get going."

"Do you think we should?" Jock looked down into the murky waters of the canal and imagined himself flailing around, the weight of his clothing pulling him under. "I can't swim."

"And I don't have my swimsuit. Don't worry, sweetheart. It's not like we're going skinny dipping."

"I know, but it's dark and we're on the water ..."

"Here, put on a life jacket if it makes you feel better."

Jock took the life jacket and pulled it on. "Shouldn't we call the police?"

"What are they going to do? Arrest him for being too tall?"

He started to follow Simon, keeping as far back as he could, without losing sight of his boat. The canal was alive in the darkness. Crickets sang from the rushes and small animals scampered in and out of the water.

"Is this the fastest he can do?" Dylan complained. "We could walk faster than this."

"Look! He's heading for the lock," Jock said. The thought of navigating the deep waters filled him with fear. "Maybe we should go back."

"No, he's slowing down. Look! He's stopping."

"What, here? Why?"

"Use the binoculars." Dylan pulled them out of the cubbyhole.

Jock put them to his eyes. Simon had stopped in front of a row of derelict buildings: warehouses by the looks of it. There were no lights on and no signs of life.

"It's perfect," Dylan said grimly, looking at the boarded-up buildings.

"You think Sapphire's in there?"

"I don't know. Why else would he come here?"

They watched as Simon secured his boat and climbed out.

"He's going inside. What shall we do?"

"I think we should follow."

Jock shivered. "We can't just go in there!"

"Maybe you can't, but I can. It's the only way to know for sure."

"But it might be dangerous!"

"She might be in there, Jock. We can't just sit around waiting. She might still be alive."

"I know …"

"I'll moor down here so he doesn't see the boat. I've got a rubber dinghy I can use to get to the warehouse. It should be easy enough to hide."

Jock stared at the creepy old warehouse, which bore a sign so faded it was impossible to read. He pictured Sapphire locked up like a princess in a dungeon, her big blue eyes pleading with him, begging him to set her free.

"Wait!"

"What?"

"I'm coming with you."

"Are you sure?"

"Yes."

"Then I hope you've got your big boy pants on." Dylan pulled out the dinghy.

He felt a flutter in his stomach. "I still think we should call the police."

"I'm telling you, they wouldn't come. They can't follow every lead."

Dylan checked the dinghy for punctures. "It could do with a bit of a pump, but I think it will do."

He lifted it down into the water and climbed in.

Jock watched him carefully. He couldn't help wondering how much he had had to drink that day. If he got into the dinghy, he would be putting his life in Dylan's hands. Could he trust him?

"Alright, Jock?"

Every nerve in Jock's body screamed at him not to go, but then he thought of Sapphire, scared and alone. What if she was in that warehouse? What if she needed him?

"Alright!"

He took a deep breath and stepped down into the little boat. The dinghy swayed precariously as he sat down.

"Careful," Dylan warned, grabbing him just in time to stop him from toppling out the other side.

"Thanks." He gripped the side.

It was harder than it had looked, rowing to the warehouse. No matter how hard they pulled, the canal seemed determined to take them in the other direction.

"Right!" Dylan hissed. "Right!"

"I'm going right."

"Other right!"

All of a sudden, the boat spun around in a circle.

"What's happening?"

"It's OK." Dylan stuck his oar in hard and punted them in the right direction.

They rowed as hard as they could. Sweat dripped from Jock's brow as he pushed his oar in again and again. Even Dylan fell quiet as he concentrated on rowing.

"It's not working," Jock moaned. He was ready to give up when the wind gave them an unexpected shunt in the right direction. "That's better! Nearly there!"

"Come on, give it some welly!" Dylan hissed as they rowed the last few yards.

Jock pulled on his oars until his arms burned with pain and they finally pulled in close enough for Dylan to grab the bank with his oar. He climbed out and hauled Jock onto the platform at the front of the building. "Careful! These planks look a bit rotten."

Dylan pulled the boat out of the water and looked about for somewhere to hide it. The platform was littered with rusting junk, so it wasn't too difficult to find a space. He set down a heavy pipe on top of it to stop it blowing away.

The warehouse wasn't any less creepy close up. There were no signs of Simon, aside from his boat. Yet he must be in there somewhere, in the darkness. What could he be doing?

"You don't carry a gun by any chance?" Jock whispered.

"No," said Dylan. "But that's probably just as well. I'm a lousy shot."

"Good to know."

Dylan gripped him by the shoulder. "Jock, if you die, promise you'll leave me your liver."

"What for? You'll only drink your way through it."

"How did you get so judgmental?"

Jock shrugged. He wondered if underneath all his bravado, Dylan was as scared as he was. No, he couldn't be or they wouldn't be doing this. Dylan was the one propelling them forward.

"Do you think that's where Simon got in?" Jock pointed to a broken window.

"Looks a bit tight for Simon, but it'll do for us," Dylan said. "Stand back a minute."

He took a loose plank and used it to knock out some of the remaining glass.

"That's better. No need to slit an artery."

Jock tried to smile but his heart was beating hard inside his chest. What if Simon had heard them? What if he was just inside, waiting for them?

He watched as Dylan climbed inside. He seemed to have no problem contorting his body to just the right angle to avoid the sharp edges of the glass. Jock wasn't sure it would be so easy for him.

"Alright?" Dylan whispered.

"Alright." The jagged edges combed his back as he pulled himself through. Dylan guided him down onto a hard, wooden floor. He looked around, but all was black.

"Now what?"

"Just listen."

"I can't hear anything."

"Shh!"

He sensed a presence. Someone or something was there. Dylan clapped a hand over his mouth, scaring him witless.

"Sorry," he whispered in his ear, "but I knew you'd scream like a girl."

"Get off me!"

He shook Dylan off and fumbled in his pocket for his phone, only now thinking to use its light. He shone it around and saw some rusty old machinery. It looked like an old factory. There were still overalls hanging from the pegs and an old crisp packet lay on the floor. There were lockers, too – signs that the warehouse had once been a big, bustling business.

"Shine your light over here," Dylan said.

Jock watched as he knelt down and touched the dusty floor with the tip of his finger. He brought the finger up to his mouth and for a moment, Jock thought he was going to lick it. Instead, he sniffed.

"What is it?"

"Rats."

"Ugh!" Jock shuddered. "Is that what smells so bad?"

"Probably. Shine your light a bit more to the left. No, other left. There! Look! There's a lift. The question is, do we trust it?"

❄

The Perfect Girl

"Quick! Stop it!" Sapphire cried, as the lift began to accelerate upwards. Any minute, the lift was going to reach its destination, delivering them into the hands of the May Queen Killer. She had to do something.

Ingrid jabbed at the buttons, but to no avail. The lift continued to climb.

"For God's sake! Do something!"

"I'm trying!"

The lights flickered off and on, off and on.

"We're stopping!"

The doors seemed to wrench themselves open. Three hungry pairs of eyes met theirs.

"Rottweilers!" Sapphire cried.

In the background, she heard the sound of laughter, but there was no time to focus on it. The dogs growled, their noses twitching as they surveyed their prey. Sapphire felt her muscles tighten. She had met Rottweilers before, but those had been well-groomed and friendly. It was hard to believe that these beasts were the same species. These dogs were ugly. There was no other word for it. Their eyes were huge and shiny and their filthy fur was knotted and patchy. There was something deeply primal about them. Looking into their eyes, it was as if history had been rewritten and the peaceful co-existence between man and dog had never happened. She jabbed the button frantically. The lift doors closed then opened again and the dogs bared their yellow teeth.

She still had the ham sandwich, she realised. She pulled it from her pocket and threw it as far as she could. The two larger dogs dived for it. The smallest could only watch as they pulled it to pieces. Ingrid retreated to the back of the lift and Sapphire would have done the same, but someone needed to press the button.

The dogs devoured the sandwich in seconds. Then the largest one licked its thick brown lips and walked slowly towards her. It looked as suspicious of her as she was of it.

"Easy," she said gently, hoping to calm the dog down with her voice.

"Nice dog! Staaay!"

The dog looked at her with contempt and swiped at her with its paw. She jumped back and to her amazement, the lift door closed. Too fast for the dog, though. Its paw was trapped.

"We're moving!" Ingrid squealed.

"What about the dog?"

They watched in morbid fascination as the trapped paw remained jammed in the door. It slid down, down, down as the lift rose and the dog howled in pain. Sapphire pressed the button, but nothing happened. She kicked at the door with her foot, but they had risen too high now. Her stomach churned. Even though the dog had been about to attack them, it didn't deserve such a brutal punishment, but there was nothing she could do. The lift had a mind of its own and no amount of jabbing the buttons made any difference.

32

The lift jumped wildly as it moved. The dog's paw lay in a grisly red puddle on the floor. Sapphire couldn't bear the sight of it, yet it was hard to look away.

"Do you think we've reached the top?" Ingrid asked, as the lift ground to a halt.

"It seems so." The doors refused to open.

"We'll have to kick the doors in," Ingrid said. She gave them a kick but the second her foot made contact with the door, the lift began to plummet. They fell to the floor and the severed paw rolled from corner to corner as they bumped their way down. The lights flashed on and off and on again.

"We're going back down to the cellar," Sapphire said.

"No!" cried Ingrid. "I can't go back there!" Her ice-blue eyes swam with tears. "I want to go home."

"We will." Sapphire pulled herself up and pressed the buttons for all she was worth. She had no idea which floor was which anymore.

The doors opened again without warning.

"Can you see anything?" Ingrid whispered.

"No. Let's get out. Quickly, before the lift moves again."

Ingrid took her hand. Together, they stepped out of the lift and into the unknown.

They stood in silence for a moment but there was nothing. No footsteps, no barking. Just the creaking of the lift as it moved away. They were in a long corridor, different from the one they had been in earlier – lighter, probably because there were more windows. Sapphire peered out but all she could see was the dark water of the canal below. It seemed a long, long way down. Definitely too far to jump. She listened, her ears alert for the sound of dogs or voices, but all was still.

"What are we going to do?" whispered Ingrid.

"We need to find a way out. There must be a better way than this."

She gripped Ingrid's arm tightly.

"Come on! This way!"

"Looks like a kitchen," Ingrid said, as they approached a large, tiled room fitted with a sink unit and cupboards. It looked newer than the rest of the warehouse, as if it had been added on as an extension. A pile of washing up lay on the draining board and an upturned cup spilt its contents, drip by drip down the counter and onto the floor.

Sapphire went to the sink and turned on the tap. "There's water!"

She filled her cupped hands and drank, again and again until her belly was full. "Aren't you thirsty?" she asked Ingrid when she came up for air.

Ingrid was opening and closing cupboards. "I thought there might be something to eat."

Sapphire joined her in her search, pulling open the cupboard nearest to her, but it contained only dust.

"They're all the same," Ingrid said. "Not a scrap of food in any of them. No wonder Claire never brings us much. Hey, what's that?"

"What?"

"That noise."

"I can't hear any–" The words were barely out of her mouth when the door burst open. She saw a wet nose and then a snout. The dog's hair stood up on end as it entered.

"No!"

Sapphire dived into the far corner, crouching behind the large, steel bin. Ingrid dove behind the door. The dog sniffed the air. The game was up.

❄

Dylan pressed the button to call the lift. It took a couple of minutes, but then the doors opened.

Jock peered in. He felt a bit like he was sticking his head in a shark's mouth. "Maybe we should take the stairs?"

"Did you see the stairs? They were completely gutted. There must have been a fire here at some point. Maybe that's why the building was abandoned."

"So should we get in the lift?"

"Absolutely not. I want to make sure it's working."

He stepped inside, pressed one of the buttons and then jumped out again before the door closed. They waited a few minutes as it went off to another floor then Dylan pressed the button to call it back again. It returned like a dog with a bone.

"Now what?" asked Jock.

"Now we can get in."

"But how do we know if it will take our weight?"

"We don't." Dylan stepped inside regardless, leaving Jock with no alternative but to follow. No way was he going to be left behind.

He looked at the burnt-out buttons. "Which way do we want to go? Up or down?"

"Up," Dylan said with certainty. "We start at the top."

The doors made a horrific grating sound as they closed and the lights flickered on and off.

"It's like a metal cage," Jock said as the lift inched slowly upward.

Their progress was very slow, as if someone were pulling them up on a rope.

A breeze blew down his neck. He moved away, but he didn't seem to be able to escape it, no matter where he stood in the lift.

"Can't you feel that?"

Dylan shook his head.

A strange tapping sound came from the walls.

He glanced at Dylan, who had his lips pressed tightly together. If he was afraid he didn't say so.

It took several minutes to reach the top floor. The doors opened automatically and Jock was about to step out when Dylan grabbed his arm.

"Watch out!"

Without warning, the lift plunged downwards with the doors still open, gaining momentum as it went.

"Brace yourself!" Dylan warned.

They threw themselves to the floor and lay there as the lift plunged down. They hit the bottom with a thump.

"Alright?" Dylan asked.

"Alright." Jock felt a bit shaky.

Dylan pulled himself to his feet with the elegance of a cat and Jock scrambled up after him and shone his light into the corridor.

"What *is* that?"

There was something wet and bloody on the floor.

"It looks like a severed paw."

"Don't touch it!" Jock begged, as Dylan inspected it. "Dylan!"

"Alright! Keep your knickers on!" Dylan kicked the offending article out of the way.

Jock looked about. "There's no one here. Let's go."

"But we haven't found Simon yet!"

The Perfect Girl

Jock shuddered. "This place gives me the heebie-jeebies."

"I think it's supposed to. That's how they keep people out."

"They?"

"Well, it can't just be Simon, can it? He doesn't exactly blend into the crowd."

They took a quick look around the corridor then returned to the lift. The doors opened immediately, almost as if it had been waiting for them. Dylan pressed the button and they plummeted downwards.

"Hang on!"

Jock felt as if the lining had come out of his stomach as they dropped and dropped. They hit the bottom with a thump and the doors flew open. He shone his light along the corridor.

"Shall we take a look?" Dylan asked.

"I thought we were going to be methodical and work our way down from the top?"

"I think the lift has other ideas."

Jock shone his light around in the darkness. There were some impressively long cobwebs that stretched all the way along the wall.

"There's no one here."

"Doesn't look like it, no."

"Look!" Jock shone his light along the far wall.

There was a clear imprint of a hand in the thick grimy dust.

"It's too small to be Simon's."

"How long does a print stay on a wall like that?"

"Wish I knew. What *is* that vile smell?"

Jock covered his mouth with a hanky. "Look, a door."

He pushed it gently and it swung open. Jock shone his light around. There was a set of stone steps leading down into a cold, dark cellar but on the top step sat a tray containing a cup and saucer. Dylan bent down and touched the cup.

"It's still warm."

❋

FEAR HUNG IN THE AIR. The dog growled and smacked its lips. Sapphire curled herself into the smallest possible ball and listened to the padding of unclipped nails on the vinyl floor. Vital seconds ticked by as she held her position, too tense to move. When she looked up, she saw Ingrid lying on the floor. The dog stood over her, prodding her with its paws. Ingrid screamed as it sank its rancid teeth into her neck. The strangest thing, the thing she would always remember, was the lack of barking. She had never known a dog not to bark before, but this vicious, angry dog hadn't barked once.

She grabbed the lid off the bin and threw it at the dog, aiming to knock it off balance. The dog released its grip on Ingrid. Its body went straight and stiff, with its head, shoulders and hips aligned. It bared its teeth. Ever so carefully, Sapphire reached down and pulled off her right shoe. She held it in her hand, waiting for the dog to pounce.

"Don't come any closer!" she warned. "Don't make me do this!"

The dog lunged at her and she shoved the shoe into its mouth. With her other hand, she peeled off her dress and threw it over the dog's head. It pawed at the material, trying to fight its way out. She knew it wouldn't hold it for long.

She sped down the corridor, shivering in her petticoat. She was weak and tired, but she knew she had to keep her legs pumping. If she stopped even for a moment, the dog would have her. The corridor was in darkness. She felt along the wall with her hands. She could hear the dog panting somewhere behind her, scratching the floor with its feet. She rounded the corner and smacked into a wall. She had come to a dead end. There was no way out.

Slowly, she looked up. The moon shone down on the dog's

face, making its teeth look even more horrific than before. It grinned, menacingly. She hit out at it, kicking it with her feet and shoving it with her fists but her efforts only stoked its anger.

"Down!" she commanded. "Down!"

The dog sank its teeth into her arm then let go, only to grab hold of her chest. It pulled her across the floor, dragging her weak, pathetic body towards the lift.

33

"Stop!" It took her a moment to register the voice as Claire's.

The dog froze.

"Heel!"

With one last growl, the dog let go. Sapphire watched as it trotted over to Claire and settled at her feet.

"How did you do that?" She was shocked that the dog had taken any notice. It had seemed so feral.

"Good girl, Petunia." Claire fed the dog a piece of dried liver. "Good job I saved some treats, eh? Don't worry, I'll shut her in my room."

Sapphire nodded mutely. Why hadn't Claire locked the dogs away in the first place? Was she still in two minds about letting them go? She watched as Claire took the dog by the collar and walked towards the lift.

"Please, don't leave me! I'm so weak and Ingrid's hurt, too."

Claire looked at her a little oddly. "I'll be right back. Just wait here."

They disappeared into the lift and the doors closed behind them. Sapphire ran her hands over her wounded body. Her chest was wet with blood and it hurt to breathe. Her arm was bleeding, too, but she had nothing to dress the wounds with. She leaned back against the wall and waited. Precious minutes ticked by and Claire did not return. What was taking so long?

Gingerly, she clambered to her feet. "Ingrid?" she called down the corridor. "You can come out now."

Ingrid didn't reply and she didn't dare call any louder. Instead, she inched her way back towards the kitchen.

"Ingrid?"

She moved as fast as she could, still clutching her bleeding chest. Ingrid lay face down in the middle of the kitchen floor.

"Oh God!" Sapphire knelt down beside her. There was blood everywhere – hers and Ingrid's. She had thought her chest hurt before, but now the ache in her heart was so raw it was unbearable. She felt desperately for a pulse, but there was none. Tears streamed down her face. "Come on!" she sobbed. "I need you! We're going to get out of here together, remember? You promised."

For several minutes, she alternated between chest compressions and breathing into Ingrid's mouth. She couldn't remember how many to do of each, but she just kept going until she could do no more. In her heart, she knew Ingrid wasn't coming back, but to accept that was to accept defeat. Ingrid was her friend, her dearest friend. What would she do without her?

"I thought I heard voices!"

Sapphire looked up. A veiled figure stood over her, surveying the damage. "What a mess!"

A gloved hand poked at her wound.

She opened her mouth to scream but managed to stop herself. She knew the May Queen Killer would relish her pain. She needed to stay strong, but she didn't have the energy to fight. There didn't seem much point now. Ingrid was dead. Their dream of getting out together was gone.

The May Queen Killer grabbed her by the elbow and

hauled her to her feet, causing fresh blood to spurt from her chest and neck.

"Get off me!" she spat, unable to take her eyes off Ingrid. "I'm not going back to that cellar."

"No, you're not. I have something much better in mind."

She was barely conscious as the May Queen Killer heaved open the door to a large walk-in cupboard and threw her in.

※

THE HARSH FLUORESCENT light made her want to puke. After so many days in the dimly lit cellar, she couldn't take such bright lighting. It was only when she uncovered her eyes that she saw that she was not alone. Fizz and Harmony lay side by side on the floor. She tried not to stare at the shackles they wore around their ankles and the chains that connected them to the ceiling. Why hadn't she been chained up with them, she wondered, or was it just a matter of time?

"Are you badly hurt?" Harmony asked.

Sapphire looked down at her wounds. She felt a jolt of pain with every breath, but it no longer seemed to matter.

"No," she lied. "I'm just tired. Are you OK?"

Harmony pulled the hair away from her face to reveal a gaping wound.

"Oh my God!" Sapphire shrieked. "Your ear!"

"They said they would let me go. I don't know why I believed them."

Sapphire reached for her and hugged her as tight as her wounded chest would allow. "I'm so sorry. I should never have left you."

"At least we're together again," Harmony said with false cheer. "And this is better than the cellar, isn't it?"

Sapphire looked around. The cupboard was a lot bigger than it had looked from the outside. It was about the size of her old garden shed.

"Does that light stay on all the time?"

She twisted to avoid its glare.

"Seems to," said Fizz, reaching down to adjust her shackles. She looked Sapphire in the eye. "What do you think's going to happen to us?"

Sapphire squeezed her hand. "I think it's best not to think about it."

Like the cellar, there were no windows in this room. The brightness came from an overhead light. She wondered if the light had been installed specifically to torture them. It was such an odd sort of a room. It was difficult to imagine what it would have been used for ordinarily. It looked a bit like a cave she had once explored, with weird formations hanging from the walls and ceiling, and yet this place was clearly man-made. It had the distinctive pong of meat. Once, she guessed, whole carcasses might have hung down from the ceiling. That would explain the hooks that dangled like sinister coat hangers, and the patches of red on the floor.

Tears streamed down her face – hot, salty tears that seemed to defy gravity, sticking to her face rather than falling down to the ground. She had been so close. Claire had given them a chance, more than a chance. She should have jumped through the window, no matter how high it was. She should have made Ingrid jump, too. They should have taken their chances in the murky waters of the canal. Anything would be better than this.

The door opened and a warm breeze blew in. Harmony screamed as Ingrid's lifeless body was hauled into the room. Sapphire felt the bile rise up in her throat as she saw her. Her skin was already blue. The door slammed shut again and Harmony fell to Ingrid's side, searching urgently for a pulse. She attempted to breathe life back into her, just as Sapphire had done, but Ingrid didn't breathe and her heart refused to start. She had been gone too long.

"Why, God?" Harmony wailed, clutching Ingrid's hand.

Sapphire rocked herself back and forth. She wanted it to be over. She wanted someone to turn out the light.

A big brown rat shot out from nowhere. It headed straight for Ingrid's body. Angrily, Sapphire shooed it away.

"Oh, Ingrid!"

She closed her tired eyes and leaned back against the wall.

"Sapphire? You have to wake up. You can't go to sleep in here," said Fizz.

She rubbed her eyes.

"Sapphire, listen to me! You need to stay awake."

"What are you talking about?" she murmured. "Just let me sleep will you? Just let me sleep."

※

Jock shone his torch down into the cellar.

"Nobody down there."

But there had been, hadn't there?

The cellar looked empty, aside from a couple of blankets. Dylan went down and had a look around, but Jock remained in the doorway. The thought of going down there was just too creepy to conceive of. Was this where Sapphire had been all this time? And if so, where was she now?

"I can hear something," he called out to Dylan, shifting his weight from one foot to the other.

"What is it?"

"The lift's moving. Someone must have called it."

"Not necessarily. That lift does what the hell it likes."

"I don't like this. I think we should get out of here."

They hurried back down the corridor. Dylan pressed the button to call the lift, but nothing happened.

Jock felt panic in his chest. "It's broken!"

"Chill!" Dylan jabbed the button again but it still didn't respond. "Maybe it needs a rest."

"What do we do?"

"We wait."

Jock fiddled with a loose thread on the sleeve of his fleece and wished he had worn something warmer. He should have left the life jacket on. That would have done.

The creaking started again.

"Thank God!"

The doors opened and he flung himself inside. "Come on!" he called to Dylan. He didn't like being alone in there.

Dylan got in and the lift slowly began to climb. Then, without warning, it stopped.

"Not again!" Dylan muttered.

The doors opened halfway between one floor and the next. Jock felt like there were little spiders crawling up and down his body. He didn't like this. It felt wrong.

"What do we do? Should we get out?"

Dylan folded his arms. "You know all those accidents you hear of? People falling to their death down lift shafts?"

He nodded.

"Well, most of those were people who climbed out of the lift. The thing to do is wait. The lift will start up again eventually."

"But what if it doesn't? Nobody even knows we're here."

"I think we can afford to wait a little longer, don't you?"

"Hey, what's that?"

"What?"

"I thought I heard a rumbling in the distance – a kind of scampering sound."

"Oh Lord!"

A dog loomed into sight. Its eyes were large and hungry. Blood dripped from its mouth.

"Do something!" Jock shrieked.

"I'm trying!" Dylan jabbed the buttons.

"We're stuck!"

Jock pressed himself against the wall while Dylan tried to out-stare the dog. The dog snarled and Jock moved further back but Dylan was not afraid. As Jock watched, he took a running jump at it, missed and fell awkwardly against the door.

"Dylan!"

The dog pounced, clamping its jaws around Dylan's head.

"Oh my God! Stop! Stop!"

He watched in horror as it hauled Dylan out of the lift and into the dimly lit corridor.

"Oh hell!"

He had no idea what to do. If he pressed the button, there was a chance the doors would shut and carry him away to safety, but if he did that, he would be leaving Dylan to the mercy of the dog.

He glanced into the corridor. There was a curtain hanging just above the dog's head. If he yanked it down, he might be able to confuse the dog with it. And if he could pull down the pole it hung from, he would have a weapon. He had never wielded a weapon before in his life but there was a first time for everything.

"I can do this," he told himself, as he crawled out of the lift. He reached up for the curtain, but just as his fingers closed around the dusty fabric, the light flickered inside the lift. The blood rushed to his ears as he realised the doors were about to close. He couldn't let that happen. He would be trapped here with Dylan and the dog. He moved back and placed his foot in the lift but he didn't like the way the doors pushed against him, as if they were trying to crush his leg. He looked again at Dylan, still trapped by the angry dog. He had to make a decision. He could jump back into the relative safety of the lift or he could stay and help his friend.

"Help!" Dylan's voice sounded weak and confused. There was so much blood it made Jock's vision swim.

Jock forced the lift doors apart and flung himself inside.

"Don't leave me!" Dylan sounded like he was choking. He

looked like the cow he had seen in Gabriella's gallery, his mouth dripping with blood.

"I'll get help!"

The doors closed behind him and the lift took off, leaving Dylan to his fate. He leaned against the metal wall and the coldness made him shiver. What had he done?

34

I walk from room to room, berating myself for thinking Claire deserved my trust. The warehouse is a labyrinth of dodgy floors and broken machinery and there are many dark corners to hide in, but the lift is the only way to travel between floors. To control the lift is to control it all.

I watch the digital display as it counts down the progress of the lift from the fourth floor. Three, two … Then the doors open and Claire gets out.

"Do you have any idea what you've done?" I demand.

She shrinks back behind Petunia, who regards me with suspicion. I hold out a biscuit and the dog snaffles it up, but she doesn't take her sad, brown eyes off me and as soon as she's swallowed the treat, she whimpers for more. I throw a second one down and she glances at Claire before she eats it, as if to ask permission.

"It's OK," Claire tells her.

Petunia continues to watch me as she chews. She is supposed to be my dog. They all are, but Claire is the one who feeds them and walks them around the warehouse. She's the one who is with them all day. She could turn those dogs against me, if she chose. That's why I'm giving them to Evan. Of course, a large weighted sack would do the trick just as well, but I've always had a soft spot for dogs.

"*Do you have any idea what you've done?*"

"*It's over. It's time to leave.*"

"*I know.*" I try to look contrite. "*I've been making plans, just like I said. I want you to come with me.*"

"*Where to?*"

"*Wherever you want.*"

"*Can't you just ... let me go?*"

"*I need you, Claire. Can't you see that?*"

Her bottom lip quivers. *We've been through so much together. I have to mean something to her.*

There is a loud creak as the lift jolts into action. *Someone else is down there – someone I hadn't accounted for.*

"*We have visitors,*" I say. "*How intriguing.*"

❄

IT TOOK Jock about ten seconds to come to his senses. He pressed the button, but the lift continued to carry him upwards. When he finally came to a stop, he pressed what he hoped was the right button to take him back to Dylan. The lift immediately hurtled off in the opposite direction and when the doors opened, the corridor was unfamiliar.

"Sod it!"

He jabbed the button below. Hopefully this time, he would get it right. The lift bumped down another floor. It was the right floor this time. The curtain fluttered like a bat in the breeze. His heart thumped like crazy as he got out. *Come on, Jock. Be a man for once.*

"Dylan?" he called into the darkness.

He crept slowly along the corridor, glad of what little light shone in through the window. He waved his phone light ahead of him, listening intently for sounds of life. He thought he heard a whimper, but he couldn't be sure if it was real or imagined. If the dog was still about, it would be on him in an instant. He edged further down the corridor, peering into what appeared to be the toilets. One of the cisterns wailed slightly, as if it had recently been flushed. He shone his light into each of the cubicles, but they were all empty. He crept out again, hating his shoes for being so squeaky. The dog would hear that, surely. A dog would hear everything.

He crept out again and was heading back towards the lift when he saw Simon lumbering towards him with Dylan slung over his shoulder like a sack of potatoes.

"Jock? Is that you?"

Simon's eyes shone in the darkness. Dylan was completely still.

"I should have known Dylan would drag you into this. Look, we have to get him to the boat. He's in a bad way."

Did he mean it? Would he really take them back to the boat?

He studied his face, but there was nothing to assure him one way or the other. Simon looked as serious as ever. His mouth was set in a solid line, his eyebrows deeply furrowed. He felt a strong hand on his shoulder.

"Jock?"

"No!"

He wrenched himself from Simon's grip and raced back towards the lift. Maybe Simon could explain all this, maybe he couldn't but his gut told him to run.

Simon was almost upon him as the lift door opened. He jumped in and pressed the button, hating those vital seconds while the lift decided whether to stay open or close.

"What are you doing here?" Jock asked through the closing door.

"What are you doing here?"

But before Jock could respond, the lift took off.

"Wait!" Simon's voice echoed through the lift as it zoomed up, up, up. It stopped on what Jock thought must be the very top floor. He got out, keeping one foot in the door, while he shone his light around the corridor. All seemed quiet, so he let the lift go and dialled 999 on his phone. He held it up high, hoping it would help him get a signal, but the phone refused to ring. He found a tiny window and stood in front of it, looking down at the water. If he were Dylan, he would probably jump, but Jock was too scared. He was always too scared.

He tried not to think about Dylan but he couldn't keep the images from his mind. How awful he had looked with blood gushing from his mangled head. He tried to breathe, but the fear was suffocating him. Before he could stop them, his knees buckled and he sank down to the ground, tears streaming down his face. How the hell was he going to get out?

Gradually, he began to feel a little stronger. He found a tube of peppermints in his pocket and chewed on one. The minty freshness made the air feel a little less stale. He pulled himself to his feet and ventured into a large kitchen. It was empty, but there was evidence of life: a couple of the cupboards were wide open and there was a stack of dirty dishes in the sink. He jumped back as something whooshed past his feet. He looked down, but it was already gone. The sink gurgled loudly and an odd thumping sound emanated from one of the cupboards.

"I don't believe in ghosts."

But it was hard not to imagine the ghoulish figures who might so easily haunt this warehouse.

There it was again, that thumping noise. His eyes widened. That was no ghost. Someone was in there.

He moved towards the cupboard. It had a strong, heavy door. At first he thought it must be locked, but when he pulled a bit harder, it started to budge. He tugged with all his might.

When the door flew open, he was met with a wall of coldness. For a moment, he thought he had found a balcony, but even the cool evening breeze wasn't this cold. He looked around at the yellow walls and the hooks on the ceiling. This was a walk-in freezer. And there was someone inside.

"Sapphire!" he gasped. "Bloody hell! It's really you!"

Sapphire stared in disbelief. She barely recognised Jock, barely remembered him. They had met in another world, another time.

"Come on! We have to get out of here."

"We need a saw," said Fizz.

"She's right," Sapphire agreed. "You have to get something to cut through the chains."

"Sapphire!" Jock seized her by the shoulders. "We have to get out of here before you freeze to death."

She shook her head. "It's not that cold."

He looked at her incredulously. "Your lips are blue and your fingers are like ice. Look at them!"

"I'm fine!"

But when she looked down at her fingers, she noticed they were a strange colour. And they wouldn't bend, no matter how much she tried. She stared at them in fascination. What was happening to her? She didn't even feel that cold. She looked at Fizz and Harmony, still chained in place and her mind whirled. There had to be a reason why she had been left unchained. Perhaps it was a test. Perhaps Jock was part of it.

"I can't leave them," she told him. She wasn't in any imminent danger. She couldn't be. She would feel it.

Jock looked confused. "Who? Sapphire, there's no one else here but you and me."

"Of course there is!"

"No! Listen to me. You're having a delusion. They're all in your head. We are alone in this freezer. Just you and me."

35

Even with the door open, Sapphire could see he was shivering.

"Come on! We have to get out of here!" he said. He made a grab for her arm but she fought him off.

"No, I can't leave them!"

"How can I convince you they're not real?"

"Who are you talking to?" asked Fizz.

Sapphire's mouth fell open. She stared at Jock and tried to picture what he would look like with a green raincoat on.

"Are you saying he's not real?"

"Who?"

Everyone was talking at once. Sapphire put her hands over her ears.

"Describe them to me," Jock said, cutting through the noise. "What do they look like?"

"They're May Queens, like me. They have blonde hair and blue eyes. Well, Fizz's hair is kind of frizzy, if you don't mind me saying? And Harmony is small and dinky, and Ingrid …" she pointed at the body on the floor. "Ingrid was Swedish."

"Sapphire, you need to listen to me. You remember that night I came up to your flat?"

She nodded.

"I had a spot of indigestion, so I opened the bathroom cabinet, looking for Rennies. Instead, I found your pills. You suffer from delusions don't you, like your mum?"

Anger swelled up inside her. "You don't know what you're talking about! I am nothing like my mum!"

"I'm sorry, I shouldn't have …"

She regarded him with suspicion. "How would you know about my mum, anyway?"

"Gabriella told me."

"Who?"

"Gabriella Helston. Claire's friend. Remember her?"

"Oh! I knew her as Gaby."

"And you were Gertrude?"

"Yes."

But how could he possibly know so much about her, unless he was just another product of her messed up mind?

"You know all about the May Queens, too," he reminded her. "You read about them in the papers, didn't you? After your sister went missing, I bet you became obsessed with the details of each and every one of them. Think about it, Sapphire. The first one, Ingrid, went missing in 1993. She was only nineteen then, but she would be into her forties by now. Take a good look at her. Does the Ingrid you're seeing look that old?"

Sapphire looked at Ingrid – really looked at her, taking in her smooth, flawless skin. Even in death, she looked young. Perfect.

"He has a point," Fizz murmured.

"So you can see him then?"

"Course I can. I was just pulling your leg."

"And what about her clothes?" Jock went on. "Are they modern, would you say? Or a bit dated?"

Sapphire looked again. Suddenly, she knew why Ingrid had seemed so familiar. She looked just like the blonde one from ABBA! There hadn't been much information about the first missing May Queen, so her imagination had had to compensate. And she didn't know much about Sweden either so …

Sapphire put her head in her hands.

"No, no, it can't be. They're not just in my mind. They can't be!"

Jock cleared his throat. "The truth is, Sapphire, those girls are probably all dead, just like Peter Helston said, and unless we get out of here, we will be, too."

"Just give me a moment."

She reached out to touch Ingrid's hand, but as her skin made contact, Ingrid evaporated, her body disintegrating into a fine dust.

"No!" Sapphire screamed. "No!"

It was like losing her all over again.

"Shh! Keep your voice down!"

She barely heard him. She grasped at the air, but there was nothing left to hold on to. All she could see was a pile of dust. She leaned down to touch it. Each tiny, sparkling particle seemed to carry the residue of life. She tried to scoop it up, but her hands felt big and clumsy, like she was wearing boxing gloves.

"Sapphire? Sapphire!" Jock broke through the silence. "You have to get up! We have to get out of here."

She was barely aware of his hands as he hauled her to her feet. She leaned against him as Fizz started to fade.

"No! Not you, too!"

Harmony reached out for her and tried to grab her hand.

"Help me!" she cried. "I'm scared! I don't want to die, Sapphire. I'm not ready!"

Sapphire tried to reach her, but the moment she made

contact, Harmony evaporated into a fine powder, just as the others had done.

"No!"

She fell to the floor and tried to gather up all the dust with her hands, but it was useless. Her hands didn't work properly anymore. She was incapable of coordination.

"Come on!" Jock said. "Time to go!"

"No, I need this!"

"I can't even see what you're talking about."

"This! This dust!"

He squinted hard at the floor. "That's ice, Sapphire. Come on! You're going to get us killed!"

"Then help me!"

"How?"

"Just sweep it into your pocket. My hands won't work."

"If I let go of this door, we'll get locked in. There's no way to open it from the inside."

"Then I'll swap places with you. Please, Jock! Just get me that dust! I need it!"

She crawled on her hands and knees to the door. Looking down, she saw that her petticoat was red with blood.

"Just sit here." He helped her sit so that she blocked the doorway. "And whatever you do, don't move. If you let that door shut, there's no way out."

He didn't take his eyes off her as he swept up the dust with his hands. He didn't trust her, she realised. Not entirely. He was worried that her madness would lead her to do mad things. Madder things.

"Can we go now?" he asked, as he slipped the remaining dust into his pocket.

"Of course."

He helped her out of the freezer. She could barely even cling to him, her body was so numb. She felt hot and cold all over and her legs felt like stumps, but looking down, she could see they were still attached to her body.

"What's happening to me?"

"It's the cold. Goodness knows how long you were in there."

"But I didn't even feel it."

"Must be down to the power of your mind. Your brain didn't register the cold, so you didn't feel it. Probably just as well."

"I could have frozen to death in there, and I wouldn't even have known."

He pulled off his fleece and wrapped it around her shoulders, shivering in his cotton T-shirt.

"Come on! We need to find a way out," he said, "and unfortunately, that means using the lift."

Sapphire shuddered. "That lift is haunted."

"Don't I know it!"

She closed her eyes as he helped her down the corridor. They stopped in front of the lift and he reached up to press the button. But before he could, a familiar, grating noise began. Someone was in there. She looked at him in panic.

"What shall we do?"

"We have to hide!"

"Where?"

They glanced round in desperation, but the corridor was more or less bare.

"It's pretty dark," Sapphire said. "Maybe if we stay very still, we won't be seen."

"What about the dog?" Jock asked, picturing the savage creature that had attacked Dylan.

"Dogs, plural."

"Shit, really?"

As they stood there, paralysed by indecision, the bell tinged.

"Run!" Sapphire hissed, her voice barely audible.

Jock looked left and right. If he let go of her, he might just get away. But he couldn't leave her, not after all it had taken to rescue her. He pushed her behind the armchair in the corner. It wasn't the greatest hiding place, but it might just work.

"Keep still," he warned her. There wasn't enough room for him, too. He looked around, desperate for a hiding place of his own, but there was no time.

Simon tore the lift doors open. He carried an LED lamp that lit up the entire corridor. If he weren't so tall, he would have easily spotted Sapphire, crouched behind the chair.

"Where is she?" His face was grim and his blue eyes blazed.

Jock stepped back towards the window. There was nowhere to go. Nowhere to run.

"I don't know."

"You're lying."

There was a loud grating sound as the lift took off again. Simon turned in the direction of the sound. There was a slight whirr as it changed direction and started climbing up again. It grew noisier the closer it came. Simon looked towards the double doors and switched off his light.

"Keep your mouth shut!" he warned.

Jock leaned back against the wall. If only his stupid legs would let him run.

The lift doors pinged and Verity got out, leaning heavily on her stick.

"What are you doing here, Mum?" Simon's voice reverberated around the lift, creating a terrifying echo. He punched the lift with his fist, leaving a dent the size of a dinner plate.

Jock heard a movement from the corner and saw Sapphire's head sticking out. If she weren't careful, Simon would see her, too.

Verity looked so tiny next to her gigantic son. And yet, her expression was resolute. She had come to reason with him, Jock realised. Perhaps she was the only person who could.

He almost didn't notice a second person emerge from the lift. The young, gaunt woman looked vaguely familiar, but it took him a moment to place her. It was Claire, of course. He recognised her from the CCTV footage. He saw Sapphire raise her head again. He tried to motion to her to stay put, but she did not heed his warning and instead, moved across the corridor towards her sister.

"You're not real, are you?" she reached out to touch her.

Claire looked at her in the same way you might look at a drunk.

"Of course I'm real!"

"I can see her," Jock said.

"You can?"

"Yes."

"Oh, God! Oh, my God!"

Sapphire reached for her with her feeble arms, but Claire did not return the gesture. She was still under the killer's spell.

Sapphire took a deep breath and lifted her head once more, summoning the last of her strength.

"What do you think he did with them, the women you took?" she asked. "The girls."

Jock looked at Simon, but it was Verity who answered.

"It was my idea," she said. "I brought them to him."

Jock blinked. What was going on?

"Only to stop him from wandering," Sapphire said. "You knew what his appetite was. You thought you could contain it. But you couldn't, could you? Peter Helston was a monster – a particularly evil one because none of his friends or family had a clue. Not even his daughter. Not even his wife."

Was this just speculation, Jock wondered, or had she got it from Claire?

The mention of Daphne turned the old woman sour. She reached out to strike Sapphire with her stick, but Simon caught it first and tossed it aside. She stood perfectly well without it, it seemed.

"How did you know?" asked Verity, turning on Simon. "I mean, how could you suspect your own mother?"

Simon's lip quivered. "It was Gabriella who put me on the right track. The minute she set eyes on Anthony, she was struck by the resemblance between him and her dad. She wanted him to take a DNA test but Anthony's parentage was never in any doubt. I was the one who had never known my father, so I took the test instead."

He watched his mother with sharp, unflinching eyes. "It turns out Gabriella is my half sister. So Peter Helston was my dad, wasn't he?"

Verity shrugged, as if the question of Simon's parentage was of no great significance.

"I just want to know why, Mum. I can understand that you had an affair with a married man, and I'm sorry that he turned out to be a bad person. But why did you take Sapphire? It doesn't make sense. Peter's dead. You were free."

"I'd developed a taste for it," Verity said. "That's what attracted me to Peter. He was the only one who understood my cravings, my desires."

She bit down hard on her lower lip, as if repelling a painful memory. "When he was arrested, he confessed to cover for me. He didn't want anyone to know I'd been involved. He wanted me to finish what we had started but much as I wanted to, I couldn't kill Claire, not on my own. So I kept her alive and in time, I came to depend on her."

Claire gave her an understanding nod.

"But I hadn't lost the taste for it. I was just pacing myself, preparing for the next kill. I thought that would be Daphne, but then Claire saw her sister in the local paper, when the May Queen contest was announced. We couldn't believe it. She was handing herself to me on a plate. She wanted me to take her. She practically invited it."

Simon closed his eyes for a moment. He must have hoped for a different outcome. Perhaps he had thought his mother would tell him he was wrong. "You're not going to get away with it this time. The police are on their way."

Verity laughed a cold, callous laugh. "You're bluffing. I can always tell."

A voice projected itself through the silence.

"Stay where you are and put your hands in the air!"

"Who's that?"

"It's the police," said Simon. "Just like I said."

"Put your hands in the air."

"I don't bloody think so!"

Too late, Jock saw the gun. He had never seen one in real life before. It looked old and rusty. Verity's eyes flashed with anger.

"Everyone stay right where you are."

"Stop! Armed police!" The voice on the loudspeaker sounded louder and clearer than before. Wherever they were, they could see everything that was happening.

"Put the gun down, Mum," Simon begged. His eyes, so like hers, were filled with fear.

Her face contorted. "This is your doing, isn't it? You brought them to me!"

"You need to give yourself up, Mum, before anyone else gets hurt."

"What's the worst they can do? Send me to prison for the rest of my life?" She let out a cackle. "Old age is not the time to go soft, Simon. It's the time to experiment, to drink and take drugs and do whatever else it is you've been holding back all those years. Because at my age, what the hell have I got to lose?"

"You're not that old, Mum. You could still–"

"I'm not that young, either."

She rubbed the back of her arthritic knee. It was feeling a little stiff. She needed to head down to the hive and get the bees to work their magic.

A tiny red dot appeared on the wall above her. She must have sensed something was up because her eyes flickered from left to right.

"What? What are you all looking at?"

She pointed the gun in Jock's direction and his fear was as forceful as a punch in the stomach.

"Tell me! Tell me!"

Words blocked his throat. He couldn't breathe. He couldn't speak. He watched, transfixed, as she eased back the trigger, but there was nothing he could do. Even after all this, his cowardice was going to kill him.

"It's a sniper," Sapphire shouted, causing Verity to swing round and point the gun at her.

"No!" Claire threw herself in front of Verity, blocking the red light with her body.

Verity let out a snort. She seemed to think it was funny that Claire would risk her life for her. And little wonder. It was a kindness so undeserved.

The red light flickered back to the wall as the police marksman waited to get a clear shot. Claire reached for the button to call the lift. The doors opened. Once again, it had stopped half on one floor, half on another.

"Press it again," Verity hissed.

Claire raised her hand but instead of hitting the button, she shoved Verity as hard as she could into the lift shaft. The old woman grasped wildly at the air, then her bony fingers clamped themselves around Claire's ankle. Claire's eyes were wide with fear as she struggled to fight her off, but the old lady held on tight, her mouth set in a hard, grim line.

"Claire!" Sapphire lunged forward, but their fingers did not quite meet. Claire's eyes bored into her and she found it hard to look away. If Jock hadn't grabbed her arm, she would have tumbled in after them.

The screams went on for longer than they should have. Down, down, down they plunged, gunshots ricocheting off the walls, arms and legs flailing with nothing to break their fall. There was a loud, sickening thud. And then nothing.

Sapphire stared down the lift shaft, desperate for a glimpse of her sister.

"Don't look," Jock warned, holding her tight.

But she had to know for sure. She grabbed his phone out of his hand and shone it down the hole. What she saw was a disgusting, mangled mess, as if someone had filled two large balloons with red paint and dropped them from a great height. Verity's face was indistinguishable from the pulp they both lay in. Claire had landed on top and her glassy eyes gazed up at them. She looked like a broken doll.

"Why did she do that?" Jock cried. "Why didn't she let the marksman take care of her?"

Sapphire stared into the abyss. "She wanted to kill her herself."

She tasted blood in her mouth and sank back against Jock, exhausted. He held her as close as he could without hurting her. The police would be with them in seconds, but it felt like eternity.

36

"They couldn't even find me a female nurse," Dylan complained, as a young man came to check his chart.

"Glad you're feeling better," the nurse said with a smile.

Jock hovered at his bedside, clutching a bag of grapes and a copy of *Bizarre* magazine.

"God, Dylan. I can't believe I left you like that. I'm so sorry. I don't know what came over me. I can't believe I was such a coward."

"That's OK. You are what you are."

"But it's not OK. I left you."

"Leave it in the past, will you? And hand me those grapes. I'm starving."

Dylan crammed a handful into his mouth and stopped to touch his head. He seemed proud of the twenty-seven stitches sewn across his skull.

"How do I look?"

"Like a cricket ball."

"Thank God for Simon, ay?"

Jock nodded. If Simon hadn't carried Dylan back to the boat, his injuries would have been much worse. And if Dylan hadn't swallowed his pride and called Stavely, who knew what would have happened.

"Poor Simon. Imagine finding out your parents are serial killers," Jock said.

"And I called him boring!" Dylan laughed.

Jock shook his head. "I still can't believe it was Verity. She seemed so nice and normal."

"She never did like me," Dylan chomped on another handful of grapes. "Should have known there was something wrong with her."

"I forgot to tell you. Simon's got a theory about who put the brick through the window," Jock said.

"Yeah?"

"He reckons it was that little turd you had a fight with in the tea shop."

Dylan frowned. "You're going to have to narrow it down."

"His name's Evan Thomas and Neil saw him talking to Verity on more than one occasion. Simon reckons she paid him to create a distraction while everyone was looking for Sapphire. It was probably his dogs that mauled the lambs, too. It doesn't seem fair that he's got away with it. That brick only just missed Morgan, and remember those poor little lambs!"

"Don't worry your pretty little head about it. Evan's none too bright. If it was him, it's just a matter of time before he trips over his own shoelaces."

❄

THE FIRST THING Sapphire did after leaving hospital was run herself a bath. While the tub was filling, she went into her bedroom to get a book.

"Hey, this is my room!" she told Claire, who was flopped out on the bed, wearing an old dressing gown Sapphire thought she had thrown away years ago. "You can have the sofa."

"We'll see about that," Claire said, lighting a cigarette.

"Hey! You can't smoke in here! You'll set off the alarm."

She picked up a dog-eared copy of *Alice in Wonderland* and went back to her bath. She wasn't that surprised Claire had made an appearance. Dr Jenkins had said it might be a while before her medication took effect.

The hot bubbles soothed her battered body. Her wounds were healing well, but it would be a while till she wore a low-cut top again. She ripped open a sachet of hot mud and massaged it into her tired face. She was just about to lie back and relax when the doorbell rang.

"Can you get that?" she asked Claire, before she remembered herself. She threw on her silk dressing gown and walked, dripping wet, to the door.

A young woman stood on the doorstep. She had one of those little suitcases that you drag along by the handle.

"Harmony?"

"No, it's Melody, actually," she led a large Afghan hound into the living room. "You had it wrong. Look it up if you don't believe me."

"Melody?"

"You don't mind if I let Kiki off the lead, do you?"

The dog ran around the room, treading her muddy paws into the carpet, before settling herself on the sofa. Sapphire bit her lip as she watched her gnaw on the remote. She turned to shut the door, only to find Fizz standing there with a large box of pizza.

"That smells amazing."

Fizz dumped the pizza on the table and produced a bottle of Buck's Fizz and a video of *Pretty Woman* from her oversized handbag.

"Sorry, I haven't got a video player."

"It'll still work," Fizz said, trying to jam the video cassette into the DVD player.

Sapphire went back to the door and peered out. She was still hoping Ingrid would show.

※

"Don't worry, I'm only here for the funeral," her mother said, as she slid into the pew beside her.

Sapphire glanced at her out of the corner of her eye, amazed to see her so well-recovered. She knew her mum had her ups and downs, but still, she hadn't thought this possible. If she had given it any thought, she would have imagined that the disappearance of both her daughters would be enough to send her into permanent catatonia.

"What happened to you?" she asked.

"I don't know. I just snapped out of it. Apparently, it happened when they told me you were missing. My memory's a bit foggy, but that's what they say."

"But where were you all that time? Do you remember anything?"

Her mum drew a breath. "I never went anywhere, Sapphire. I was still there, just muted. I did a lot of listening - the conversations I could repeat for you. You wouldn't believe how much I heard. But it just exhausted me, the effort of being, and listening, taking it all in."

Sapphire leaned a little closer. She didn't even smell like Mum. She smelt of soap and shampoo and just a touch of Lillies of the Valley – just how a mother was supposed to smell, one who could wash and dress herself, one who took pride in her appearance.

It confounded her. Since her own diagnosis, Sapphire had seen herself as a functioning schizophrenic, not a lunatic like her mother. She knew what she was doing. She took her medication and she controlled her illness. It didn't control her. She had her rules and her coping mechanisms and she lived with it. She still saw people who were not there – the man in the green raincoat was her most frequent tormentor – but she knew what he was and she only acknowledged him when there was no one else around. He was like an unfriendly ghost, but he had no power unless she gave it to him.

But her abduction had meant such an abrupt cessation of her medication that it was no wonder she had been confused. Anyone would have struggled to adapt to life in a dark, rat-infested cellar, and Sapphire had retreated into her schizophrenia. Her mind had dreamed up companions for her. Her illness hadn't been a menace. It had been her saviour. It had meant that she was never truly alone.

Her mother sat beside her, an unexpected shoulder to cry on throughout Claire's service.

"Don't be afraid." She took Sapphire's hand in hers. "Who knows, maybe we'll even see her again one day."

Sapphire closed her free hand around the pills that waited in her pocket. It was exactly at that moment that Gertrude climbed out of her body and walked up the aisle to the altar. No one else seemed to notice as she stood beside the vicar, nodding politely as he conducted his sermon. She waited until they sang Claire's favourite hymn, then opened the casket. Sapphire forced herself not to scream as Claire climbed out and Gertrude lay down in her place.

She looked down at her hands, surprised to find that she was still there. She had separated so completely from the person who used to be Gertrude that the two of them were now separate entities: one dead and the other alive.

She looked back at the church door to see if her father would also appear, but even in her hallucinations, he was absent.

Angie and Simon sat close together on the pew opposite. She sensed it wouldn't be long until Angie fell pregnant. In fact, if she looked closely, she thought she could make out the outline of a foetus through the swell of her dress. Gabriella sat on the other side of Simon. She glanced dubiously in

Sapphire's direction, like she wasn't sure if she should be there. Sapphire gave her a cursory nod to let her know it was OK.

As they moved outside, Sapphire looked up at the heavens and willed it to rain down on Claire's awful grey grave. The man in the green raincoat marched by, crashing dustbin lids together as the vicar spoke comforting words about people he didn't know and circumstances he couldn't begin to imagine. His words floated to the ground, covering the coffin in a pile of baby blue feathers. The man in the green raincoat crashed his dustbin lids louder and louder until he created thunder. The heavens opened and colourful raindrops poured down. Sapphire brushed the water from her face, smudging the landscape with purples and oranges that only she could see. A huge rainbow smiled across the sky, and the clouds shimmered like they had been tossed in glitter and lit up from the insides with halogen lamps. She reached for Jock's hand. Once she had craved control, but now she chose to live life in full, technicolour glory. The pills would remain in her suit pocket for many years to come.

※

"We'd better ask someone how to find the Metro," Jock said, as he and Dylan emerged from customs at Prague's Václav Havel Airport.

"That's OK. I've arranged for someone to meet us," Dylan said, scanning the room.

"Oh, OK."

He had been a little sceptical about allowing Dylan to arrange this lads' break for the two of them, but he seemed to have everything in hand.

"Ah, there we go," Dylan said, pointing towards a stern-looking lady with a placard bearing their names. Dylan waved her over.

"Why's she wearing a nurse's uniform?"

"I paid extra for that!" Dylan said with a smirk.

Jock rolled his eyes, wondering what other little surprises Dylan had in store for him.

"Ambulance was busy," she said in clipped English. "We must take my car."

"What's she talking about an ambulance for?" he asked, looking at Dylan with concern. "Are you ill?"

"Quite on the contrary. In a few hours, I'll be getting my new liver."

Jock zipped his jumper up all the way to the top. "But I thought you said I wasn't a match?"

"You're not."

"Come on! Are you getting in or what?" the nurse asked.

Jock climbed in the back and fastened his seatbelt. Dylan sat in the front.

"So, what's going on, Dylan? How did you find a donor?"

"I found this website called Liverswap.com."

"Really?"

He nodded. "I found a woman on there who's willing to give me a piece of her liver."

"And she's a match?"

"That's right."

"That's amazing, Dylan. But why didn't you say so?"

"Well, here's the thing, Jock. She's willing to donate because her boyfriend also needs a transplant, and as it happens, his blood type matches yours. It's a painless procedure, really it is. We're all going to get it done here in Prague then we get to recuperate in the beautiful Czech capital. Alright, Jock?"

Jock clutched the door handle as the car sped along at 60 mph, on what felt like the wrong side of the road.

"You'd better be bloody joking."

ALSO BY LORNA DOUNAEVA
MCBRIDE VENDETTA SERIES BOOK ONE

FRY

She acts like she's your new best friend, but is she really a deadly enemy?

When Isabel nearly runs over mysterious Alicia, she is filled with guilt. She helps Alicia get a job at the supermarket where she works and soon, Alicia is acting like her new best friend. Then fires break out all over town and she suspects Alicia knows more than she's letting on, but it's Isabel the police suspect. In order to survive, Isabel must question her own innocence, her sanity and the very fabric of her morality.

Lorna Dounaeva's debut novel is a sizzling psychological thriller that will make you question how well you can ever really know a person.

FRY is a very British fast paced psychological thriller.

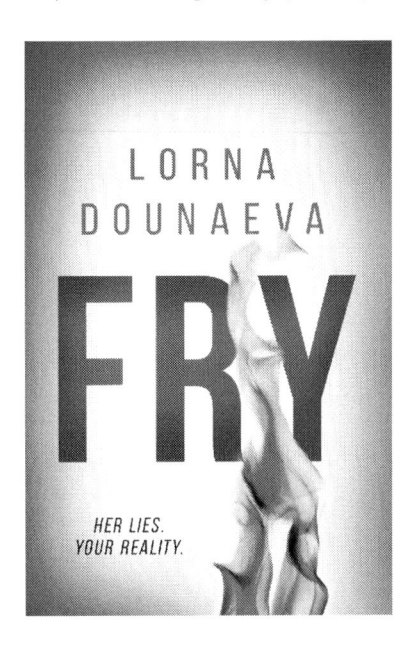

ALSO BY LORNA DOUNAEVA
MCBRIDE VENDETTA SERIES BOOK TWO

Angel Dust

It's every parent's worst nightmare…

When Isabel's daughter, Lauren is snatched from outside her school, she suspects Jody McBride is behind the kidnapping. Yet the detective in charge of Lauren's case seems more interested in picking apart her statement, and investigating members of her family.

Can Isabel persuade the police to take her seriously, or will she have to take matters into her own hands? In order to save Lauren, she must take a stark look at her own relationships, and consider how well she really knows her daughter.

ALSO BY LORNA DOUNAEVA
MCBRIDE VENDETTA SERIES BOOK THREE

Cold Bath Lane

Who will pay the price for her silence?

Nine-year-old Jody is does well in school, despite living in a run-down part of East London.

Then one terrible night, her life changes forever, and Jody is forced to make an impossible choice between telling the truth and keeping her family together.

The police bring her in for questioning, and pressure her to tell them what really happened but is Jody ready to admit it, even to herself? Will the truth win out, or will Jody be sucked into a web of lies in order to protect her family?

This disturbing crime novel is utterly gripping and impossible to put down.

A BURDEN NO CHILD SHOULD BEAR.

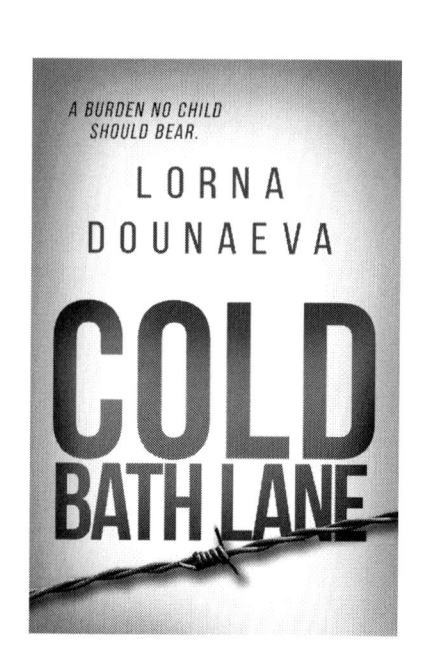

LORNA DOUNAEVA

COLD BATH LANE

AFTERWORD

If you've enjoyed this book, I'd be eternally grateful if you'd consider posting a review. A couple of lines are plenty and it makes all the difference to authors, as we rely on word of mouth to get our books known.

Thank you!
    Lorna

P.S. I hope you'll consider joining my readers' club to receive updates on new releases and giveaways at www.lornadounaeva.com

You can also contact me at info@LornaDounaeva.com

ABOUT THE AUTHOR

Lorna Dounaeva is a quirky British crime writer who once challenged a Flamenco troupe to a dance-off. She is a politics graduate, who worked for the British Home Office for a number of years, before turning to crime fiction. She loves books and films with strong female characters and her influences include *Single White Female* and *Sleeping with the Enemy*. She lives in Surrey, England with her husband and their three children, who keep her busy wiping food off the ceiling and removing mints from USB sockets.

facebook.com/LornaDounaevaAuthor
twitter.com/LornaDounaeva
instagram.com/lorna_dounaeva

Made in the USA
Middletown, DE
15 May 2024